Managing in the New Economy

The Harvard Business Review Book Series

Managing in the New Economy

Edited with an Introduction by
Joan Magretta

A Harvard Business Review Book

Printed in the United States of America

03 02 01 00 99   5 4 3 2 1

The *Harvard Business Review* articles in this collection are available as individual reprints. Discounts apply to quantity purchases. For information and ordering contact Customer Service, Harvard Business School Publishing, Boston, MA 02163. Telephone: (617) 496-1449, 8 A.M. to 6 P.M. Eastern Time, Monday through Friday. Fax: (617) 496-1029, 24 hours a day. E-mail: custserv@hbsp.harvard.edu.

Library of Congress Cataloging-in-Publication Data

Managing in the new economy / edited with an introduction by Joan
    Magretta.
        p.   cm. — (A Harvard business review book)
    Includes index.
    ISBN 1-57851-186-0 (alk. paper)
    1. Knowledge management. 2. Competition, International.
    3. Business forecasting. I. Magretta, Joan. II. Series: Harvard
    business review book series.
    HD30.2.M362   1999
    658—dc21   99-24214
                                                           CIP

The paper used in this publication meets the requirements of the American National Standard for Permanence of Paper for Printed Library Materials Z39.48-1984.

Contents

Introduction

Joan Magretta

There has been so much hype on the subject of the so-called new economy that it's tempting to join forces with the economists who dismiss the notion as mere wishful thinking. No less an authority than U.S. Federal Reserve Chairman Alan Greenspan is among the skeptics: "Our economy, of course, is changing every day, and in that sense it is always 'new.'" The deeper question, says Greenspan, is whether there has been a fundamental, discontinuous change in the way our economy works that promises significantly higher growth. In this more profound sense, his answer to the question "Is there a new economy?" is no.[1]

But if the new economy tends to evaporate when viewed from the lofty perspective of the macroeconomy, it looks more solid when the sight line shifts. As even Greenspan acknowledges, down in the economic trenches "important technological changes . . . are altering, in ways with few precedents, the manner in which we organize production, trade across countries, and deliver value to consumers."

Those three categories cover a good deal of what goes on in the pragmatic realm of managerial work. For those who worry day in and day out about creating value for customers, and buying and selling in the global marketplace, there surely is a new economy—or at least a new set of activities, a new set of issues, a new set of priorities that simply did not exist 15 years ago and that today constitute a significant piece of the managerial agenda.

While some industries are more immediately affected by that new agenda than others, it is relevant to leaders across the full spectrum of organizations—high tech or low, large or small, old or new, businesses or social enterprises. The new agenda is taking shape at the intersection of three long-term trends, which will continue to gather momentum in the decades ahead.

1. **The rise of networks.** Information technology, by breaking the trade-off between richness and reach, is changing the economics that underlie industry and organizational structures. The scope of an organization's activities is one of the fundamental questions of strategy. As more individuals and businesses connect electronically, the economics of scope will continue to shift, and with that shift come changes in relationships within an organization, in who competes with whom, and in what is made internally versus bought from outside.

2. **The growth of knowledge work.** Increasingly, value creation is a function of information and ideas, and this is true across a wide spectrum of businesses including those firmly rooted in the world of tangible products. Knowledge can turn products into services, or it can make physical products more valuable and smaller at the same time (think about cell phones, for example). The result is that much of our economic growth in recent years has been "weightless." Along with this fundamental shift in how value is created comes a new management challenge: managing knowledge work and innovation.

3. **The globalization of trade.** As political and logistical barriers to global trade and competition drop, every organization needs to reexamine its own economic landscape. Who are the relevant customers, suppliers, and competitors in a reconfigured world? What shifts in strategy and organization are required to manage effectively across geographic and cultural boundaries?

Every industry will feel the impact of these three forces in its own way. But the direction in which these forces drive industries is always the same: toward more dynamic, faster-paced competition and change. In some industries, new competitors have already emerged; in others, major restructuring is underway. Most industries have felt and will continue to feel growing pressure to innovate and to increase the pace of innovation. Uncertainty—always a constant of business decision making—appears to be on the rise.

Much of the writing about the new economy fuels this heightened sense of uncertainty. With its numbing incantation about relentless forces and continual reinvention, such writing lulls us into accepting uncritically that *everything*—including the fundamental logic of business—has changed and that all the old rules are useless. In their place, a set of punchy aphorisms is served up as a new recipe for success.

Such writing is misleading on two counts. First, it is simply non-sense that everything is changed. Neither the basic principles of business economics nor the enduring realities of human nature have been abolished. If anything, they are more relevant today than ever before, because anyone struggling to lead an organization through the maze of changes wrought by the new economy needs to know where the ground is solid.

Second, people who have to make real business decisions every day and then live with the consequences know that there is no list of five, or seven, or ten rules that will guarantee success, however clever the alliteration. They also know that there are few absolutes in management and that frameworks are helpful only if you know how and when to apply them.

There are no silver bullets in this collection of articles from the *Harvard Business Review*. What it offers instead is some of the best recent thinking in print about managing in the new economy. As the *Review*'s strategy editor over the past five years, I had the privilege of editing almost all of the pieces I have selected for this volume. Read as a book, rather than as individual pieces, the collection is intended to help readers make sense of the new managerial agenda. It suggests there is a good deal more continuity and coherence to the new work of management than would appear on the surface.

The book has three parts. Part I, "Competition and Strategy," frames the strategic issues of the new economy. How do changes in information technology alter the familiar structures of industries and of organizations? How do companies create value in a knowledge-based economy? How does globalization change the way companies compete and the way they are managed? How should executives develop strategies in light of the huge uncertainties they face and the information they have?

Written by authors often associated with different "camps" in the strategy wars, I find these articles remarkable for what they have in common. All are grounded in the bedrock of economic thinking that is as relevant to the new economy as to the old. Each in its way teaches us to apply robust analytic models of strategy and competition—value chain thinking, for example—to new conditions in the business environment.

Part II, as the title suggests, turns to issues of "Leadership and Organization." The knowledge economy makes new demands on managers. More than ever, it is critical for an organization to tap the creative energies of its people. What does effective leadership of knowledge work look like? Will free agency obsolete big organizations? In an economy where organizations are temporary, how can individuals take more responsibility for their own effectiveness? In a culturally diverse global economy, what become the foundations for ethical leadership?

So much of the buzz about managing in the new economy has left the impression that all companies must be run the same way—with empowered workforces in flat organizations. The articles here go deeper, beyond the contemporary fads. There is a good deal of wisdom—coupled with hardheaded economic thinking—about enduring values, about people as people and not as "human resources," and about the purposes organizations serve.

In Part III, "Ideas at Work," all of the themes and theories discussed earlier come to life as we listen to three CEOs describe how they and their organizations are tackling the challenges of managing in the new economy. Articles about management tend to be analytic, focusing on one dimension of what we all know to be a multidimensional beast. They enrich our intellectual understanding of one piece of the puzzle.

These interviews attempt to capture the whole puzzle. Each of the CEOs faces opportunities and obstacles in one way or another characteristic of the new economy. Each has crafted a unique and coherent competitive strategy. Each is leading an organization in creative ways tailored to execute that strategy.

Part I: Competition and Strategy

The collection begins with "Strategy and the New Economics of Information" by Philip B. Evans and Thomas S. Wurster of the Boston Consulting Group. It is the most lucid account I have read about why the revolution in information technology is having and will continue to have such a profound impact on all businesses, and not just on high-tech or information companies. It provides a framework for understanding the "deep structure" of the network economy and the principles underlying the massive restructuring of industries, which will continue well into the next century.

The fundamental shift in the economics of information currently underway is less about technology than about the fact that a new behavior is reaching critical mass. Millions of people at home and at work are connecting electronically. When information is carried by things—by a salesperson or by a piece of direct mail, for example—it goes where the things go and no further. But once everyone is connected electronically, information can travel by itself. What is truly revolutionary about the explosion in connectivity is the possibility it offers to unbundle information from its physical carrier. And that, in turn, allows companies to create new value propositions and to split apart and reconfigure existing value chains.

Value chain thinking—one of many seminal ideas in strategy we owe to the earlier work of Michael E. Porter of the Harvard Business School—underlies many of the articles in this collection. The concept captures the fundamental and enduring economic logic of business. A company's value chain consists of all the activities a company performs to design, produce, market, deliver, and support its products. The value chains of companies that supply and buy from one another collectively make up the industry's value chain, its particular configuration of competitors, suppliers, distribution channels, and customers.

While we tend to think of value chains as a succession of physical activities, Evans and Wurster remind us that value chains also include all the information that flows within a company and between a company and its suppliers, distributors, and customers. They explain how the cost of information, especially the trade-off between richness and reach, plays a determining role in the structure of any company or industry. The new connectivity breaks that old trade-off.

Rethinking strategy in light of the new economics of information is one of the core issues of the new economy. Rethinking how value is created in a knowledge-based economy—and how that affects competition—is a second major issue and the subject of Porter's "Clusters and the New Economics of Competition."

Today's economic map of the world offers striking evidence that innovation and competitive success in many fields is geographically concentrated in clusters. Silicon Valley and Hollywood are among the best-known examples, but there are hundreds of similarly configured clusters around the globe. By demonstrating how clusters work, Porter shows us the dynamism of modern competition: Competitive advantage rests on productivity, which in turn demands a steady drumbeat of innovation.

Vibrant clusters stimulate innovation. They function as an alternative organizational form to vertical integration, allowing individual enterprises to coordinate effectively with each other without sacrificing the flexibility so critical to the fast pace of global competition. Within the confines of a cluster, specialized know-how and the transfer of knowledge across organizations and institutions help individual companies to innovate continually and to stay at the productivity frontier.

Clusters offer a pool of skilled employees and specialized suppliers, as well as access to information and new ideas. Local rivalry and peer pressure play an important role, motivating executives to outdo each other. What Porter describes as a paradox of the global economy is at the same time a truism of the knowledge economy: Competitive advantage lies increasingly in local things—knowledge, relationships, and motivation that distant rivals cannot match.

Clusters highlight the uniqueness of a location as a source of competitive advantage. Looking at the global economy through a different lens, C.K. Prahalad and Kenneth Lieberthal see the uniqueness of locations as both an opportunity and a threat. Their focus is new markets. Specifically, they lay out what it will take for Western companies to succeed in the four biggest emerging markets, which together promise the lion's share of future economic growth. "The End of Corporate Imperialism"—the title refers to the assumption that everyone must be just like "us"—tackles globalization, the third of the defining issues of the new economy.

Many observers worry that Western multinationals will overrun traditional local cultures in places like China and India. Prahalad and Lieberthal, professors at the University of Michigan, turn this familiar concern on its head. The question they urge business leaders to ask is how the multinationals themselves will be changed. Success in the emerging markets, they argue, will require new business models and resource shifts on such a scale that the multinationals themselves will be transformed. Hence the end of corporate imperialism. The cultural and economic realities of the major emerging markets, combined with their sheer size, will demand radically different approaches to strategy and organization.

In describing markets such as China, India, Brazil, and Indonesia, the operative word is *emerging*. No one, least of all the authors, is suggesting that such huge opportunities come without huge risks. In fact, all of the three defining shifts of the new economy—in the economics of information, in the relative value of knowledge, and in the globalization of trade—combine to create uncertainty, to destabilize existing strategies and industry structures. Decision making in the face of uncertainty has always been the major challenge of strategy. The next two articles are about the information and the tools needed to think strategically in the new economy.

Traditional approaches to strategic planning lead executives to view uncertainty in a binary way, according to McKinsey's Hugh Courtney, Jane Kirkland, and Patrick Viguerie in "Strategy under Uncertainty." They assume that the world is either certain, and therefore open to precise cash flow predictions about the future, or uncertain, and completely unpredictable. Either extreme can lead to bad decisions and missed opportunities.

Even the most uncertain environments contain a good deal of strategically relevant information. "Strategy under Uncertainty" offers a framework for sifting through that information. Most strategic decisions, the authors argue, fall into one of four discrete levels of uncertainty. The kind of analysis companies rely on and the strategic postures they choose must be tailored to the level of uncertainty they face.

Options thinking is one of the most promising and potentially powerful of the new tools for decision making under uncertainty. Traditional corporate finance, with its reliance on net present value (NPV) calculations, offers only two possible actions: invest or don't invest. But decision making in the real world is more textured. As soon as we start executing a strategy, we begin learning—about business conditions, competitors' actions, technical developments—and we need to respond flexibly to what we learn.

Options thinking addresses the issues an active manager will care about: not only whether to invest or not, but when to invest, and what to do in the meantime. In financial terms, then, a business strategy is much more like a series of options than it is like a series of static cash flows. That insight underlies Timothy A. Luehrman's "Strategy as a Portfolio of Real Options." Luehrman has written a series of articles for the *Harvard Business Review* on valuation.

The discounted cash flow approach used almost universally to estimate the value of a strategy locks managers into a static and a passive mind-set. It is built on the assumption that a company will follow a predetermined plan, regardless of how events unfold. Options, on the other hand, reflect the more active role managers play in adjusting their decisions as they learn. By aligning the financial model for valuation with the nature of the uncertainties managers face, options deliver the extra insight to help executives think strategically on their feet.

For a generation of professionally trained business leaders, net present value has been more than a financial tool. In essence, it embodied a whole managerial mind-set. "Strategy as a Portfolio of Real Options" also heralds a new way of thinking. As Luehrman describes it, the options approach is more than a technical tool for finance specialists; it is a way of conceptualizing business problems that encourages active and flexible management of future opportunities.

Part II: Leadership and Organization

Trust has always been important in organizations, but in the new economy—where value creation depends increasingly on ideas and innovation—it is essential. "Fair Process: Managing in the Knowledge Economy" by INSEAD's W. Chan Kim and Renée Mauborgne describes a management tool for companies struggling to make the transition from a production-based to a knowledge-based economy.

Unlike the traditional factors of production—land, labor, and capital—knowledge is a resource locked in the human mind. Creating and sharing knowledge are intangible activities that can be neither supervised nor forced on people. They happen only when people cooperate willingly. Traditional management science has an arsenal of tools to promote efficiency and consistency by controlling behavior and compelling people to comply with management dictates—tools for allocating resources, creating economic incentives and rewards, monitoring and measuring performance, and manipulating organizational structures to set lines of authority.

These conventional levers still have a role to play, but they have little to do with engendering trust, which encourages the exchange of ideas, which, in turn, promotes innovation. Kim and Mauborgne note that individuals are most likely to trust and cooperate freely with systems—whether they themselves win or lose by those systems—when *fair process* is observed. Not to be confused with consensus building or empowerment, fair process is a way to approach decision making that follows three principles: engage people in the decisions that affect them; explain the thinking underlying decisions once they have been taken; and set clear expectations about the new rules of the game.

"When people are trusted," writes Henry Mintzberg, "they do not have to be empowered." Knowledge workers need to be trusted, and leading them is more about inspiring than supervising. In "Covert Leadership: Notes on Managing Professionals," Mintzberg, who teaches at McGill and INSEAD, observes that in a good deal of knowledge work, the profession itself, not the manager, supplies much of the structure, coordination, and control.

Leaders in professional organizations often face a special challenge—leading among ostensible equals. Thus they must learn to manage under a set of constraints that leave them neither in absolute control of others nor completely powerless, but functioning somewhere in between. Mintzberg urges a greater appreciation in all managerial work of what he calls covert leadership: not leadership actions in and of themselves—motivating, coaching, directing—but rather unobtrusive actions that infuse all the other things managers do, that inspire others. He describes such leadership as managing by doing, which he warns can be done only by someone with an intimate understanding of what is being managed.

Both "Fair Process" and "Covert Leadership" have to do with how individuals within organizations are treated, especially by their managers. In "The Dawn of the E-Lance Economy," Thomas W. Malone and Robert J. Laubacher of MIT question whether individuals will continue to work within organizations as we know them today.

While the authors acknowledge that an economy consisting of electronically connected freelancers is a radical concept, they note that in many ways it is already upon us. We see it in the emergence of virtual companies, in the rise of outsourcing and telecommuting, and in the proliferation of freelance and temporary workers. Even within large organizations, we see it in the increasing importance of ad hoc project teams, in the rise of "intrapreneurs," and in the formation of independent business units.

At the heart of the "e-lance" economy is the idea that by changing the way work is done, electronic networks may lead to a new kind of economy centered on the individual. Consider the development of Linux software. A temporary community of self-managed individuals came together, connected by the Internet, to engage in a common task. Their job complete, the network disbanded.

Malone and Laubacher discuss the organizational implications of networks and connectivity, picking up where Evans and Wurster leave off in "Strategy and the New Economics of Information." When it is cheaper to conduct transactions internally, within the bounds of a corporation, organizations grow larger. But when it is cheaper to conduct them externally, in the open market, organizations stay small or shrink. Such new coordination technologies as powerful personal computers and broad electronic networks enable us to return to the preindustrial model of tiny autonomous businesses conducting transactions with one another in the market. The one crucial difference is that electronic networks allow small companies to tap into the global reservoirs of information, expertise, and financing that used to be available only to large companies.

Malone and Laubacher say we need a new mind-set for thinking about the transformation of management that these new organizational models imply. When we see a flock of birds in formation, they write, we assume the bird in front is the leader, somehow determining the organization of all the other birds. In fact, biologists tell us, the bird in front is no more important than any other. Each is simply flying by a set of rules, and they are all essential to the pattern they are forming.

In "The Post-Capitalist Executive," a *Harvard Business Review* interview by T George Harris, Peter F. Drucker certainly heeds the call for a new mind-set for thinking about the relationship between individuals and organizations. Drucker began writing about the knowledge worker more than 30 years ago, and he has been consistently provocative and insightful about the transformation of industrial economies into knowledge economies.

To build achieving organizations today, Drucker says, you must replace rank and power with responsibility and mutual understanding. Drucker explains with characteristic directness and sense just what that means. Contrary to popular thinking, the answer is neither "participation" nor "empowerment." Instead, the key is self-awareness, the difficult and demanding discipline of thinking about who you are and what you do best. While self-awareness has always been important, Drucker notes, in the knowledge economy it is essential for survival.

Not long ago, most people were either farmers, factory workers, tradesmen, or domestic servants; it was easy to know what others did at work. This is no longer true. As knowledge work has become more specialized, the burden has shifted to individuals not only to define what their own contribution to the organization will be, but also to take responsibility for telling others around them what their priorities are. "When you don't communicate," Drucker writes, "you don't get to do the things you are good at."

Values are an important part of self-management and self-awareness. While ethics are universal, values are matters of deep belief about which honest people, and organizations, can disagree. As Drucker has previously stated, to work in an organization whose value system is unacceptable or incompatible with one's own condemns a person both to frustration and to poor performance.

Moving from the personal to the universal, Part II ends with "Values in Tension: Ethics Away from Home" by Thomas Donaldson. Even the best-informed, best-intentioned executives must rethink their assumptions about business practice in foreign settings. Donaldson, who teaches business ethics at Wharton, offers a set of guiding principles to help executives answer the questions, When is different just different, and When is different wrong? He doesn't shrink from the especially thorny (and common) problem of what to do when a host country's ethical standards are lower than the home country's.

Part III: Ideas at Work

Part III begins with "The Power of Virtual Integration: An Interview with Dell Computer's Michael Dell." When Michael Dell dropped out of school to start his company in 1984, he might not have been able to tell you what the term "value chain" meant, but he certainly grasped the basic economics. His simple business insight was that he could bypass the dealer channel through which personal computers were then sold. Instead, he would sell directly to customers and build customized products to order. In one swoop, Dell eliminated the reseller's markup and the costs and risks associated with carrying large inventories of finished goods. The formula became known as the direct business model, and it gave Dell a substantial cost advantage.

Dell's product line has expanded over the years. In addition to desktop personal computers, the company now sells a broader range of hardware—laptops, servers, and workstations. But make no mistake, Dell sells physical *things*, manufactured goods that must be assembled and transported and delivered and serviced. It sounds a lot like the old, tangible economy.

Is Dell, then, stuck in the past of material goods and physical flows? Or is it the quintessential new economy company, creating wealth through ideas and information, and doing so with incredible speed and flexibility? In fact, Dell is both.

Companies have always thrived by offering customers superior value, giving them more for less. For the most part, they offer better value by shrinking the time and the resources consumed in meeting customers' needs. (Recall that the adage "Time is money" appeared in 1748, in Ben Franklin's *Advice to a Young Tradesman*.) The basic economics of business haven't changed, but like many other companies today, Dell is harnessing the tools of the knowledge economy—

information and technology—to bring new levels of efficiency and productivity to the old world of tangible goods.

Dell stays nimble by focusing on only a few elements of the value chain and letting its suppliers worry about the rest. It has found ways to work across organizational boundaries with suppliers and with customers that Michael Dell calls "virtual integration," a term which suggests his company is getting the best of both worlds: the coordination of vertical integration plus the flexibility of a virtual organization.

Dell's strategy has been remarkably consistent over the company's 15-year life, a fact that contradicts the shibboleth of the new economy that the world simply moves too fast for strategy to matter. Hypercompetition and turbulence, the argument goes, will obsolete any strategy as soon as it is articulated. Tell that to Michael Dell. Under his leadership, continuity in strategy has driven ongoing innovation in execution, and it has created great wealth for shareholders.

As Dell has grown, it has rapidly recut its customer base into successively finer segments—and it has changed the structure of its own organization in order to map onto those new customer segments. This flexible approach to organization keeps the company close to its customers and holds businesses to a manageable size.

Halfway around the globe, Victor Fung, chairman of a large Hong Kong–based export trading company, shares Michael Dell's obsession with serving customers, with speed and flexibility. His company, Li & Fung, was founded in China 90 years ago by his grandfather. Today, however, it is anything but a staid family enterprise. Part of a new breed of focused Asian multinationals, Li & Fung has been an innovator in the development of supply chain management.

On behalf of its customers, primarily American and European retailers, Li & Fung works with an ever-expanding network of thousands of suppliers—mostly in emerging markets—sourcing clothing and other consumer goods ranging from toys to fashion accessories to luggage. The goal is to deliver a new type of value added, the best products on a global scale. Instead of asking which country does the best job overall, Li & Fung dissects the manufacturing value chain and looks at each step for the solution best tailored to the customers' needs. Thus, in effect, Li & Fung creates a customized value chain for every customer order.

The result, as the title of my interview with him suggests, is "Fast, Global, and Entrepreneurial: Supply Chain Management Hong Kong Style." Supply chain management—buying the right things and shortening delivery cycles—is critical for any time-sensitive product. What

Li & Fung does for its retailing customers many large manufacturing companies are increasingly doing for themselves. Supply chain management is not just an inflated title for yesterday's purchasing department; it is new work, requiring expertise in a host of information-intensive service functions, including product development, sourcing, financing, shipping, handling, and logistics.

For anyone trying to make sense of the new economy, Li & Fung is a fascinating case study blending the old and the new. Information and relationships—coupled with entrepreneurial drive and motivation—are the core of its competitive strategy. As the emerging markets open up new sources of supply, Li & Fung's role as an information node becomes ever more valuable.

As the company grows and becomes more multinational, it seeks to maintain its entrepreneurial roots. "The last thing we want to do," says Victor Fung, "is to run the company like the big multinationals." One way to remain entrepreneurial is to organize around small divisions, each focused solely on the needs of one customer. Such divisions can be easily created or collapsed, allowing Li & Fung to change course rapidly when demand dictates.

Both Dell and Li & Fung use information to move things faster, thus taking time and cost out of the value chain. As Michael Dell puts it, "We substitute information for inventory." "Growth through Global Sustainability: An Interview with Monsanto's CEO, Robert B. Shapiro" takes this idea one giant step further. Information, says Shapiro, is the key to reconciling economic growth and environmental sustainability. We can grow without destroying the planet if we "create value and satisfy people's needs by increasing the information component of what's produced and diminishing the amount of stuff."

That's the thinking behind Monsanto's decision to divest the company's chemicals business in order to focus instead on biotechnology. The latter, Shapiro explains, is really a subset of information technology because it is about DNA-encoded information. In Monsanto's agricultural business, the old chemicals model was to spray a plant with pesticides. The new biotech model is to genetically code the plant so it repels harmful insects. It's the essence of the knowledge economy, productivity growth that is essentially weightless. Putting the right information in the plant replaces making, distributing, and applying tons of chemicals.

Thus Monsanto is using high technology to transform one of the oldest activities of mankind, agriculture. The company is placing big bets on new businesses built around the concept of environmental sustainability. The world cannot avoid needing sustainability in the long run, Shapiro argues. It represents a strategic discontinuity, the kind of shift that determines the future of a business.

In the interview Shapiro explains the thought process behind Monsanto's massive shift in strategy, arguing that it's critical to distinguish what's knowable about the future from what isn't. Sometimes major discontinuities are predictable because they are implicit in today's demographics. Thus, far from being a "soft" emotional or ethical issue, Shapiro sees sustainable development as a piece of rational business logic. Billions of people in the developing world expect the quality of their lives to improve—and it must. At the same time, the earth's closed physical system can't withstand a systematic increase of material things. It can, however, support exponential increases of information and knowledge. Environmentally sustainable businesses will substitute information for stuff, and services for products.

Nowhere is this more critical than in the emerging markets. Shapiro argues that we must help the developing economies avoid reliving "the entire industrial revolution with all its waste, its energy use, and its pollution." Companies like Monsanto can help, Shapiro explains, but only if strong intellectual property rights let them reconcile environmental and economic goals.

For Victor Fung, the entrepreneurial challenge is to stay responsive to customers and to continue to uncover new sources of supply. For Shapiro, the challenge is even more fundamental, creating new businesses. Most organizations today, he maintains, struggle with innovation and creativity. There's no longer a script you can ask people to follow. Instead, people will be most effective when they organize themselves around tasks and goals that they care about passionately. Shapiro's description of how Monsanto has embraced sustainable development echoes Drucker's self-management and Mintzberg's covert leadership. People, Shapiro says, will give more if they can figure out what they can contribute out of their own authentic abilities and beliefs. As long as someone else predetermines what they are going to do all day, you're asking them to behave inauthentically.

And in the new economy, that appears to be a managerial approach with a limited future.

Note

1. See Alan Greenspan, "Is There a New Economy?" *California Management Review* 41, no. 1 (Fall 1998): 75–76.

PART

I

Competition
and Strategy

1
Strategy and the New Economics of Information

Philip B. Evans and Thomas S. Wurster

A fundamental shift in the economics of information is under way—a shift that is less about any specific new technology than about the fact that a new behavior is reaching critical mass. Millions of people at home and at work are communicating electronically using universal, open standards. This explosion in connectivity is the latest—and, for business strategists, the most important—wave in the information revolution.

Over the past decade, managers have focused on adapting their operating processes to new information technologies. Dramatic as those *operating* changes have been, a more profound transformation of the business landscape lies ahead. Executives—and not just those in high-tech or information companies—will be forced to rethink the *strategic* fundamentals of their businesses. Over the next decade, the new economics of information will precipitate changes in the structure of entire industries and in the ways companies compete.

Early signs of this change are not hard to find. Consider the recent near-demise of Encyclopædia Britannica, one of the strongest and best-known brand names in the world. Since 1990, sales of Britannica's multivolume sets have plummeted by more than 50%. CD-ROMs came from nowhere and devastated the printed encyclopedia business as we traditionally understand it.

How was that possible? The *Encyclopædia Britannica* sells for somewhere in the region of $1,500 to $2,200. An encyclopedia on CD-ROM, such as Microsoft Encarta, sells for around $50. And many people get Encarta for free because it comes with their personal computers or CD-ROM drives. The cost of producing a set of encyclopedias—printing, binding, and physical distribution—is about $200 to $300. The cost of producing a CD-ROM is about $1.50. This is a spectacular, if small, example of the way information technologies and new competition can disrupt the conventional value proposition of an established business.

Imagine what the people at Britannica thought was happening. The editors probably viewed CD-ROMs as nothing more than electronic versions of inferior products. Encarta's content is licensed from the Funk & Wagnalls encyclopedia, which was historically sold in supermarkets. Microsoft merely spruced up that content with public-domain illustrations and movie clips. The way *Britannica*'s editors must have seen it, Encarta was not an encyclopedia at all. It was a toy.

Judging from their initial inaction, Britannica's executives failed to understand what their customers were really buying. Parents had been buying *Britannica* less for its intellectual content than out of a desire to do the right thing for their children. Today when parents want to "do the right thing," they buy their kids a computer.

The computer, then, is *Britannica*'s real competitor. And along with the computer come a dozen CD-ROMs, one of which happens to be— as far as the customer is concerned—a more-or-less perfect substitute for the *Britannica*.

When the threat became obvious, Britannica did create a CD-ROM version—but to avoid undercutting the sales force, the company included it free with the printed version and charged $1,000 to anyone buying the CD-ROM by itself. Revenues continued to decline. The best salespeople left. And Britannica's owner, a trust controlled by the University of Chicago, finally sold out. Under new management, the company is now trying to rebuild the business around the Internet.

Britannica's downfall is more than a parable about the dangers of complacency. It demonstrates how quickly and drastically the new economics of information can change the rules of competition, allowing new players and substitute products to render obsolete such traditional sources of competitive advantage as a sales force, a supreme brand, and even the world's best content.

When managers hear this story, many respond, "Interesting, but it has nothing to do with *my* business. Britannica is in an information business. Thank goodness I'm not." They feel less secure, however, when they learn that the largest chunk of Britannica's cost structure was not the editorial content—which constituted only about 5% of costs—but the direct sales force. Britannica's vulnerability was due mainly to its dependence on the economics of a different kind of information: the economics of intensive personal selling. Many businesses fit that description, among them automobiles, insurance, real estate, and travel.

Every Business Is an Information Business

In many industries not widely considered information businesses, information actually represents a large percentage of the cost structure. About one-third of the cost of health care in the United States—some $300 billion—is the cost of capturing, storing, and processing such information as patients' records, physicians' notes, test results, and insurance claims.

More fundamentally, information is the glue that holds together the structure of all businesses. A company's value chain consists of all the activities it performs to design, produce, market, deliver, and support its product. The value chains of companies that supply and buy from one another collectively make up an industry's value chain, its particular configuration of competitors, suppliers, distribution channels, and customers.[1]

When we think about a value chain, we tend to visualize a linear flow of physical activities. But the value chain also includes all the information that flows within a company and between a company and its suppliers, its distributors, and its existing or potential customers. Supplier relationships, brand identity, process coordination, customer loyalty, employee loyalty, and switching costs all depend on various kinds of information.

When managers talk about the value of customer relationships, for example, what they really mean is the proprietary information that they have about their customers and that their customers have about the company and its products. Brands, after all, are nothing but the information—real or imagined, intellectual or emotional—that consumers have in their heads about a product. And the tools used to build brands—advertising, promotion, and even shelf space—are themselves information or ways of delivering information.

Similarly, information defines supplier relationships. Having a relationship means that two companies have established certain channels of communication built around personal acquaintance, mutual understanding, shared standards, electronic data interchange (EDI) systems, or synchronized production systems.

In any buyer-seller relationship, information can determine the relative bargaining power of the players. Auto dealers, for example, know the best local prices for a given model. Customers—unless they invest a lot of time shopping around—generally do not. Much of the dealer's margin depends on that *asymmetry* of information.

Not only does information define and constrain the relationship among the various players in a value chain, but in many businesses it also forms the basis for competitive advantage—even when the cost of that information is trivial and the product or service is thoroughly physical. To cite some of the best-known examples, American Airlines for a long time used its control of the SABRE reservation system to achieve higher levels of capacity utilization than its competitors. Wal-Mart has exploited its EDI links with suppliers to increase its inventory turns dramatically. And Nike has masterfully employed advertising, endorsements, and the microsegmentation of its market to transform sneakers into high-priced fashion goods. All three companies compete as much on information as they do on their physical product.

In many ways, then, information and the mechanisms for delivering it stabilize corporate and industry structures and underlie competitive advantage. But the informational components of value are so deeply embedded in the physical value chain that, in some cases, we are just beginning to acknowledge their separate existence.

When information is carried by things—by a salesperson or by a piece of direct mail, for example—it goes where the things go and no further. It is constrained to follow the linear flow of the physical value chain. But once everyone is connected electronically, information can travel by itself. The traditional link between the flow of product-related information and the flow of the product itself, between the economics of information and the economics of things, can be broken. What is truly revolutionary about the explosion in connectivity is the possibility it offers to unbundle information from its physical carrier.

The Trade-Off between Richness and Reach

Let's back up for a minute to consider why this is such a revolutionary proposition. To the extent that information is embedded in physical modes of delivery, its economics are governed by a basic law: the trade-off between richness and reach. *Reach* simply means the number of people, at home or at work, exchanging information. *Richness* is defined by three aspects of the information itself. The first is *bandwidth*, or the amount of information that can be moved from sender to receiver in a given time. Stock quotes are narrowband; a film is broadband. The second aspect is the degree to which the information can be *customized*. For example, an advertisement on television is far less customized than a personal sales pitch but reaches far more people. The third aspect is *interactivity*. Dialogue is possible for a small group, but to reach millions of people the message must be a monologue.

In general, the communication of rich information has required proximity and dedicated channels whose costs or physical constraints have limited the size of the audience to which the information could be sent. Conversely, the communication of information to a large audience has required compromises in bandwidth, customization, and interactivity. (See Exhibit 1-1 "The Traditional Economics of Information.") This pervasive trade-off has shaped how companies communicate, collaborate, and conduct transactions internally and with customers, suppliers, and distributors.

A company's marketing mix, for example, is determined by apportioning resources according to this trade-off. A company can embed its message in an advertisement, a piece of customized direct mail, or a personal sales pitch—alternatives increasing in richness but diminishing in reach.

When companies conduct business with one another, the number of parties they deal with is inversely proportional to the richness of the information they need to exchange: Citibank can trade currencies with hundreds of other banks each minute because the data exchange requires little richness; conversely, Wal-Mart has narrowed its reach by moving to fewer and larger long-term supplier contracts to allow a richer coordination of marketing and logistical systems.

Within a corporation, traditional concepts of span of control and hierarchical reporting are predicated on the belief that communication cannot be rich and broad simultaneously. Jobs are structured to channel rich communication among a few people standing in a hierarchical relationship to one another (upward or downward), and broader communication is effected through the indirect routes of the organizational pyramid. Indeed, there is an entire economic theory (pioneered by Ronald H. Coase and Oliver E. Williamson[2]) suggesting that the boundaries of the corporation are set by the economics of exchanging information: organizations enable the exchange of rich information among a narrow, internal group; markets enable the exchange of thinner information among a larger, external group. The point at which one mode becomes less cost-effective than the other determines the boundaries of the corporation.

The trade-off between richness and reach, then, not only governs the old economics of information but also is fundamental to a whole

Exhibit 1-1   The Traditional Economics of Information

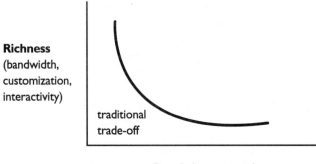

set of premises about how the business world works. And it is precisely this trade-off that is now being blown up.

The rapid emergence of universal technical standards for communication, allowing everybody to communicate with everybody else at essentially zero cost, is a sea change. And it is as much the agreement on standards as the technology itself that is making this change possible. It's easy to get lost in the technical jargon, but the important principle here is that the *same* technical standards underlie all the so-called Net technologies: the *Internet*, which connects everyone; *extranets*, which connect companies to one another; and *intranets*, which connect individuals within companies.

Those emerging open standards and the explosion in the number of people and organizations connected by networks are freeing information from the channels that have been required to exchange it, making those channels unnecessary or uneconomical. Although the standards may not be ideal for any individual application, users are finding that they are good enough for most purposes today. And they are improving exponentially. Over time, organizations and individuals will be able to extend their reach by many orders of magnitude, often with a negligible sacrifice of richness.

Where once a sales force, a system of branches, a printing press, a chain of stores, or a delivery fleet served as formidable barriers to entry because they took years and heavy investment to build, in this new world, they could suddenly become expensive liabilities. New competitors on the Internet will be able to come from nowhere to steal customers. Similarly, the replacement of expensive, proprietary, legacy systems with inexpensive, open extranets will make it easier and cheaper for companies to, for example, bid for supply contracts, join a virtual factory, or form a competing supply chain.

Inside large corporations, the emergence of universal, open standards for exchanging information over intranets fosters cross-functional teams and accelerates the demise of hierarchical structures and their proprietary information systems. (See Exhibit 1-2 "The End of Channels and Hierarchies.")

The Deconstruction of the Value Chain

The changing economics of information threaten to undermine established value chains in many sectors of the economy, requiring virtually every company to rethink its strategy—not incrementally, but fundamentally. What will happen, for instance, to category killers such as Toys "R" Us and Home Depot when a search engine on the Internet gives consumers more choice than any store? What will be the point of having a supplier relationship with General Electric when it posts its purchasing requirements on an Internet bulletin board and entertains bids from anybody inclined to respond? What will happen to health care providers and insurers if a uniform electronic format for patient records eliminates a major barrier that today discourages patients from switching hospitals or doctors?

Consider the future of newspapers, which like most businesses are built on a vertically integrated value chain. Journalists and advertisers supply copy, editors lay it out, presses create the physical product, and an elaborate distribution system delivers it to readers each morning.

Newspaper companies exist as intermediaries between the journalist and the reader because there are enormous economies of scale in printing and distribution. But when high-resolution electronic tablets advance to the point where readers consider them a viable alternative to newsprint, those traditional economies of scale will become irrelevant. Editors—or even journalists—will be able to E-mail content directly to readers.

Freed from the necessity of subscribing to entire physical newspapers, readers will be able to mix and match content from a virtually unlimited number of sources. News could be downloaded daily from different electronic-news services. Movie reviews, recipes, and travel features could come just as easily from magazine or book publishers. Star columnists, cartoonists, or the U.S. Weather Service could send

Exhibit 1-2 The End of Channels and Hierarchies

In today's world, rich content passes through media, which we call channels, *that can reach only a limited audience. The existence of channels creates hierarchy, both of choice (people have to gather rich information in an order dictated by the structure of the channels) and of power (some people have better access to rich infor-*
(continued at top of facing page)

Hierarchical Decision Tree

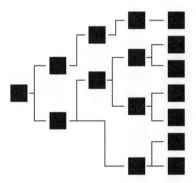

Hierarchy of power is illustrated by the traditional organization chart, in which senior executives have a wider span of knowledge than do their subordinates.

Hierarchical Organization

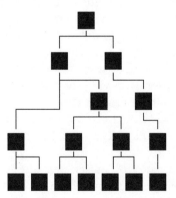

Hierarchy enables richness but constrains choice and creates asymmetries in information. The alternative to hierarchy is *markets,* which are symmetrical and open to the extent that they are *perfect.* But traditional markets trade only in less rich information.

(continued from top of previous page)
mation than others do). Hierarchy of choice is illustrated by the decision tree along which consumers are compelled to do their shopping in the physical world: they must choose a street, then a shop, then a department, then a shelf, then a product. They cannot select in any other sequence. They can return to the street and search along a different path, of course, but only by expending time and effort.

When the trade-off between richness and reach is eliminated, channels are no longer necessary: everyone communicates richly with everyone else on the basis of shared standards. This might be termed *hyperarchy* after the hyperlinks of the World Wide Web.

Hyperarchy

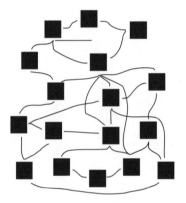

The World Wide Web is a hyperarchy. So are a deconstructed value chain within a business and a deconstructed supply chain within an industry. So are intranets. So are structures allowing fluid, team-based collaboration at work. So, too, is the pattern of amorphous and permeable corporate boundaries characteristic of the companies in Silicon Valley. (So, too, incidentally, are the architectures of object-oriented programming in software and of packet switching in telecommunications.)

Hyperarchy challenges *all* hierarchies, whether of logic or of power, with the possibility (or the threat) of random access and information symmetry. It challenges all markets with the possibility that far richer information can be exchanged than that involved in trading products and certificates of ownership. When the principles of hyperarchy are thoroughly understood, they will provide a way to understand not only positioning strategies within businesses and industries but also more fundamental questions of corporate organization and identity.

their work directly to subscribers. Intermediaries—search engines, alert services, formatting software, or editorial teams—could format and package the content to meet readers' individual interests. It does not follow that all readers will choose to unbundle all the current content of the physical newspaper, but the principal logic for that bundle—the economics of printing—will be gone.

This transformation is probably inevitable but distant. As newspaper executives correctly point out, the broadsheet is still an extraordinarily cheap and user-friendly way to distribute information. Little electronic tablets are not going to replace it very soon.

However, the timing of total deconstruction is not really the issue. *Pieces* of the newspaper can be unbundled today. Classified advertising is a natural on-line product. Think how much easier it would be to submit, pay for, update, search through, and respond to classified ads electronically. Stripping away classifieds, however, would remove 25% of the typical newspaper's revenues but less than 10% of its costs.

Newspaper companies have moved aggressively into the electronic-classifieds business. They have exploited their advantage as makers of the original print marketplace to provide an integrated print and electronic offering that reaches the widest population of buyers and sellers. This electronic offering preserves the margins of 60% to 80% that newspapers need from the classifieds to cover their fixed printing costs.

But as more and more people use the electronic medium, companies focused on targeted segments of the electronic-classifieds market (operating on, say, 15% margins) will gain share. The greater their share, by definition, the more attractive they will become to buyers and sellers. Eventually, the newspapers will either lose business or (more likely) retain it by settling for much lower margins.

Either way, the subsidy that supports the fixed costs of the print product will be gone. So newspapers will cut content or raise prices for readers and advertisers, accelerating their defection. That, in turn, will create opportunities for another focused competitor to pick off a different part of the value chain. Thus the greatest vulnerability for newspapers is not the total substitution of a new business model but a steady erosion through a sequence of partial substitutions that will make the current business model unsustainable.

Retail banking is ripe for a similar upheaval. The current business model depends on a vertically integrated value chain through which multiple products are originated, packaged, sold, and cross-sold through proprietary distribution channels. The high costs of distribution drive economies of utilization and scale and thus govern strategy in retail banking as it works today.

Home electronic banking looks at first glance like another, but cheaper, distribution channel. Many banks see it that way, hoping that its wide-spread adoption might enable them to scale down their higher-cost physical channels. Some banks are even offering proprietary software and electronic transactions for free. But something much deeper has happened than the emergence of a new distribution channel. Customers now can access information and make transactions in a variety of new ways.

Some 10 million people in the United States regularly use personal-financial-management software such as Intuit's Quicken or Microsoft Money to manage their checkbooks and integrate their personal financial affairs. Current versions of these programs can use modems to access electronic switches operated by CheckFree or VISA Interactive, which in turn route instructions or queries to the customers' banks. Such a system lets customers pay bills, make transfers, receive electronic statements, and seamlessly integrate account data into their personal financial plans. In addition, almost all financial institutions supply information at their Web sites, which anybody on-line can access using a browser.

No single software program can achieve both richness and reach, yet. Quicken, Money, and proprietary bank software permit *rich* exchanges but only with the customer's own bank. Web browsers do much less but *reach* the entire universe of financial institutions. However, the software vendors and switch providers have the resources, and ultimately will be motivated, to form alliances with financial institutions to eliminate this artificial trade-off. Bridges between financial management software and the Web, combined with advances in reliability, security, digital signatures, and legally binding electronic contracts, will enable financial Web sites to provide the full range of banking services.

If that happens, the trade-off between richness and reach will be broken. Customers will be able to contact any financial institution for any kind of service or information. They will be able to maintain a balance sheet on their desktop, drawing on data from multiple institutions. They will be able to compare alternative product offerings and to sweep funds automatically between accounts at different institutions. Bulletin boards or auctioning software will allow customers to announce their product requirements and accept bids. Chat rooms will permit customers to share information with each other or get advice from experts.

The sheer breadth of choice available to potential customers will create the need for third parties to play the role of navigator or facilitating agent. For example, some companies will have an incentive to create (or simply make available) databases on interest rates, risk ratings, and service histories. Others will create insurance and mortgage calculators or intelligent-agent software that can search for and evaluate products. Still other companies will authenticate the identity of counterparties or serve as guarantors of performance, confidentiality, or creditworthiness. (See Exhibit 1-3 "The Transformation of Retail Banking.")

As it becomes easier for customers to switch from one supplier to another, the competitive value of one-stop shopping and established relationships will drop. Cross-selling will become more difficult. Information about customers' needs or behavior will be harder for companies to obtain. Competitive advantage will be determined product by product, and therefore providers with broad product lines will lose ground to focused specialists.

In this new world, distribution will be done by the phone company, statements by financial management software, facilitation by different kinds of agent software, and origination by any number of different kinds of product specialists. The integrated value chain of retail banking will have been deconstructed.

Deconstructed but not destroyed. All the old functions will still be performed, as well as some new ones. Banks will not become obsolete, but their current business definition will—specifically, the concept that a bank is an integrated business where multiple products are originated, packaged, sold, and cross-sold through proprietary distribution channels.

Many bankers—like encyclopedia executives—deny all this. They argue that most customers do not have personal computers and that many who do are not choosing to use them for banking. They point out that people worry about the security of on-line transactions and that consumers trust banks more than they trust software companies. All true. However, on-line technology is advancing inexorably. And because they generate a disproportionate share of deposits and fees, the 10% of the population that currently use personal-financial-management software probably account for 75% of the profits of the banking system.

Market research suggests that Quicken users are more likely to be loyal to their software than to their banks. In one study, half of them said that if they were changing banks *anyway*, they would require their new bank to support the software—that is, allow them to transact their business on-line using Quicken. Now, bank accounts churn at the rate of about 10% per year. If a bank that doesn't support Quicken loses half of the new Quicken-using customers it might otherwise attract every year, and if such customers churn at the average rate, then it follows that the bank will lose 3% to 5% of its retail-customer margin per year. Refusal to support Quicken (or provide an acceptable alternative) could undermine the entire value of a franchise within just a few years.

The deconstruction of the value chain in banking is not unprecedented. Fifteen years ago, *corporate* banking was a spread business—that is, banks made money by charging a higher interest rate for loans than they paid for deposits. Their business model required them to form deep relationships with their corporate customers so that they could pump their own products through that distribution system. But then, thanks to technology, corporate customers gained access to the same financial markets that the banks used. Today, corporate banking consists of small businesses that largely stand alone (even when they function under the umbrella of a big bank) and compete product by product. Credit flows directly from the ultimate lender to the ultimate borrower, facilitated by bankers who rate the risk, give advice, make markets, and serve as custodians. The bankers make money through the fees they charge for those individual services. Clients no longer bundle their purchases, and relationships are more volatile. Once critical, an advantage in distribution today counts for little.

Newspapers and banking are not special cases. The value chains of scores of other industries will become ripe for unbundling. The logic is most compelling—and therefore likely to strike soonest—in information businesses where the cost of physical distribution is high: newspapers, ticket sales, insurance, financial information, scientific publishing, software, and of course encyclopedias. But in any business whose physical value chain has been compromised for the sake of delivering information, there is an opportunity to unbundle the two, creating a separate information business and allowing (or compelling) the physical one to be streamlined. All it will take to deconstruct a business is a

Exhibit 1-3 *The Transformation of Retail Banking*

In today's integrated business model, the retail bank stands between the customer and the full range of financial services. But soon, through Internet technologies, customers will have direct access to product providers. As choices proliferate, totally new businesses will arise to help customers navigate through the expanded range of banking options.

Integrated Business Model

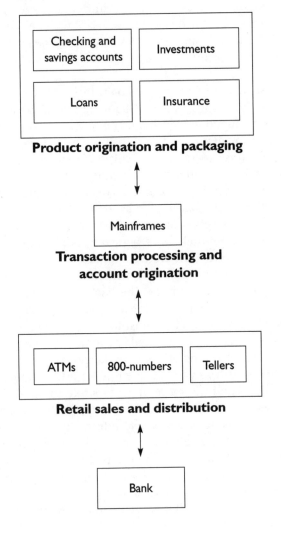

Reconfigured Business Model

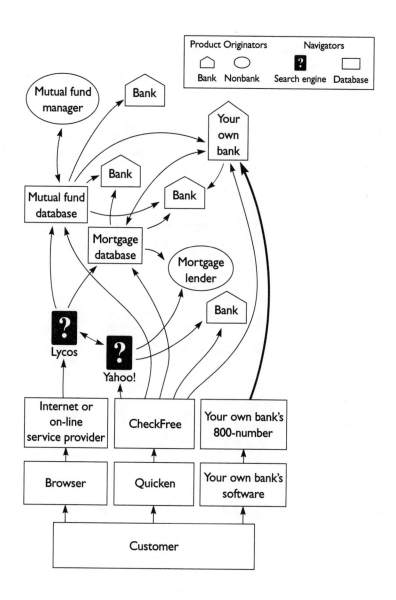

competitor that focuses on the vulnerable sliver of information in its value chain. (See "What Will Happen to Your Business?")

What Will Happen to Your Business?

All businesses will eventually be affected by the shifting economics of information, but not all at the same rate or in the same way. Answers to the following questions are a first step in determining how a business could be restructured:

1. How and where in the current value chain of this business is information a component of value?
2. Where are trade-offs currently being made between richness and reach in this business?
3. In what situations will these trade-offs be eliminated?
4. Which critical activities—especially informational activities—could be peeled off as stand-alone businesses?
5. Could the underlying physical business be run more efficiently if the information functions were stripped away?
6. What new activities—especially facilitating-agent roles—might be required?
7. Among the successor businesses, how would risks and rewards be distributed?
8. How would losing control over key activities affect the profitability of the current business model?
9. Which current strategic assets could become liabilities?
10. What new capabilities are needed to dominate the new businesses that will emerge?

Implications for Competitive Advantage

Deconstructing a vertically integrated value chain does more than transform the structure of a business or an industry—it alters the sources of competitive advantage. The new economics of information therefore not only present threats to established businesses but also represent a new set of opportunities. Every industry will shift according to its own dynamics, and those shifts will occur at different speeds and with varying intensity. No single set of predictions can be applied across the board, but some fundamental strategic implications of the changing economics of information can be drawn:

EXISTING VALUE CHAINS WILL FRAGMENT INTO MULTIPLE BUSINESSES, EACH OF WHICH WILL HAVE ITS OWN SOURCES OF COMPETITIVE ADVANTAGE. When individual functions having different economies of scale or scope are bundled together, the result is a compromise of each—an averaging of the effects. When the bundles of functions are free to re-form as separate businesses, however, each can exploit its own sources of competitive advantage to the fullest.

Take, for example, car retailing in the United States. Dealerships provide information about products in showrooms and through test-drives. They hold inventory and distribute cars. They broker financing. They make a market in secondhand cars. They operate maintenance and repair services. Although most of these activities are physical, the bundle of functions is held together by the classic *informational* logic of one-stop shopping. A dealer's competitive advantage is therefore based on a mixture of location, scale, cost, sales force management, quality of service, and affiliations with car manufacturers and banks.

Bundling these functions creates compromises. Each step in the value chain has different economies of scale. If the functions were unbundled, specialty companies that offer test-drives could take cars to prospective buyers' homes. Distributors of new cars could have fewer and larger sites in order to minimize inventory and transportation costs. Providers of after-sales service would be free to operate more and smaller local facilities to furnish better service. Auto manufacturers could deliver product information over the Internet. And car purchasers could obtain financing by putting their business out for bid via an electronic broker. Eliminate the informational glue that combines all these functions in a single, compromised business model, and the multiple businesses that emerge will evolve in radically different directions.

SOME NEW BUSINESSES WILL BENEFIT FROM NETWORK ECONOMIES OF SCALE, WHICH CAN GIVE RISE TO MONOPOLIES. In a networked market, the greater the number of people connected, the greater the value of being connected, thus creating *network economies of scale*. There is no point, for example, in being the only person in the world who owns a telephone. As the number of people who own telephones rises, the value to any one individual of hooking up increases progressively.

This self-reinforcing dynamic builds powerful monopolies. Businesses that broker information, make markets, or set standards are all taking advantage of this dynamic. The implication: the first company to achieve critical mass will often take all, or nearly all—although the continuing battle between first-mover Netscape and Microsoft in the market for network browsers illustrates that the lead of the first mover is not always definitive.

Reaching critical mass can be an enormous challenge. General Electric may have solved the problem by using its own huge purchasing power. GE has opened its internal electronic-procurement system to other buyers of industrial goods, turning its own sourcing system into a market-making business.

AS VALUE CHAINS FRAGMENT AND RECONFIGURE, NEW OPPORTUNITIES WILL ARISE FOR PURELY PHYSICAL BUSINESSES.   In many businesses today, the efficiency of the physical value chain is compromised for the purpose of delivering information. Shops, for example, try to be efficient warehouses and effective merchandisers simultaneously and are often really neither. The new economics of information will create opportunities to rationalize the physical value chain, often leading to businesses whose physically based sources of competitive advantage will be more sustainable.

Consider the current battle in bookselling. Amazon.com, an electronic retailer on the Web, has no physical stores and very little inventory. It offers an electronic list of 2.5 million books, ten times larger than that of the largest chain store, and customers can search through that list by just about any criterion. Amazon orders most of its books from two industry wholesalers in response to customers' requests. It then repacks and mails them from a central facility.

Amazon cannot offer instant delivery; nor can customers physically browse the shelves the way they can in a traditional bookstore. Its advantages are based on superior information and lower physical costs. Customers can, for example, access book reviews. They have greater choice and better searching capabilities. And Amazon saves money on inventory and retail space.

But Amazon's success is not a given. The discount chains are aggressively launching their own Web businesses. There is nothing defensible about Amazon's wide selection since it really comes from publishers' and wholesalers' databases. By double-handling the books, Amazon still incurs unnecessary costs.

In fact, the wholesalers in the book industry could probably create the lowest-cost distribution system by filling customers' orders directly. If competition pushes the industry in that direction, electronic retailers would become mere search engines connected to somebody else's database—and that would not add much value or confer on them much of a competitive advantage. The wholesalers could be the big winners.

WHEN A COMPANY FOCUSES ON DIFFERENT ACTIVITIES, THE VALUE PROPOSITION UNDERLYING ITS BRAND IDENTITY WILL CHANGE.   Because a brand reflects its company's value chain, deconstruction will require new brand strategies. For instance, the importance of branches and automated teller machines today leads many banks to emphasize *ubiquity* in their brand image (Citibank, for example). However, the reconfiguration of financial services might lead a company to focus on being a product provider. For such a strategy, *performance* becomes the key message, as it is for Fidelity. Another brand strategy might focus on helping customers navigate the universe of third-party products. The key message would be *trust*, as it is for Charles Schwab.

NEW BRANDING OPPORTUNITIES WILL EMERGE FOR THIRD PARTIES THAT NEITHER PRODUCE A PRODUCT NOR DELIVER A PRIMARY SERVICE.   Navigator or agent brands have been around for a long time. The Zagat guide to restaurants and *Consumer Reports* are two obvious examples. It's Zagat's own brand—its credibility in restaurant reviewing—that steers its readers toward a particular establishment. A more recent example is the Platform for Internet Content Selection (PICS), a programming standard that allows browsers to interpret third-party rating labels on Web sites. With it a parent might search for sites that have been labeled "safe for children" by EvaluWeb. PICS enables anybody to rate anything, and it makes those ratings ubiquitous, searchable, sortable, and costless. The dramatic proliferation of networked markets increases the need for such navigators and other facilitating agents, those that guarantee a product's performance or assume risk, for example. Thus there will be many new opportunities to develop brands. (See "Where the New Businesses Will Emerge.")

BARGAINING POWER WILL SHIFT AS A RESULT OF A RADICAL REDUCTION IN THE ABILITY TO MONOPOLIZE THE CONTROL OF INFORMATION.   Market power often comes from controlling a choke point in an information channel and extracting tolls from those dependent on the flow of information through it. For example, sellers to retail customers today use their control over the information available to those customers to minimize comparison shopping and maximize cross-selling. But when richness and reach extend to the point where such channels are unnecessary, that game will stop. Any choke point could then be circumvented. Buyers will know their alternatives as well as the seller does. Some new intermediaries—organizers of virtual markets—may even evolve into aggregators of buying power, playing suppliers off against one another for the benefit of the purchasers they represent.

CUSTOMERS' SWITCHING COSTS WILL DROP, AND COMPANIES WILL HAVE TO DEVELOP NEW WAYS OF GENERATING CUSTOMER LOYALTY. Common standards for exchanging and processing information and the growing numbers of individuals accessing networks will drastically reduce switching costs.

Proprietary EDI systems, for example, lock companies into supply relationships. But extranets linking companies with their suppliers using the Internet's standard protocols make switching almost costless. The U.S. auto industry is creating such an extranet called the Automotive Network eXchange (ANX). Linking together auto manufacturers with several thousand automotive suppliers, the system is expected to save its participants around a billion dollars a year, dramatically reduce ordering and billing errors, and speed the flow of information to second- and third-tier suppliers. By reducing switching costs and creating greater symmetry of information, ANX will intensify competition at every level of the supply chain.

INCUMBENTS COULD EASILY BECOME VICTIMS OF THEIR OBSOLETE PHYSICAL INFRASTRUCTURES AND THEIR OWN PSYCHOLOGY. Assets that traditionally offered competitive advantages and served as barriers to entry will become liabilities. The most vulnerable companies are those currently providing information that could be delivered more effectively and inexpensively electronically—for example, the physical parts of sales and distribution systems, such as branches, shops, and sales forces. As with newspapers, the loss of even a small portion of customers to new distribution channels or the migration of a high-margin product to the electronic domain can throw a business with high fixed costs into a downward spiral.

It may be easy to grasp this point intellectually, but it is much harder for managers to act on its implications. In many businesses, the assets in question are integral to a company's core competence. It is not easy psychologically to withdraw from assets so central to a company's identity. It is not easy strategically to downsize assets that have high fixed costs when so many customers still prefer the current business model. It is not easy financially to cannibalize current profits. And it is certainly not easy to squeeze the profits of distributors to whom one is tied by long-standing customer relationships or by franchise laws.

Newcomers suffer from none of these inhibitions. They are unconstrained by management traditions, organizational structures, customer relationships, or fixed assets. Recall the cautionary tale of Encyclopædia Britannica. Executives must mentally deconstruct their own businesses. If they don't, someone else will.

Where the New Businesses Will Emerge

In a world of limited connectivity, choices at each point in the value chain are, by definition, finite. In contrast, broadband connectivity means infinite choice. But infinite choice also means infinite bewilderment. This navigation problem can be solved in all sorts of ways, and each solution is a potential business.

The navigator could be a database. The navigator could be a search engine. The navigator could be intelligent-agent software. The navigator could be somebody giving advice. The navigator could be a brand providing recommendations or endorsements.

The logic of navigation can be observed in a number of businesses in which choice has proliferated. People often react to clutter by going back to the tried and true. Customer research indicates that people faced with complex choices either gravitate toward dominant brands or confine their search to narrow formats, each offering a presorted set of alternatives. In the grocery store, for example, where the number of products has quadrupled over the last 15 years, hundreds of segmented specialty brands have gained market share in almost every category. But so have the one or two leading brands. The proliferation of choice has led to the fragmentation of the small brands and the simultaneous concentration of the large ones. The losers are the brands in the middle.

Similarly, television viewers seem to flock to the hit shows without caring which network those shows are on. But they select specialty programming, such as nature documentaries or music videos, by tuning in to a cable channel offering that format. In essence, the viewer selects the channel, and the channel selects the content. In the first case, the product's brand pulls volume through the channel; in the second, the channel's brand pushes content toward receptive viewers.

Those two approaches by the consumer yield different patterns of competitive advantage and profitability. Networks need hit shows more than the hit shows need any network: the producers have the bargaining power and therefore receive the higher return. Conversely, producers of low-budget nature documentaries need a distributor more than the distributor needs any program, and the profit pattern is, therefore, the reverse. In one year, the popular comedian Bill Cosby earned more than the entire CBS network; the Discovery Channel probably earns more than all of its content providers put together. Despite the fact that CBS's 1996 revenues were about six times those of the Discovery Channel, Discovery's 52% profit margin dwarfed CBS's 4%.

The economics playing out in the television industry are a model for what will likely emerge in the world of universal connectivity. Think of it as two different value propositions: one is a focus on popular content; the other, a focus on navigation.

Navigation might have been the right strategy for Encyclopædia Britannica in responding to the threat from CD-ROMs. Its greatest competitive asset, after all, was a brand that certified high-quality, objective information. Given the clutter of cyberspace, what could be more compelling than a Britannica-branded guide to valuable information on the Internet?

If Britannica's executives had written off their sales force, if they had built alliances with libraries and scientific journals, if they had built a Web site that had hot links directly to original sources, if they had created a universal navigator to valuable and definitive information validated by the Encyclopædia Britannica brand, they would have been heroes. They might have established a monopoly, following the example of Bill Gates. In fact, he might have been forced to acquire them.

Notes

1. For a complete discussion of the value chain concept, see Michael Porter's *Competitive Advantage* (New York: The Free Press, 1985). Differences in value chains—that is, differences in how competitors perform strategic activities or differences in which activities they choose to perform—are the basis for competitive advantage.

2. Ronald H. Coase, "The Nature of the Firm," *Economica*, vol. 4, no. 4, 1937, p. 386; Oliver E. Williamson, *Markets and Hierarchies: Analysis and Antitrust Implications* (New York: Free Press, 1975).

2

Clusters and the New Economics of Competition

Michael E. Porter

Now that companies can source capital, goods, information, and technology from around the world, often with the click of a mouse, much of the conventional wisdom about how companies and nations compete needs to be overhauled. In theory, more open global markets and faster transportation and communication should diminish the role of location in competition. After all, anything that can be efficiently sourced from a distance through global markets and corporate networks is available to any company and therefore is essentially nullified as a source of competitive advantage.

But if location matters less, why, then, is it true that the odds of finding a world-class mutual-fund company in Boston are much higher than in most any other place? Why could the same be said of textile-related companies in North Carolina and South Carolina, of high-performance auto companies in southern Germany, or of fashion shoe companies in northern Italy?

Today's economic map of the world is dominated by what I call *clusters*: critical masses—in one place—of unusual competitive success in particular fields. Clusters are a striking feature of virtually every national, regional, state, and even metropolitan economy, especially in more economically advanced nations. Silicon Valley and Hollywood may be the world's best-known clusters. Clusters are not unique, however; they are highly typical—and therein lies a paradox: the

---

Extensive additional discussion of clusters and cluster development can be found in Michael E. Porter's two new essays—"Clusters and Competition" and "Competing Across Locations"—in his new collection titled On Competition *(Harvard Business School Press, Boston, MA: 1998).*

enduring competitive advantages in a global economy lie increasingly in local things—knowledge, relationships, motivation—that distant rivals cannot match.

Although location remains fundamental to competition, its role today differs vastly from a generation ago. In an era when competition was driven heavily by input costs, locations with some important endowment—a natural harbor, for example, or a supply of cheap labor—often enjoyed a *comparative advantage* that was both competitively decisive and persistent over time.

Competition in today's economy is far more dynamic. Companies can mitigate many input-cost disadvantages through global sourcing, rendering the old notion of comparative advantage less relevant. Instead, competitive advantage rests on making more productive use of inputs, which requires continual innovation.

Untangling the paradox of location in a global economy reveals a number of key insights about how companies continually create competitive advantage. What happens *inside* companies is important, but clusters reveal that the immediate business environment *outside* companies plays a vital role as well. This role of locations has been long overlooked, despite striking evidence that innovation and competitive success in so many fields are geographically concentrated—whether it's entertainment in Hollywood, finance on Wall Street, or consumer electronics in Japan.

Clusters affect competitiveness within countries as well as across national borders. Therefore, they lead to new agendas for all business executives—not just those who compete globally. More broadly, clusters represent a new way of thinking about location, challenging much of the conventional wisdom about how companies should be configured, how institutions such as universities can contribute to competitive success, and how governments can promote economic development and prosperity.

What Is a Cluster?

Clusters are geographic concentrations of interconnected companies and institutions in a particular field. Clusters encompass an array of linked industries and other entities important to competition. They include, for example, suppliers of specialized inputs such as components, machinery, and services, and providers of specialized infrastructure. Clusters also often extend downstream to channels and customers and laterally to manufacturers of complementary products and to companies in industries related by skills, technologies, or common inputs. Finally, many clusters include governmental and other institutions—such as universities, standards-setting agencies, think tanks, vocational training providers, and trade associations—that provide specialized training, education, information, research, and technical support.

The California wine cluster is a good example. It includes 680 commercial wineries as well as several thousand independent wine grape growers. (See Exhibit 2-1 "Anatomy of the California Wine Cluster.") An extensive complement of industries supporting both wine making and grape growing exists, including suppliers of grape stock, irrigation and harvesting equipment, barrels, and labels; specialized public relations and advertising firms; and numerous wine publications aimed at consumer and trade audiences. A host of local institutions is involved with wine, such as the world-renowned viticulture and enology program at the University of California at Davis, the Wine Institute, and special committees of the California senate and assembly. The cluster also enjoys weaker linkages to other California clusters in agriculture, food and restaurants, and wine-country tourism.

Consider also the Italian leather fashion cluster, which contains well-known shoe companies such as Ferragamo and Gucci as well as a host of specialized suppliers of footwear components, machinery, molds, design services, and tanned leather. (See Exhibit 2-2 "Mapping the Italian Leather Fashion Cluster.") It also consists of several chains of related industries, including those producing different types of leather goods (linked by common inputs and technologies) and different types of footwear (linked by overlapping channels and technologies). These industries employ common marketing media and compete with similar images in similar customer segments. A related Italian cluster in textile fashion, including clothing, scarves, and accessories, produces complementary products that often employ common channels. The extraordinary strength of the Italian leather fashion cluster can be attributed, at least in part, to the multiple linkages and synergies that participating Italian businesses enjoy.

A cluster's boundaries are defined by the linkages and complementarities across industries and institutions that are most important to competition. Although clusters often fit within political boundaries, they may cross state or even national borders. In the United States, for example, a pharmaceuticals cluster straddles New Jersey and Pennsylvania near Philadelphia. Similarly, a chemicals cluster in Germany crosses over into German-speaking Switzerland.

Exhibit 2-1   Anatomy of the California Wine Cluster

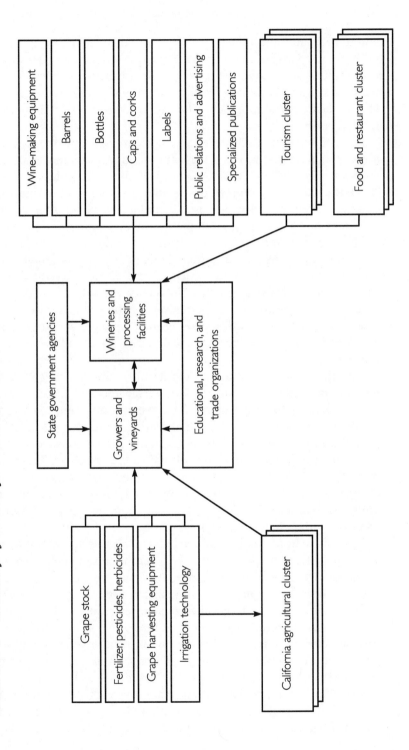

Exhibit 2-2   Mapping the Italian Leather Fashion Cluster

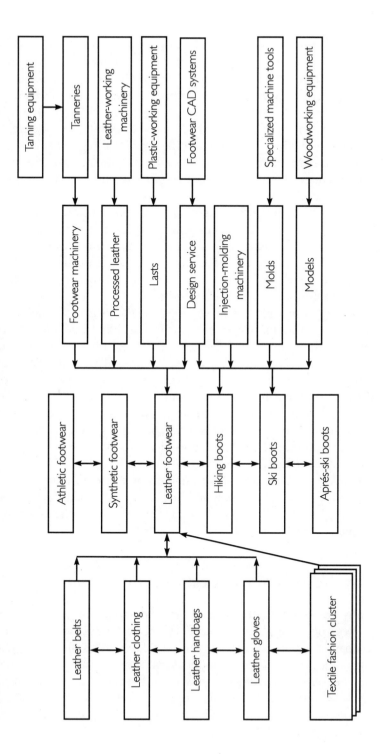

Clusters rarely conform to standard industrial classification systems, which fail to capture many important actors and relationships in competition. Thus significant clusters may be obscured or even go unrecognized. In Massachusetts, for example, more than 400 companies, representing at least 39,000 high-paying jobs, are involved in medical devices in some way. The cluster long remained all but invisible, however, buried within larger and overlapping industry categories such as electronic equipment and plastic products. Executives in the medical devices cluster have only recently come together to work on issues that will benefit them all.

Clusters promote both competition and cooperation. Rivals compete intensely to win and retain customers. Without vigorous competition, a cluster will fail. Yet there is also cooperation, much of it vertical, involving companies in related industries and local institutions. Competition can coexist with cooperation because they occur on different dimensions and among different players.

Clusters represent a kind of new spatial organizational form in between arm's-length markets on the one hand and hierarchies, or vertical integration, on the other. A cluster, then, is an alternative way of organizing the value chain. Compared with market transactions among dispersed and random buyers and sellers, the proximity of companies and institutions in one location—and the repeated exchanges among them—fosters better coordination and trust. Thus clusters mitigate the problems inherent in arm's-length relationships without imposing the inflexibilities of vertical integration or the management challenges of creating and maintaining formal linkages such as networks, alliances, and partnerships. A cluster of independent and informally linked companies and institutions represents a robust organizational form that offers advantages in efficiency, effectiveness, and flexibility.

Why Clusters Are Critical to Competition

Modern competition depends on productivity, not on access to inputs or the scale of individual enterprises. Productivity rests on *how* companies compete, not on the particular fields they compete in. Companies can be highly productive in any industry—shoes, agriculture, or semiconductors—if they employ sophisticated methods, use advanced technology, and offer unique products and services. All industries can employ advanced technology; all industries can be knowledge intensive.

The sophistication with which companies compete in a particular location, however, is strongly influenced by the quality of the local business environment.[1] Companies cannot employ advanced logistical techniques, for example, without a high-quality transportation infrastructure. Nor can companies effectively compete on sophisticated service without well-educated employees. Businesses cannot operate efficiently under onerous regulatory red tape or under a court system that fails to resolve disputes quickly and fairly. Some aspects of the business environment, such as the legal system, for example, or corporate tax rates, affect all industries. In advanced economies, however, the more decisive aspects of the business environment are often cluster specific; these constitute some of the most important microeconomic foundations for competition.

Clusters affect competition in three broad ways: first, by increasing the productivity of companies based in the area; second, by driving the direction and pace of innovation, which underpins future productivity growth; and third, by stimulating the formation of new businesses, which expands and strengthens the cluster itself. A cluster allows each member to benefit *as if* it had greater scale or *as if* it had joined with others formally—without requiring it to sacrifice its flexibility.

CLUSTERS AND PRODUCTIVITY

Being part of a cluster allows companies to operate more productively in sourcing inputs; accessing information, technology, and needed institutions; coordinating with related companies; and measuring and motivating improvement.

Better access to employees and suppliers. Companies in vibrant clusters can tap into an existing pool of specialized and experienced employees, thereby lowering their search and transaction costs in recruiting. Because a cluster signals opportunity and reduces the risk of relocation for employees, it can also be easier to attract talented people from other locations, a decisive advantage in some industries.

A well-developed cluster also provides an efficient means of obtaining other important inputs. Such a cluster offers a deep and specialized supplier base. Sourcing locally instead of from distant suppliers lowers transaction costs. It minimizes the need for inventory, eliminates importing costs and delays, and—because local reputation is important—lowers the risk that suppliers will overprice or renege on commitments. Proximity improves communications and makes it easier for suppliers to provide ancillary or support services such as installation and debugging. Other things being equal, then, local outsourcing is a better solution than distant outsourcing, especially for advanced and specialized inputs involving embedded technology, information, and service content.

Formal alliances with distant suppliers can mitigate some of the disadvantages of distant outsourcing. But all formal alliances involve their own complex bargaining and governance problems and can inhibit a company's flexibility. The close, informal relationships possible among companies in a cluster are often a superior arrangement.

In many cases, clusters are also a better alternative to vertical integration. Compared with in-house units, outside specialists are often more cost effective and responsive, not only in component production but also in services such as training. Although extensive vertical integration may have once been the norm, a fast-changing environment can render vertical integration inefficient, ineffective, and inflexible.

Even when some inputs are best sourced from a distance, clusters offer advantages. Suppliers trying to penetrate a large, concentrated market will price more aggressively, knowing that as they do so they can realize efficiencies in marketing and in service.

Working against a cluster's advantages in assembling resources is the possibility that competition will render them more expensive and scarce. But companies do have the alternative of outsourcing many inputs from other locations, which tends to limit potential cost penalties. More important, clusters increase not only the demand for specialized inputs but also their supply.

Access to specialized information. Extensive market, technical, and competitive information accumulates within a cluster, and members have preferred access to it. In addition, personal relationships and community ties foster trust and facilitate the flow of information. These conditions make information more transferable.

Complementarities. A host of linkages among cluster members results in a whole greater than the sum of its parts. In a typical tourism cluster, for example, the quality of a visitor's experience depends not only on the appeal of the primary attraction but also on the quality and efficiency of complementary businesses such as hotels, restaurants, shopping outlets, and transportation facilities. Because members of the cluster are mutually dependent, good performance by one can boost the success of the others.

Complementarities come in many forms. The most obvious is when products complement one another in meeting customers' needs, as the tourism example illustrates. Another form is the coordination of activities across companies to optimize their collective productivity. In wood products, for instance, the efficiency of sawmills depends on a reliable supply of high-quality timber and the ability to put all the timber to use—in furniture (highest quality), pallets and boxes (lower quality), or wood chips (lowest quality). In the early 1990s, Portuguese sawmills suffered from poor timber quality because local landowners did not invest in timber management. Hence most timber was processed for use in pallets and boxes, a lower-value use that limited the price paid to landowners. Substantial improvement in productivity was possible, but only if several parts of the cluster changed simultaneously. Logging operations, for example, had to modify cutting and sorting procedures, while sawmills had to develop the capacity to process wood in more sophisticated ways. Coordination to develop standard wood classifications and measures was an important enabling step. Geographically dispersed companies are less likely to recognize and capture such linkages.

Other complementarities arise in marketing. A cluster frequently enhances the reputation of a location in a particular field, making it more likely that buyers will turn to a vendor based there. Italy's strong reputation for fashion and design, for example, benefits companies involved in leather goods, footwear, apparel, and accessories. Beyond reputation, cluster members often profit from a variety of joint marketing mechanisms, such as company referrals, trade fairs, trade magazines, and marketing delegations.

Finally, complementarities can make buying from a cluster more attractive for customers. Visiting buyers can see many vendors in a single trip. They also may perceive their buying risk to be lower because one location provides alternative suppliers. That allows them to multisource or to switch vendors if the need arises. Hong Kong thrives as a source of fashion apparel in part for this reason.

Access to institutions and public goods. Investments made by government or other public institutions—such as public spending for specialized infrastructure or educational programs—can enhance a company's productivity. The ability to recruit employees trained at local programs, for example, lowers the cost of internal training. Other quasi-public goods, such as the cluster's information and technology pools and its reputation, arise as natural by-products of competition.

It is not just governments that create public goods that enhance pro-ductivity in the private sector. Investments by companies—in training programs, infrastructure, quality centers, testing laboratories, and so on—also contribute to increased productivity. Such private invest-ments are often made collectively because cluster participants recog-nize the potential for collective benefits.

Better motivation and measurement. Local rivalry is highly motivating. Peer pressure amplifies competitive pressure within a cluster, even among noncompeting or indirectly competing companies. Pride and the desire to look good in the local community spur executives to at-tempt to outdo one another.

Clusters also often make it easier to measure and compare perfor-mances because local rivals share general circumstances—for example, labor costs and local market access—and they perform similar activi-ties. (See Exhibit 2-3 "Mapping Selected U.S. Clusters.") Companies within clusters typically have intimate knowledge of their suppliers' costs. Managers are able to compare costs and employees' perfor-mance with other local companies. Additionally, financial institutions can accumulate knowledge about the cluster that can be used to mon-itor performance.

CLUSTERS AND INNOVATION

In addition to enhancing productivity, clusters play a vital role in a company's ongoing ability to innovate. Some of the same characteris-tics that enhance current productivity have an even more dramatic ef-fect on innovation and productivity growth.

Because sophisticated buyers are often part of a cluster, companies inside clusters usually have a better window on the market than iso-lated competitors do. Computer companies based in Silicon Valley and Austin, Texas, for example, plug into customer needs and trends with a speed difficult to match by companies located elsewhere. The ongo-ing relationships with other entities within the cluster also help com-panies to learn early about evolving technology, component and ma-chinery availability, service and marketing concepts, and so on. Such learning is facilitated by the ease of making site visits and frequent face-to-face contact.

Clusters do more than make opportunities for innovation more visi-ble. They also provide the capacity and the flexibility to act rapidly. A

Exhibit 2-3   *Mapping Selected U.S. Clusters*

Here are just some of the clusters in the United States. A few—Hollywood's entertainment cluster and High Point, North Carolina's household-furniture cluster—are well known. Others are less familiar, such as golf equipment in Carlsbad, California, and optics in Phoenix, Arizona. A relatively small number of clusters usually account for a major share of the economy within a geographic area as well as for an overwhelming share of its economic activity that is "exported" to other locations. *Exporting clusters*—those that export products or make investments to compete outside the local area—are the primary source of an area's economic growth and prosperity over the long run. The demand for local industries is inherently limited by the size of the local market, but exporting clusters can grow far beyond that limit.

Seattle
Aircraft equipment and design
Boat and ship building
Metal fabrication

Oregon
Electrical measuring equipment
Woodworking equipment
Logging and lumber supplies

Boise
Sawmills
Farm machinery

Las Vegas
Amusements and casinos
Small airlines

Phoenix
Helicopters
Semiconductors
Electronic testing labs
Optics

Carlsbad
Golf equipment

Los Angeles area
Defense and aerospace
Entertainment

Silicon Valley
Microelectronics
Biotechnology
Venture capital

Colorado
Computer-integrated systems and programming
Engineering services
Mining and oil and gas exploration

Wisconsin/Iowa/Illinois
Agricultural equipment

Minneapolis
Cardiovascular equipment and services

Omaha
Telemarketing
Hotel reservations
Credit card processing

Wichita
Light aircraft
Farm equipment

Dallas
Real estate development

Warsaw, Indiana
Orthopedic devices

Western Michigan
Office and institutional furniture

Michigan
Clocks

Nashville/Louisville
Hospital management

Baton Rouge/New Orleans
Specialty foods

Southeastern Texas/Louisiana
Chemicals

Cleveland/Louisville
Paints and coatings

Dalton, Georgia
Carpets

Pittsburgh
Advanced materials
Energy

Detroit
Auto equipment and parts

Western Massachusetts
Polymers

Rochester
Imaging equipment

Providence
Jewelry
Marine equipment

Boston
Mutual funds
Biotechnology
Software and networking
Venture capital

Hartford
Insurance

New York City
Financial services
Advertising
Publishing
Multimedia

Pennsylvania/New Jersey
Pharmaceuticals

North Carolina
Household furniture
Synthetic fibers
Hosiery

Southern Florida
Health technology
Computers

company within a cluster often can source what it needs to implement innovations more quickly. Local suppliers and partners can and do get closely involved in the innovation process, thus ensuring a better match with customers' requirements.

Companies within a cluster can experiment at lower cost and can delay large commitments until they are more assured that a given innovation will pan out. In contrast, a company relying on distant suppliers faces greater challenges in every activity it coordinates with other organizations—in contracting, for example, or securing delivery or obtaining associated technical and service support. Innovation can be even harder in vertically integrated companies, especially in those that face difficult trade-offs if the innovation erodes the value of in-house assets or if current products or processes must be maintained while new ones are developed.

Reinforcing the other advantages for innovation is the sheer pressure—competitive pressure, peer pressure, constant comparison—that occurs in a cluster. Executives vie with one another to set their companies apart. For all these reasons, clusters can remain centers of innovation for decades.

CLUSTERS AND NEW BUSINESS FORMATION

It is not surprising, then, that many new companies grow up within an existing cluster rather than at isolated locations. New suppliers, for example, proliferate within a cluster because a concentrated customer base lowers their risks and makes it easier for them to spot market opportunities. Moreover, because developed clusters comprise related industries that normally draw on common or very similar inputs, suppliers enjoy expanded opportunities.

Clusters are conducive to new business formation for a variety of reasons. Individuals working within a cluster can more easily perceive gaps in products or services around which they can build businesses. Beyond that, barriers to entry are lower than elsewhere. Needed assets, skills, inputs, and staff are often readily available at the cluster location, waiting to be assembled into a new enterprise. Local financial institutions and investors, already familiar with the cluster, may require a lower risk premium on capital. In addition, the cluster often presents a significant local market, and an entrepreneur may benefit from established relationships. All of these factors reduce the perceived risks of entry—and of exit, should the enterprise fail.

The formation of new businesses within a cluster is part of a positive feedback loop. An expanded cluster amplifies all the benefits I have described—it increases the collective pool of competitive resources, which benefits all the cluster's members. The net result is that companies in the cluster advance relative to rivals at other locations.

Birth, Evolution, and Decline

A cluster's roots can often be traced to historical circumstances. In Massachusetts, for example, several clusters had their beginnings in research done at MIT or Harvard. The Dutch transportation cluster owes much to Holland's central location within Europe, an extensive network of waterways, the efficiency of the port of Rotterdam, and the skills accumulated by the Dutch through Holland's long maritime history.

Clusters may also arise from unusual, sophisticated, or stringent local demand. Israel's cluster in irrigation equipment and other advanced agricultural technologies reflects that nation's strong desire for self-sufficiency in food together with a scarcity of water and hot, arid growing conditions. The environmental cluster in Finland emerged as a result of pollution problems created by local process industries such as metals, forestry, chemicals, and energy.

Prior existence of supplier industries, related industries, or even entire related clusters provides yet another seed for new clusters. The golf equipment cluster near San Diego, for example, has its roots in southern California's aerospace cluster. That cluster created a pool of suppliers for castings and advanced materials as well as engineers with the requisite experience in those technologies.

New clusters may also arise from one or two innovative companies that stimulate the growth of many others. Medtronic played this role in helping to create the Minneapolis medical-device cluster. Similarly, MCI and America Online have been hubs for growing new businesses in the telecommunications cluster in the Washington, D.C., metropolitan area.

Sometimes a chance event creates some advantageous factor that, in turn, fosters cluster development—although chance rarely provides the sole explanation for a cluster's success in a location. The telemarketing cluster in Omaha, Nebraska, for example, owes much to the decision by the U.S. Air Force to locate the Strategic Air Command

(SAC) there. Charged with a key role in the country's nuclear deterrence strategy, SAC was the site of the first installation of fiber-optic telecommunications cables in the United States. The local Bell operating company (now U.S. West) developed unusual capabilities through its dealings with such a demanding customer. The extraordinary telecommunications capability and infrastructure that consequently developed in Omaha, coupled with less unique attributes such as its central-time-zone location and easily understandable local accent, provided the underpinnings of the area's telemarketing cluster.

Once a cluster begins to form, a self-reinforcing cycle promotes its growth, especially when local institutions are supportive and local competition is vigorous. As the cluster expands, so does its influence with government and with public and private institutions.

A growing cluster signals opportunity, and its success stories help attract the best talent. Entrepreneurs take notice, and individuals with ideas or relevant skills migrate in from other locations. Specialized suppliers emerge; information accumulates; local institutions develop specialized training, research, and infrastructure; and the cluster's strength and visibility grow. Eventually, the cluster broadens to encompass related industries. Numerous case studies suggest that clusters require a decade or more to develop depth and real competitive advantage.[2]

Cluster development is often particularly vibrant at the intersection of clusters, where insights, skills, and technologies from various fields merge, sparking innovation and new businesses. An example from Germany illustrates this point. The country has distinct clusters in both home appliances and household furniture, each based on different technologies and inputs. At the intersection of the two, though, is a cluster of built-in kitchens and appliances, an area in which Germany commands a higher share of world exports than in either appliances or furniture.

Clusters continually evolve as new companies and industries emerge or decline and as local institutions develop and change. They can maintain vibrancy as competitive locations for centuries; most successful clusters prosper for decades at least. However, they can and do lose their competitive edge due to both external and internal forces. Technological discontinuities are perhaps the most significant of the external threats because they can neutralize many advantages simultaneously. A cluster's assets—market information, employees' skills, scientific and technical expertise, and supplier bases—may all become irrelevant. New England's loss of market share in golf equipment is a good example. The New England cluster was based on steel shafts, steel irons, and wooden-headed woods. When companies in California began making golf clubs with advanced materials, East Coast producers had difficulty competing. A number of them were acquired or went out of business.

A shift in buyers' needs, creating a divergence between local needs and needs elsewhere, constitutes another external threat. U.S. companies in a variety of clusters, for example, suffered when energy efficiency grew in importance in most parts of the world while the United States maintained low energy prices. Lacking both pressure to improve and insight into customer needs, U.S. companies were slow to innovate, and they lost ground to European and Japanese competitors.

Clusters are at least as vulnerable to internal rigidities as they are to external threats. Overconsolidation, mutual understandings, cartels, and other restraints to competition undermine local rivalry. Regulatory inflexibility or the introduction of restrictive union rules slows productivity improvement. The quality of institutions such as schools and universities can stagnate.

Groupthink among cluster participants—Detroit's attachment to gas-guzzling autos in the 1970s is one example—can be another powerful form of rigidity. If companies in a cluster are too inward looking, the whole cluster suffers from a collective inertia, making it harder for individual companies to embrace new ideas, much less perceive the need for radical innovation.

Such rigidities tend to arise when government suspends or intervenes in competition or when companies persist in old behaviors and relationships that no longer contribute to competitive advantage. Increases in the cost of doing business begin to outrun the ability to upgrade. Rigidities of this nature currently work against a variety of clusters in Switzerland and Germany.

As long as rivalry remains sufficiently vigorous, companies can partially compensate for some decline in the cluster's competitiveness by outsourcing to distant suppliers or moving part or all of production elsewhere to offset local wages that rise ahead of productivity. German companies in the 1990s, for example, have been doing just that. Technology can be licensed or sourced from other locations, and product development can be moved. Over time, however, a location will decline if it fails to build capabilities in major new technologies or needed supporting firms and institutions.

Implications for Companies

In the new economics of competition, what matters most is not inputs and scale, but productivity—and that is true in all industries. The term *high tech*, normally used to refer to fields such as information technology and biotechnology, has distorted thinking about competition, creating the misconception that only a handful of businesses compete in sophisticated ways.

In fact, there is no such thing as a low-tech industry. There are only low-tech companies—that is, companies that fail to use world-class technology and practices to enhance productivity and innovation. A vibrant cluster can help any company in any industry compete in the most sophisticated ways, using the most advanced, relevant skills and technologies. (See "Clusters, Geography, and Economic Development.")

Clusters, Geography, and Economic Development

Poor countries lack well-developed clusters; they compete in the world market with cheap labor and natural resources. To move beyond this stage, the development of well-functioning clusters is essential. Clusters become an especially controlling factor for countries moving from a middle-income to an advanced economy. Even in high-wage economies, however, the need for cluster upgrading is constant. The wealthier the economy, the more it will require innovation to support rising wages and to replace jobs eliminated by improvements in efficiency and the migration of standard production to low-cost areas.

Promoting cluster formation in developing economies means starting at the most basic level. Policymakers must first address the foundations: improving education and skill levels, building capacity in technology, opening access to capital markets, and improving institutions. Over time, additional investment in more cluster-specific assets is necessary.

Government policies in developing economies often unwittingly work against cluster formation. Restrictions on industrial location and subsidies to invest in distressed areas, for example, can disperse companies artificially. Protecting local companies from competition leads to excessive vertical integration and blunted pressure for innovation, retarding cluster development.

In the early stages of economic development, countries should expand internal trade among cities and states and trade with neighboring countries as important stepping stones to building the skills to compete globally. Such trade greatly enhances cluster development. Instead, attention is typically riveted on the large, advanced markets, an orientation that has often been reinforced by protectionist policies restricting trade with nearby markets. However, the kinds of goods developing countries can trade with advanced economies are limited to commodities and to activities sensitive to labor costs.

While it is essential that clusters form, *where* they form also matters. In developing economies, a large proportion of economic activity tends to concentrate around capital cities such as Bangkok and Bogotá. That is usually because outlying areas lack infrastructure, institutions, and suppliers. It may also reflect an intrusive role by the central government in controlling competition, leading companies to locate near the seat of power and the agencies whose approval they require to do business.

This pattern of economic geography inflicts high costs on productivity. Congestion, bottlenecks, and inflexibility lead to high administrative costs and major inefficiencies, not to mention a diminished quality of life. Companies cannot easily move out from the center, however, because neither infrastructure nor rudimentary clusters exist in the smaller cities and towns. (The building of a tourism cluster in developing economies can be a positive force in improving the outlying infrastructure and in dispersing economic activity.)

Even in advanced economies, however, economic activity may be geographically concentrated. Japan offers a particularly striking case, with nearly 50% of total manufacturing shipments located around Tokyo and Osaka. This is due less to inadequacies in infrastructure in outlying areas than to a powerful and intrusive central government, with its centralizing bias in policies and institutions. The Japanese case vividly illustrates the major inefficiencies and productivity costs resulting from such a pattern of economic geography, even for advanced nations. It is a major policy issue facing Japan.

An economic geography characterized by specialization and dispersion—that is, a number of metropolitan areas, each specializing in an array of clusters—appears to be a far more productive industrial organization than one based on one or two huge, diversified cities. In nations such as Germany, Italy, Switzerland, and the United States, this kind of internal specialization and trade—and internal competition among locations—fuels productivity growth and hones the ability of companies to compete effectively in the global arena.

Thus executives must extend their thinking beyond what goes on inside their own organizations and within their own industries. Strategy must also address what goes on outside. Extensive vertical integration may once have been appropriate, but companies today must forge close linkages with buyers, suppliers, and other institutions.

Specifically, understanding clusters adds the following four issues to the strategic agenda.

1. CHOOSING LOCATIONS.   Globalization and the ease of transportation and communication have led many companies to move some or all of their operations to locations with low wages, taxes, and utility costs. What we know about clusters suggests, first, that some of those cost advantages may well turn out to be illusory. Locations with those advantages often lack efficient infrastructure, sophisticated suppliers, and other cluster benefits that can more than offset any savings from lower input costs. Savings in wages, utilities, and taxes may be highly visible and easy to measure up front, but productivity penalties remain hidden and unanticipated.

More important to ongoing competitiveness is the role of location in innovation. Yes, companies have to spread activities globally to source inputs and gain access to markets. Failure to do so will lead to a competitive *disadvantage*. And for stable, labor-intensive activities such as assembly and software translation, low factor costs are often decisive in driving locational choices. (See Exhibit 2-4 "Mapping Portugal's Clusters.")

For a company's "home base" for each product line, however, clusters are critical. Home base activities—strategy development, core product and process R&D, a critical mass of the most sophisticated production or service provision—create and renew the company's product, processes, and services. Therefore locational decisions must be based on both total systems costs and innovation potential, not on input costs alone. Cluster thinking suggests that every product line needs a home base, and the most vibrant cluster will offer the best location. Within the United States, for example, Hewlett-Packard has chosen cluster locations for the home bases of its major product lines: California, where almost all of the world's leading personal computer and workstation businesses are located, is home to personal computers and workstations; Massachusetts, which has an extraordinary concentration of world-renowned research hospitals and leading medical instrument companies, is home to medical instruments.

As global competition nullifies traditional comparative advantages and exposes companies to the best rivals from around the world, a growing number of multinationals are shifting their home bases to

Exhibit 2-4   Mapping Portugal's Clusters

In a middle-income economy like Portugal, exporting clusters tend to be more natural-resource or labor intensive.

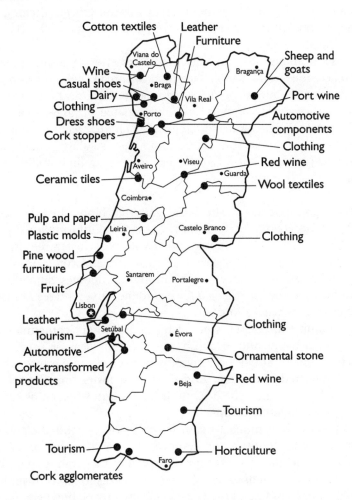

more vibrant clusters—often using acquisitions as a means of establishing themselves as insiders in a new location. Nestlé, for example, after acquiring Rowntree Mackintosh, relocated its confectionary business to York, England, where Rowntree was originally based, because a vibrant food cluster thrives there. England, with its sweet-toothed consumers, sophisticated retailers, advanced advertising agencies, and highly competitive media companies, constitutes a more dynamic environment for competing in mass-market candy than Switzerland did. Similarly, Nestlé has moved its headquarters for bottled water to France, the most competitive location in that industry. Northern Telecom has relocated its home base for central office switching from Canada to the United States—drawn by the vibrancy of the U.S. telecommunications-equipment cluster.

Cluster thinking also suggests that it is better to move groups of linked activities to the same place than to spread them across numerous locations. Colocating R&D, component fabrication, assembly, marketing, customer support, and even related businesses can facilitate internal efficiencies in sourcing and in sharing technology and information. Grouping activities into campuses also allows companies to extend deeper roots into local clusters, improving their ability to capture potential benefits.

2. ENGAGING LOCALLY.   The social glue that binds clusters together also facilitates access to important resources and information. Tapping into the competitively valuable assets within a cluster requires personal relationships, face-to-face contact, a sense of common interest, and "insider" status. The mere colocation of companies, suppliers, and institutions creates the *potential* for economic value; it does not necessarily ensure its realization.

To maximize the benefits of cluster involvement, companies must participate actively and establish a significant local presence. They must have a substantial local investment even if the parent company is headquartered elsewhere. And they must foster ongoing relationships with government bodies and local institutions such as utilities, schools, and research groups.

Companies have much to gain by engaging beyond their narrow confines as single entities. Yet managers tend to be wary, at least initially. They fear that a growing cluster will attract competition, drive up costs, or cause them to lose valued employees to rivals or spin-offs. As their understanding of the cluster concept grows, however, managers realize that many participants in the cluster do not compete directly and that the offsetting benefits, such as a greater supply of better trained people, for example, can outweigh any increase in competition.

3. UPGRADING THE CLUSTER.   Because the health of the local business environment is important to the health of the company, upgrading the

cluster should be part of management's agenda. Companies upgrade their clusters in a variety of ways.

Consider Genzyme. Massachusetts is home to a vibrant biotechnology cluster, which draws on the region's strong universities, medical centers, and venture capital firms. Once Genzyme reached the stage in its development when it needed a manufacturing facility, CEO Henri Termeer initially considered the pharmaceuticals cluster in the New Jersey and Philadelphia area because it had what Massachusetts lacked: established expertise in drug manufacturing. Upon further reflection, however, Termeer decided to influence the process of creating a manufacturing capability in Genzyme's home base, reasoning that if his plans were successful, the company could become more competitive.

Thus Genzyme deliberately chose to work with contractors committed to the Boston area, bypassing the many specialized engineering firms located near Philadelphia. In addition, it undertook a number of initiatives, with the help of city and state government, to improve the labor force, such as offering scholarships and internships to local youth. More broadly, Genzyme has worked to build critical mass for its cluster. Termeer believes that Genzyme's success is linked to the cluster's—and that all members will benefit from a strong base of supporting functions and institutions.

4. WORKING COLLECTIVELY.   The way clusters operate suggests a new agenda of collective action in the private sector. Investing in public goods is normally seen as a function of government, yet cluster thinking clearly demonstrates how companies benefit from local assets and institutions.

In the past, collective action in the private sector has focused on seeking government subsidies and special favors that often distort competition. But executives' long-term interests would be better served by working to promote a higher plane of competition. They can begin by rethinking the role of trade associations, which often do little more than lobby government, compile some statistics, and host social functions. The associations are missing an important opportunity.

Trade associations can provide a forum for the exchange of ideas and a focal point for collective action in overcoming obstacles to productivity and growth. Associations can take the lead in such activities as establishing university-based testing facilities and training or research programs; collecting cluster-related information; offering forums on common managerial problems; investigating solutions to environmental issues; organizing trade fairs and delegations; and managing purchasing consortia.

For clusters consisting of many small and midsize companies—such as tourism, apparel, and agriculture—the need is particularly great for collective bodies to assume scale-sensitive functions. In the Netherlands, for instance, grower cooperatives built the specialized auction and handling facilities that constitute one of the Dutch flower cluster's greatest competitive advantages. The Dutch Flower Council and the Association of Dutch Flower Growers Research Groups, in which most growers participate, have taken on other functions as well, such as applied research and marketing.

Most existing trade associations are too narrow; they represent industries, not clusters. In addition, because their role is defined as lobbying the federal government, their scope is national rather than local. National associations, however, are rarely sufficient to address the local issues that are most important to cluster productivity.

By revealing how business and government together create the conditions that promote growth, clusters offer a constructive way to change the nature of the dialogue between the public and private sectors. With a better understanding of what fosters true competitiveness, executives can start asking government for the right things. The example of MassMEDIC, an association formed in 1996 by the Massachusetts medical-devices cluster, illustrates this point. It recently worked successfully with the U.S. Food and Drug Administration to streamline the approval process for medical devices. Such a step clearly benefits cluster members and enhances competition at the same time.

What's Wrong with Industrial Policy

Productivity, not exports or natural resources, determines the prosperity of any state or nation. Recognizing this, governments should strive to create an environment that supports rising productivity. Sound macroeconomic policy is necessary but not sufficient. The microeconomic foundations for competition will ultimately determine productivity and competitiveness.

Governments—both national and local—have new roles to play. They must ensure the supply of high-quality inputs such as educated citizens and physical infrastructure. They must set the rules of competition—by protecting intellectual property and enforcing antitrust laws, for example—so that productivity and innovation will govern success in the economy. Finally, governments should promote cluster formation and upgrading and the buildup of public or quasi-public goods that have a significant impact on many linked businesses.

This sort of role for government is a far cry from industrial policy. In industrial policy, governments target "desirable" industries and intervene—through subsidies or restrictions on investments by foreign companies, for example—to favor local companies. In contrast, the aim of cluster policy is to reinforce the development of *all* clusters. This means that a traditional cluster such as agriculture should not be abandoned; it should be upgraded. Governments should not choose among clusters, because each one offers opportunities to improve productivity and support rising wages. Every cluster not only contributes directly to national productivity but also affects the productivity of *other* clusters. Not all clusters will succeed, of course, but market forces—not government decisions—should determine the outcomes.

Government, working with the private sector, should reinforce and build on existing and emerging clusters rather than attempt to create entirely new ones. Successful new industries and clusters often grow out of established ones. Businesses involving advanced technology succeed not in a vacuum but where there is already a base of related activities in the field. In fact, most clusters form independently of government action—and sometimes in spite of it. They form where a foundation of locational advantages exists. To justify cluster development efforts, some seeds of a cluster should have already passed a market test.

Cluster development initiatives should embrace the pursuit of competitive advantage and specialization rather than simply imitate successful clusters in other locations. This requires building on local sources of uniqueness. Finding areas of specialization normally proves more effective than head-on competition with well-established rival locations.

New Public-Private Responsibilities

Economic geography in an era of global competition, then, poses a paradox. In a global economy—which boasts rapid transportation, high-speed communication, and accessible markets—one would expect location to diminish in importance. But the opposite is true. The enduring competitive advantages in a global economy are often heavily local, arising from concentrations of highly specialized skills and knowledge, institutions, rivals, related businesses, and sophisticated customers. Geographic, cultural, and institutional proximity leads to special access, closer relationships, better information, powerful incentives, and other advantages in productivity and innovation that are difficult to tap from a distance. The more the world economy becomes complex, knowledge based, and dynamic, the more this is true.

Leaders of businesses, government, and institutions all have a stake—and a role to play—in the new economics of competition. Clusters reveal the mutual dependence and collective responsibility of all these entities for creating the conditions for productive competition. This task will require fresh thinking on the part of leaders and the willingness to abandon the traditional categories that drive our thinking about who does what in the economy. The lines between public and private investment blur. Companies, no less than governments and universities, have a stake in education. Universities have a stake in the competitiveness of local businesses. By revealing the process by which wealth is actually created in an economy, clusters open new public-private avenues for constructive action.

Notes

1. I first made this argument in *The Competitive Advantage of Nations* (New York: Free Press, 1990). I modeled the effect of the local business environment on competition in terms of four interrelated influences, graphically depicted in a diamond: factor conditions (the cost and quality of inputs); demand conditions (the sophistication of local customers); the context for firm strategy and rivalry (the nature and intensity of local competition); and related and supporting industries (the local extent and sophistication of suppliers and related industries). Diamond theory stresses how these elements combine to produce a dynamic, stimulating, and intensely competitive business environment.

   A cluster is the manifestation of the diamond at work. Proximity—the colocation of companies, customers, and suppliers—amplifies all of the pressures to innovate and upgrade.

2. Selected case studies are described in "Clusters and Competition" in my book *On Competition* (Boston: Harvard Business School Press, 1998), which also includes citations of the published output of a number of cluster initiatives. Readers can also find a full treatment of the intellectual roots of cluster thinking, along with an extensive bibliography.

3
The End of Corporate Imperialism

C.K. Prahalad and Kenneth Lieberthal

As they search for growth, multinational corporations will have to compete in the big emerging markets of China, India, Indonesia, and Brazil. The operative word is *emerging*. A vast consumer base of hundreds of millions of people is developing rapidly. Despite the uncertainty and the difficulty of doing business in markets that remain opaque to outsiders, Western MNCs will have no choice but to enter them. (See Table 3-1 "Market Size: Emerging Markets versus the United States.")

During the first wave of market entry in the 1980s, MNCs operated with what might be termed an imperialist mind-set. They assumed that the big emerging markets were new markets for their old products. They foresaw a bonanza in incremental sales for their existing products or the chance to squeeze profits out of their sunset technologies. Further, the corporate center was seen as the sole locus of product and process innovation. Many multinationals did not consciously look at emerging markets as sources of technical and managerial talent for their global operations. As a result of this imperialist mind-set, multinationals have achieved only limited success in those markets.

Many corporations, however, are beginning to see that the opportunity that big emerging markets represent will demand a new way of thinking. Success will require more than simply developing greater cultural sensitivity. The more we understand the nature of these markets, the more we believe that multinationals will have to rethink and reconfigure every element of their business models.

So while it is still common today to question how corporations like General Motors and McDonald's will change life in the big emerging

*Table 3-1   Market Size: Emerging Markets versus the
United States*

Product	China	India	Brazil	United States
Televisions (million units)	13.6	5.2	7.8	23.0
Detergent (kilograms per person)	2.5	2.7	7.3	14.4
(million tons)	3.5	2.3	1.1	3.9
Shampoo (in billions of dollars)	1.0	0.8	1.0	1.5
Pharmaceuticals (in billions of dollars)	5.0	2.8	8.0	60.6
Automotive (million units)	1.6	0.7	2.1	15.5
Power (megawatt capacity)	236,542	81,736	59,950	810,964

markets, Western executives would be smart to turn the question around. Success in the emerging markets will require innovation and resource shifts on such a scale that life within the multinationals themselves will inevitably be transformed. In short, as MNCs achieve success in those markets, they will also bring corporate imperialism to an end.

We would not like to give the impression that we think markets such as China, India, Brazil, and Indonesia will enjoy clear sailing. As Indonesia is showing, these markets face major obstacles to continued high growth; political disruptions, for example, can slow down and even reverse trends toward more open markets. But given the long-term growth prospects, MNCs will have to compete in those markets. Having studied in depth the evolution of India and China over the past 20 years, and having worked extensively with MNCs competing in these and other countries, we believe that there are five basic questions that MNCs must answer to compete in the big emerging markets:

- Who is the emerging middle-class market in these countries, and what kind of business model will effectively serve their needs?
- What are the key characteristics of the distribution networks in these markets, and how are the networks evolving?
- What mix of local and global leadership is required to foster business opportunities?

- Should the MNC adopt a consistent strategy for all its business units within one country?
- Will local partners accelerate the multinational's ability to learn about the market?

What Is the Business Model for the Emerging Middle Class?

What is big and emerging in countries like China and India is a new consumer base consisting of hundreds of millions of people. Starved of choice for over 40 years, the rising middle class is hungry for consumer goods and a better quality of life and is ready to spend. The emerging markets have entered a new era of product availability and choice. In India alone, there are 50 brands of toothpaste available today and more than 250 brands of shoes.

Consumers are experimenting and changing their choice of products rapidly. Indians, for example, will buy any product once, but brand switching is common. One survey found that Indian consumers tried on average 6.2 brands of the same packaged-goods product in one year, compared with 2.0 for American consumers. But does this growth of consumer demand add up to a wealth of opportunity for the MNCs?

The answer is yes . . . but. Consider the constitution of the middle class itself. When managers in the West hear about the emerging middle class of India or China, they tend to think in terms of the middle class in Europe or the United States. This is one sign of an imperialist mind-set—the assumption that everyone must be just like "us." True, consumers in the emerging markets today are much more affluent than they were before their countries liberalized trade, but they are not affluent by Western standards. This is usually the first big miscalculation that MNCs make.

When these markets are analyzed, moreover, they turn out to have a structure very unlike that of the West. Income levels that characterize the Western middle class would represent a tiny upper class of consumers in any of the emerging markets. Today the active consumer market in the big emerging markets has a three-tiered pyramid structure. (See Exhibit 3-1 "The Market Pyramid in China, India, and Brazil.")

Exhibit 3-1   The Market Pyramid in China, India, and Brazil

Purchasing power parity in U.S. dollars		Population in millions		
		China	India	Brazil
tier I	greater than $20,000	2	7	9
tier 2	$10,000 to $20,000	60	63	15
tier 3	$5,000 to $10,000	330	125	27
	less than $5,000	800	700	105

Consider India. At the top of the pyramid, in tier one, is a relatively small number of consumers who are responsive to international brands and have the income to afford them. Next comes tier two, a much larger group of people who are less attracted to international brands. Finally, at the bottom of the pyramid of consumers is tier three—a massive group that is loyal to local customs, habits, and often to local brands. Below that is another huge group made up of people who are unlikely to become active consumers anytime soon.

MNCs have tended to bring their existing products and marketing strategies to the emerging markets without properly accounting for these market pyramids. They end up, therefore, becoming high-end niche players. That's what happened to Revlon, for example, when it introduced its Western beauty products to China in 1976 and to India in 1994. Only the top tier valued and could afford the cachet of Revlon's brand. And consider Ford's recent foray into India with its Escort, which Ford priced at more than $21,000. In India, anything over $20,000 falls into the luxury segment. The most popular car, the Maruti-Suzuki, sells for $10,000 or less. Fiat learned to serve that tier of the market in Brazil, designing a new model called the Palio specifically for Brazilians. Fiat is now poised to transfer that success from Brazil to India.

While it is seductive for companies like Ford to think of big emerging markets as new outlets for old products, a mind-set focused on incremental volume misses the real opportunity. To date, MNCs like Ford and Revlon have either ignored tier two of the pyramid or conceded it to local competitors. But if Ford wants to be more than a small, high-end player, it will have to design a robust and roomy $9,000 car to compete with Fiat's Palio or with a locally produced car.

Tailoring products to the big emerging markets is not a trivial task. Minor cultural adaptations or marginal cost reductions will not do the job. Instead, to overcome an implicit imperialism, companies must undergo a fundamental rethinking of every element of their business model.

RETHINKING THE PRICE-PERFORMANCE EQUATION. Consumers in big emerging markets are getting a fast education in global standards, but they often are unwilling to pay global prices. In India, an executive in a multinational food-processing company told us the story of a man in Delhi who went to McDonald's for a hamburger. He didn't like the food or the prices, but he liked the ambience. Then he went to Nirula's, a successful Delhi food chain. He liked the food and the prices there, but he complained to the manager because Nirula's did not have the same pleasant atmosphere as McDonald's. The moral of the story? Price-performance expectations are changing, often to the consternation of both the multinationals and the locals. McDonald's has been forced to adapt its menu to local tastes by adding vegetable burgers. Local chains like Nirula's have been pushed to meet global standards for cleanliness and ambience.

Consumers in the big emerging markets are far more focused than their Western counterparts on the price-performance equation. That focus tends to give low-cost local competitors the edge in hotly contested markets. MNCs can, however, learn to turn this price sensitivity to their advantage. Philips Electronics, for example, introduced a combination video-CD player in China in 1994. Although there is virtually no market for this product in Europe or the United States, the Chinese quickly embraced it as a great two-for-one bargain. More than 15 million units have been sold in China, and the product seems likely to catch on in Indonesia and India. Consumers in those countries see the player as good value for the money.

RETHINKING BRAND MANAGEMENT. Armed with powerful, established brands, multinationals are likely to overestimate the extent of

Westernization in the emerging markets and the value of using a consistent approach to brand management around the world.

In India, Coca-Cola overvalued the pull of its brand among the tier-two consumers. Coke based its advertising strategy on its worldwide image and then watched the advantage slip to Pepsi, which had adopted a campaign that was oriented toward the Indian market. As one of Coke's senior executives recently put it in the *Wall Street Journal*, "We're so successful in international business that we applied a tried and true formula . . . and it was the wrong formula to apply in India."

It took Coke more than two years to get the message, but it is now repositioning itself by using local heroes, such as popular cricket players, in its advertising. Perhaps more important, it is heavily promoting a popular Indian brand of cola—Thums Up—which Coke bought from a local bottler in 1993, only to scorn it for several years as a poor substitute for the Real Thing.

RETHINKING THE COSTS OF MARKET BUILDING.   For many MNCs, entering an emerging market means introducing a new product or service category. But Kellogg, for example, found that introducing breakfast cereals to India was a slow process because it meant creating new eating habits. Once the company had persuaded Indians to eat cereal, at great expense, local competitors were able to ride on Kellogg's coattails by introducing breakfast cereals with local flavors. As a result, Kellogg may discover in the long run that they paid too high a price for too small a market. Sampling, celebrity endorsements, and other forms of consumer education are expensive: regional tastes vary and language barriers can create difficulties. India, for example, has 13 major languages and pronounced cultural differences across regions.

Multinationals would do well to rethink the costs of building markets. Changing developed habits is difficult and expensive. Providing consumers with a new product that requires no reeducation can be much easier. For example, consider the rapid adoption of pagers in China. Because telephones are not widely available there, pagers have helped fill the void as a means of one-way communication.

RETHINKING PRODUCT DESIGN.   Even when consumers in emerging markets appear to want the same products as are sold elsewhere, some redesign is often necessary to reflect differences in use, distribution, or selling. Because the Chinese use pagers to send entire messages—which is not how they were intended to be used—Motorola developed pagers capable of displaying more lines of information. The result: Motorola encountered the enviable problem of having to scramble to keep up with exploding demand for its product.

In the mid-1980s, a leading MNC in telecommunications began exporting its electronic switching systems to China for use in the phone system. The switching systems had been designed for the company's home market, where there were many customers but substantial periods when the phones were not in use. In China, on the other hand, there were very few phones, but they were in almost constant use. The switching system, which worked flawlessly in the West, simply couldn't handle the load in China. Ultimately, the company had to redesign its software.

Distribution can also have a huge impact on product design. A Western maker of frozen desserts, for example, had to reformulate one of its products not because of differences in consumers' tastes, but because the refrigerators in most retail outlets in India weren't cold enough to store the product properly. The product had been designed for storage at minus 15 degrees centigrade, but the typical retailer's refrigerator operates at minus 4 degrees. Moreover, power interruptions frequently shut down the refrigerators.

RETHINKING PACKAGING. Whether the problem is dust, heat, or bumpy roads, the distribution infrastructure in emerging markets places special strains on packaging. One glass manufacturer, for example, was stunned at the breakage it sustained as a result of poor roads and trucks in India.

And consumers in tiers two and three are likely to have packaging preferences that are different from consumers in the West. Single-serve packets, or sachets, are enormously popular in India. They allow consumers to buy only what they need, experiment with new products, and conserve cash at the same time. Products as varied as detergents, shampoos, pickles, cough syrup, and oil are sold in sachets in India, and it is estimated that they make up 20% to 30% of the total sold in their categories. Sachets are spreading as a marketing device for such items as shampoos in China as well.

RETHINKING CAPITAL EFFICIENCY. The common wisdom is that the infrastructure problems in emerging markets—inefficient distribution systems, poor banking facilities, and inadequate logistics—will require companies to use more capital than in Western markets, not less. But that is the wrong mind-set. Hindustan Lever, a subsidiary of Unilever in India, saw a low-cost Indian detergent maker, Nirma, become the largest branded detergent maker in the world over a seven-year period by courting the tier-two and tier-three markets. Realizing that it could not compete by making marginal changes, Hindustan Lever rethought every aspect of its business, including production, distribution, marketing, and capital efficiency.

Today Hindustan Lever operates a $2 billion business with effectively zero working capital. Consider just one of the practices that makes this possible. The company keeps a supply of signed checks from its dealers. When it ships an order, it simply writes in the correct amount for the order. This practice is not uncommon in India. The Indian agribusiness company, Rallis, uses it with its 20,000 dealers in rural India. But this way of doing things is unheard of in Unilever's home countries, the United Kingdom and the Netherlands.

Hindustan Lever also manages to operate with minimal fixed capital. It does so in part through an active program of supplier management; the company works with local entrepreneurs who own and manage plants whose capacity is dedicated to Hindustan Lever's products. Other MNCs will find that there is less need for vertical integration in emerging markets than they might think. Quality suppliers can be located and developed. Their lower overhead structure can help the MNCs gain a competitive cost position. Supply chain management is an important tool for changing the capital efficiency of a multinational's operations.

Rather than concede the market, Hindustan Lever radically changed itself and is today successfully competing against Nirma with a low-cost detergent called Wheel. The lesson learned in India has not been lost on Unilever. It is unlikely to concede tier-two and tier-three markets in China, Indonesia, or Brazil without a fight.

How Does the Distribution System Work?

One of the greatest regrets of multinational executives, especially those we spoke with in China, was that they had not invested more in distribution before launching their products. Access to distribution is often critical to success in emerging markets, and it cannot be taken for granted. There is no substitute for a detailed understanding of the unique characteristics of a market's distribution system and how that system is likely to evolve.

Consider the differences between China and India. Distribution in China is primarily local and provincial. Under the former planned economy, most distribution networks were confined to political units, such as counties, cities, or provinces. Even at present, there is no real national distribution network for most products. Many MNCs have gained access to provincial networks by creating joint ventures. But these JVs are now impediments to the creation of the badly needed national network. Chinese JV partners protect their turf. This gap between the MNCs' need for a national, cost-effective distribution system and the more locally oriented goals of their partners is creating serious tensions. We expect that many JVs formed originally to allow multinationals market and distribution access will be restructured because of this very issue during the next five to seven years.

In India, on the other hand, individual entrepreneurs have already put together a national distribution system in a wide variety of businesses. Established companies such as Colgate-Palmolive and Godrej in personal care, Hindustan Lever in packaged goods, Tatas in trucks, Bajaj in scooters—the list is long—control their own distribution systems. Those systems take the form of long-standing arrangements with networks of small-scale distributors throughout the country, and the banking network is part of those relationships. Many of the established packaged-goods companies reach more than 3 million retail outlets—using trains, trucks, bullock-drawn carts, camels, and bicycles. And many companies claim to service each one of those outlets once a week.

Any MNC that wants to establish its own distribution system in India inevitably runs up against significant obstacles and costs. Ford, for example, is trying to establish a new, high-quality dealer network to sell cars in India. To obtain a dealership, each prospective dealer is expected to invest a large amount of his own money and must undergo special training. In the long haul, Ford's approach may prove to be a major source of advantage to the company, but the cost in cash and managerial attention of building the dealers' network will be substantial.

Ironically, the lack of a national distribution system in China may be an advantage. MNCs with patience and ingenuity can more easily build distribution systems to suit their needs, and doing so might confer competitive advantages. As one manager we talked to put it, "The trick to sustained, long-term profitability in China lies not in technology or in savvy advertising or even in low pricing, but rather in building a modern distribution system." Conceivably, China may see consolidation of the retail market earlier than India.

The Chinese and Indian cases signal the need for MNCs to develop a market-specific distribution strategy. In India, MNCs will have to determine who controls national distribution in order to distinguish likely partners from probable competitors. In China, multinationals seeking national distribution of their products must consider the motivations of potential partners before entering relationships that may frustrate their intentions.

Will Local or Expatriate Leadership Be More Effective?

Leadership of a multinational's venture in an emerging market requires a complex blend of local sensitivity and global knowledge. Getting the balance right is critical but never easy. MNCs frequently lack the cultural understanding to get the mix of expatriate and local leaders right.

Expatriates from the MNCs' host country play multiple roles. They transfer technology and management practices. They ensure that local employees understand and practice the corporate culture. In the early stages of market development, expatriates are the conduits for information flow between the multinational's corporate office and the local operation. But while headquarters staff usually recognizes the importance of sending information to the local operation, they tend to be less aware that information must also be received from the other direction. Expatriates provide credibility at headquarters when they convey information, especially information concerning the adaptations the corporation must make in order to be successful in the emerging market. Given these important roles, the large number of expatriates in China—170,000 by one count—is understandable.

Every multinational operation we observed in China had several expatriates in management positions. In India, by contrast, we rarely saw expatriate managers, and the few that we did see were usually of Indian origin. That's because among the big emerging markets, India is unique in that it has developed, over time, a cadre of engineers and managers. The Indian institutes of technology and institutes of management turn out graduates with a high degree of technical competence.

Perhaps more important from the perspective of a multinational, Indian managers speak English fluently and seem adept at learning a new corporate culture. At the same time, they have a much better appreciation of local nuances and a deeper commitment to the Indian market than any expatriate could have.

Those seeming advantages may be offset, however, by two disadvantages. First, a management team of native-born managers may not have the same "share of voice" at corporate headquarters that expatriate managers have. Yet maintaining a strong voice is essential, given the difficulty most managers at corporate headquarters have in understanding the dynamics and peculiar requirements of operating in emerging markets. Second, the "soft technology" that is central to Western competitive advantage—the bundle of elements that creates a dynamic, cost-effective, market-sensitive organization—is hard to develop when the management team consists of people who have worked only briefly, if at all, in such an organization.

Several multinationals have sent expatriates of Chinese or Indian origin from their U.S. or European base back to their Chinese or Indian operations in order to convey the company's soft technology in a culturally sensitive way. But that strategy has not, in general, been successful. As one manager we spoke to noted, "Indians from the United States who are sent back as expatriates are frozen in time. They remember the India they left 20 years ago. They are totally out of sync. But they do not have the humility to accept that they have to learn." We heard the same sentiment echoed in China, both for Chinese-Americans and, less frequently, for Chinese who had obtained a higher education in the United States and then returned as a part of a multinational management team.

Using American or West European expatriates during the early years of market entry can make sense, but this approach has its own set of problems. Cultural and language difficulties in countries like China and India typically limit expats' interaction with the locals as well as their effectiveness. In addition, the need to understand how to deal with the local political system, especially in China, makes long-term assignments desirable. It often takes an expatriate manager two years to get fully up to speed. From the company's perspective, it makes sense to keep that manager in place for another three years to take full advantage of what he or she has learned. But few Western expatriates are willing to stay in China that long; many feel that a long assignment keeps them out of the loop and may impose a high career cost. Multinationals, therefore, need to think about how to attract and retain high-quality expatriate talent, how to maintain expats' links to the parent company, and how to use and pass along expats' competencies once they move on to another post.

Is It Necessary to "Present One Face"?

Beyond the normal organizational questions that would exist wherever a company does business, there is a question of special importance in emerging markets: Do local political considerations require the multinational to adopt a uniform strategy for each of its business units operating in the country, or can it permit each unit to act on its own?

As with the issue of distribution, the contrasts between China and India make clear why there is no one right answer to this question. In China, massive governmental interference in the economy makes a uniform country strategy necessary. The Chinese government tends to view the activities of individual business units as part of a single company's effort, and therefore concessions made by any one unit—such as an agreement to achieve a certain level of local sourcing—may well become requirements for the others. An MNC in China must be able to articulate a set of principles that conforms to China's announced priorities, and it should coordinate the activities of its various business units so that they resonate with those priorities.

Given the way most multinationals operate, "presenting one face" to China is very difficult. Business units have their own P&L responsibilities and are reluctant to lose their autonomy. Reporting lines can become overly complex. Although we observed many organizational approaches, not a single MNC we looked at is completely satisfied with its approach to this difficult issue.

Is it any wonder? Consider the life of one MNC executive we visited in China. As the head of his company's China effort, he has to coordinate with the company's regional headquarters in Japan, report to international headquarters in Europe, and maintain close contact with corporate headquarters in North America. He also has to meet with members of the Chinese government, with the MNC's business-unit executives in China, and with the leaders of the business units' Chinese partners. Simply maintaining all of these contacts is extraordinarily taxing and time consuming.

There is somewhat less need to present one face to India. Since 1991, the Indian government has scaled back its efforts to shape what

MNCs do in the country. Business units may therefore act more independently than would be appropriate in China. The strategy for India can be developed on a business-by-business basis. Nonetheless, the market is large and complex. National regulations are onerous, and state-level governments are still so different from one another that MNCs are well advised to develop knowledge that they can share with all their business units in India.

Do Partners Foster Valuable Learning?

In the first wave of market entry, multinationals used joint ventures extensively as a way not only to navigate through bureaucratic processes but also to learn about new markets. With few exceptions, however, JVs in emerging markets have been problematic. In some cases, executives of the multinationals mistakenly thought the JVs would do their strategic thinking for them. In most cases, tensions in JV relationships have diverted management attention away from learning about the market.

One consistent problem is that companies enter joint ventures with very different expectations. One Chinese manager described the situation in terms of an old saying: We are sleeping in the same bed, with different dreams. The local partner sees the MNC as a source of technology and investment, and the multinational sees the partner as a means to participate in the domestic market.

When they come to an emerging market, multinationals usually are still building their manufacturing and marketing infrastructures, and they don't expect immediate returns. Local partners, however, often want to see short-term profit. This disparity of aims leads to enormous strain in the relationship. The costs associated with expatriate managers also become a bone of contention. Who controls what can be yet another source of trouble—especially when the domestic partner has experience in the business. And when new investment is needed to grow the business, local partners often are unable to bring in the matching funds, yet they resent the dilution of their holding and the ensuing loss of control.

MNCs are finally learning that their local partners often do not have adequate market knowledge. The experience of most local partners predates the emergence of real consumer markets, and their business practices can be archaic. But as markets evolve toward greater transparency, as MNCs develop senior managers who understand how "the

system" works, and as the availability of local talent increases, multinationals have less to gain by using intermediaries as a vehicle for
learning.

The MNCs' need for local partners clearly is diminishing. In 1997, a
consulting firm surveyed 67 companies invested in China and found
that the percentage of their projects that became wholly foreign-
owned enterprises grew steadily from 18% in 1992 to 37% in 1996. A
passive partner that can provide a local face may still be important in
some industries, but this is a very different matter from the JV.

Success Will Transform the Multinationals

As executives look for growth in the big emerging markets, they
tend quite naturally to focus on the size of the opportunity and the
challenges that lie ahead. Few, however, stop to think about how success will transform their companies. But consider the magnitude of
the changes we have been describing and the sheer size of the markets
in question. Success in the big emerging markets will surely change
the shape of the modern multinational as we know it today.

For years, executives have assumed they could export their current
business models around the globe. That assumption has to change.
Citicorp, for example, aims to serve a billion banking customers by
2010. There is no way Citicorp, given its current cost structure, can
profitably serve someone in Beijing or Delhi whose net wealth is less
than $5,000. But if Citicorp creates a new business model—rethinking
every element of its cost structure—it will be able to serve not only average Chinese people but also inner-city residents in New York. In
short, companies must realize that the innovation required to serve
the large tier-two and tier-three segments in emerging markets has the
potential to make them more competitive in their traditional markets—and therefore in *all* markets.

Over time, the imperialist assumption that innovation comes from
the center will gradually fade away and die. Increasingly, as multinationals develop products better adapted to the emerging markets, they
are finding that those markets are becoming an important source of
innovation. Telecommunications companies, for example, are discovering that people in markets with no old technology to "forget" may
accept technological changes faster. MNCs such as Texas Instruments
and Motorola are assigning responsibility for software-oriented

business development to their Indian operations. China has become such a significant market for video-CD players that the Chinese are likely to be major players in introducing the next round of video-CD standards around the world.

The big emerging markets will also have a significant influence on the product development philosophy of the MNCs. One major multinational recognized to its surprise that the Chinese have found a way of producing high-quality detergents with equipment and processes that cost about one-fifth of what the MNC spends. Stories like that get repeated in a wide variety of businesses, including fine chemicals, cement, textile machinery, trucks, and television sets.

As product development becomes decentralized, collaboration between labs in Bangalore, London, and Dallas, for example, will gradually become the rule, not the exception. New-product introductions will have to take into consideration nontraditional centers of influence. Thus in the CD business at Philips, new-product introductions, which previously occurred almost exclusively in Europe, now also take place in Shanghai and California.

As corporate imperialism draws to a close, multinationals will increasingly look to emerging markets for talent. India is already recognized as a source of technical talent in engineering, sciences, and software, as well as in some aspects of management. All high-tech companies recruit in India not only for the Indian market but also for the global market. China, given its growth and its technical and managerial-training infrastructure, has not yet reached that stage, but it may well reach it in the not-too-distant future.

A major shift in geographical resources will take place within the next five years. Philips is already downsizing in Europe and reportedly employs more Chinese than Dutch workers. Over 40% of the market for Coke, Gillette, Lucent, Boeing, and GE power systems is in Asia. And in the last two years, ABB has shrunk its European head count by more than 40,000 while adding 45,000 people in Asia.

In addition to these changes, an increasing percentage of the investment in plant and equipment and marketing will go to the emerging markets. As those markets grow to account for 30% to 40% of capital invested—and even a larger percentage of market share and profits—they will attract much more attention from top management.

The importance of these markets will inevitably be reflected in the ethnic and national origin of senior management. At present, with a few exceptions such as Citicorp and Unilever, senior management ranks are filled with nationals from the company's home country. By the year 2010, however, the top 200 managers from around the world for any multinational will have a much greater cultural and ethnic mix.

How many of today's multinationals are prepared to accommodate 30% to 40% of their top team of 200 coming from China, India, and Brazil? How will that cultural mix influence decision making, risk taking, and team building? Diversity will put an enormous burden on top-level managers to articulate clearly the values and behaviors expected of senior managers, and it will demand large investments in training and socialization. The need for a single company culture will also become more critical as people from different cultures begin to work together. Providing the right glue to hold companies together will be a big challenge.

That challenge will be intensified by an impending power shift within multinationals. The end of corporate imperialism suggests more than a new relationship between the developed and the emerging economies. It also suggests an end to the era of centralized corporate power—embodied in the attitude that "headquarters knows best"—and a shift to a much more dispersed base of power and influence.

Consider the new patterns of knowledge transfer we are beginning to see. Unilever, for example, is transferring Indian managers with experience in low-cost distribution to China, where they will build a national distribution system and train Chinese managers. And it has transferred Indian managers with knowledge of tier-two markets to Brazil. The phenomenon of using managers from outside the home country to transfer knowledge is relatively new. It will grow over time to the point where the multinational becomes an organization with several centers of expertise and excellence.

Multinationals will be shaped by a wide variety of forces in the coming decades. The big emerging markets will be one of the major forces they come up against. And the effect will be nothing short of dramatic change on both sides. Together, they will challenge each other to change for the better as a truly global twenty-first century economy takes shape. The MNCs will create a higher standard of products, quality, technology, and management practices. Large, opaque markets will gradually become more transparent. The process of transition to market economies will be evolutionary, uneven, and fraught with uncertainties. But the direction is no longer in question.

In order to participate effectively in the big emerging markets, multinationals will increasingly have to reconfigure their resource base, rethink their cost structure, redesign their product development process, and challenge their assumptions about the cultural mix of their top managers. In short, they will have to develop a new mind-set and adopt new business models to achieve global competitiveness in the postimperialist age.

4
Strategy under Uncertainty

Hugh Courtney, Jane Kirkland, and Patrick Viguerie

What makes for a good strategy in highly uncertain business environments? Some executives seek to shape the future with high-stakes bets. Eastman Kodak Company, for example, is spending $500 million per year to develop an array of digital photography products that it hopes will fundamentally change the way people create, store, and view pictures. Meanwhile, Hewlett-Packard Company is investing $50 million per year to pursue a rival vision centered around home-based photo printers. The business press loves to hype such industry-shaping strategies because of their potential to create enormous wealth, but the sober reality is that most companies lack the industry position, assets, or appetite for risk necessary to make such strategies work.

More risk-averse executives hedge their bets by making a number of smaller investments. In pursuit of growth opportunities in emerging markets, for example, many consumer-product companies are forging limited operational or distribution alliances. But it's often difficult to determine if such limited investments truly reserve the right to play in these countries or just reserve the right to lose.

Alternatively, some executives favor investments in flexibility that allow their companies to adapt quickly as markets evolve. But the costs of establishing such flexibility can be high. Moreover, taking a wait-and-see strategy—postponing large investments until the future becomes clear—can create a window of opportunity for competitors.

This article is based on research sponsored by McKinsey's ongoing Strategy Theory Initiative (STI). The authors would like to thank their STI colleagues for their significant contributions to this article.

How should executives facing great uncertainty decide whether to bet big, hedge, or wait and see? Chances are, traditional strategic-planning processes won't help much. The standard practice is to lay out a vision of future events precise enough to be captured in a discounted-cash-flow analysis. Of course, managers can discuss alternative scenarios and test how sensitive their forecasts are to changes in key variables, but the goal of such analysis is often to find the most likely outcome and create a strategy based on it. That approach serves companies well in relatively stable business environments. But when there is greater uncertainty about the future, it is at best marginally helpful and at worst downright dangerous.

One danger is that this traditional approach leads executives to view uncertainty in a binary way—to assume that the world is either certain, and therefore open to precise predictions about the future, or uncertain, and therefore completely unpredictable. Planning or capital-budgeting processes that require point forecasts force managers to bury underlying uncertainties in their cash flows. Such systems clearly push managers to underestimate uncertainty in order to make a compelling case for their strategy.

Underestimating uncertainty can lead to strategies that neither defend against the threats nor take advantage of the opportunities that higher levels of uncertainty may provide. In one of the most colossal underestimations in business history, Kenneth H. Olsen, then president of Digital Equipment Corporation, announced in 1977 that "there is no reason for any individual to have a computer in their home." The explosion in the personal computer market was not inevitable in 1977, but it was certainly within the range of possibilities that industry experts were discussing at the time.

At the other extreme, assuming that the world is entirely unpredictable can lead managers to abandon the analytical rigor of their traditional planning processes altogether and base their strategic decisions primarily on gut instinct. This "just do it" approach to strategy can cause executives to place misinformed bets on emerging products or markets that result in record write-offs. Those who took the plunge and invested in home banking in the early 1980s immediately come to mind.

Risk-averse managers who think they are in very uncertain environments don't trust their gut instincts and suffer from decision paralysis. They avoid making critical strategic decisions about the products, markets, and technologies they should develop. They focus instead on reengineering, quality management, or internal cost-reduction programs. Although valuable, those programs are not substitutes for strategy.

Making systematically sound strategic decisions under uncertainty requires a different approach—one that avoids this dangerous binary view. It is rare that managers know absolutely nothing of strategic importance, even in the most uncertain environments. In fact, they usually can identify a range of potential outcomes or even a discrete set of scenarios. This simple insight is extremely powerful because determining which strategy is best, and what process should be used to develop it, depend vitally on the level of uncertainty a company faces.

What follows, then, is a framework for determining the level of uncertainty surrounding strategic decisions and for tailoring strategy to that uncertainty. No approach can make the challenges of uncertainty go away, but this one offers practical guidance that will lead to more informed and confident strategic decisions.

Four Levels of Uncertainty

Even the most uncertain business environments contain a lot of strategically relevant information. First, it is often possible to identify clear trends, such as market demographics, that can help define potential demand for future products or services. Second, there is usually a host of factors that are currently *unknown* but that are in fact *knowable*—that could be known if the right analysis were done. Performance attributes for current technologies, elasticities of demand for certain stable categories of products, and competitors' capacity-expansion plans are variables that are often unknown, but not entirely unknowable.

The uncertainty that remains after the best possible analysis has been done is what we call *residual uncertainty*—for example, the outcome of an ongoing regulatory debate or the performance attributes of a technology still in development. But often, quite a bit can be known about even those residual uncertainties. In practice, we have found that the residual uncertainty facing most strategic-decision makers falls into one of four broad levels (see Exhibit 4-1 "How to Use the Four Levels of Uncertainty"):

Exhibit 4-1   How to Use the Four Levels of Uncertainty

	A Clear-Enough Future	**Alternate Futures**
What Can Be Known?	• A single forecast precise enough for determining strategy	• A few discrete outcomes that define the future
Analytic Tools	• "Traditional" strategy tool kit	• Decision analysis • Option valuation models • Game theory
Examples	• Strategy against low-cost airline entrant	• Long-distance telephone carriers' strategy to enter deregulated local-service market • Capacity strategies for chemical plants

LEVEL 1: A CLEAR-ENOUGH FUTURE

At level 1, managers can develop a single forecast of the future that is precise *enough* for strategy development. Although it will be inexact to the degree that all business environments are inherently uncertain, the forecast will be sufficiently narrow to point to a single strategic direction. In other words, at level 1, the residual uncertainty is irrelevant to making strategic decisions.

Consider a major airline trying to develop a strategic response to the entry of a low-cost, no-frills competitor into one of its hub airports. Should it respond with a low-cost service of its own? Should it cede the low-cost niche segments to the new entrant? Or should it compete aggressively on price and service in an attempt to drive the entrant out of the market?

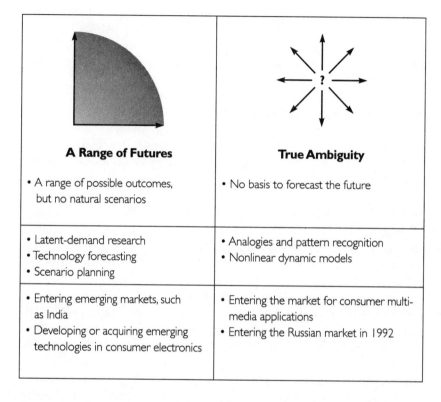

A Range of Futures	**True Ambiguity**
• A range of possible outcomes, but no natural scenarios	• No basis to forecast the future
• Latent-demand research • Technology forecasting • Scenario planning	• Analogies and pattern recognition • Nonlinear dynamic models
• Entering emerging markets, such as India • Developing or acquiring emerging technologies in consumer electronics	• Entering the market for consumer multi-media applications • Entering the Russian market in 1992

To make that strategic decision, the airline's executives need market research on the size of different customer segments and the likely response of each segment to different combinations of pricing and service. They also need to know how much it costs the competitor to serve, and how much capacity the competitor has for, every route in question. Finally, the executives need to know the new entrant's competitive objectives to anticipate how it would respond to any strategic moves their airline might make. In today's U.S. airline industry, such information is either known already or is possible to know. It might not be easy to obtain—it might require new market research, for example—but it is inherently knowable. And once that information is known, residual uncertainty would be limited, and the incumbent airline would be able to build a confident business case around its strategy.

LEVEL 2: ALTERNATE FUTURES

At level 2, the future can be described as one of a few alternate outcomes, or *discrete scenarios*. Analysis cannot identify which outcome will occur, although it may help establish probabilities. Most important, some, if not all, elements of the strategy would change if the outcome were predictable.

Many businesses facing major regulatory or legislative change confront level 2 uncertainty. Consider U.S. long-distance telephone providers in late 1995, as they began developing strategies for entering local telephone markets. By late 1995, legislation that would fundamentally deregulate the industry was pending in Congress, and the broad form that new regulations would take was fairly clear to most industry observers. But whether or not the legislation was going to pass and how quickly it would be implemented in the event it did pass were uncertain. No amount of analysis would allow the long-distance carriers to predict those outcomes, and the correct course of action—for example, the timing of investments in network infrastructure—depended on which outcome occurred.

In another common level 2 situation, the value of a strategy depends mainly on competitors' strategies, and those cannot yet be observed or predicted. For example, in oligopoly markets, such as those for pulp and paper, chemicals, and basic raw materials, the primary uncertainty is often competitors' plans for expanding capacity: Will they build new plants or not? Economies of scale often dictate that any plant built would be quite large and would be likely to have a significant impact on industry prices and profitability. Therefore, any one company's decision to build a plant is often contingent on competitors' decisions. This is a classic level 2 situation: The possible outcomes are discrete and clear. It is difficult to predict which one will occur. And the best strategy depends on which one does occur.

LEVEL 3: A RANGE OF FUTURES

At level 3, a range of potential futures can be identified. That range is defined by a limited number of key variables, but the actual outcome may lie anywhere along a continuum bounded by that range. There are no natural discrete scenarios. As in level 2, some, and possibly all, elements of the strategy would change if the outcome were predictable.

Companies in emerging industries or entering new geographic markets often face level 3 uncertainty. Consider a European consumer-goods company deciding whether to introduce its products to the Indian market. The best possible market research might identify only a broad range of potential customer-penetration rates—say, from 10% to 30%—and there would be no obvious scenarios within that range. Such a broad range of estimates would be common when introducing completely new products and services to a market, and therefore determining the level of latent demand is very difficult. The company entering India would be likely to follow a very different and more aggressive entry strategy if it knew for certain that its customer penetration rates would be closer to 30% than to 10%.

Analogous problems exist for companies in fields driven by technological innovation, such as the semiconductor industry. When deciding whether to invest in a new technology, producers can often estimate only a broad range of potential cost and performance attributes for the technology, and the overall profitability of the investment depends on those attributes.

LEVEL 4: TRUE AMBIGUITY

At level 4, multiple dimensions of uncertainty interact to create an environment that is virtually impossible to predict. Unlike in level 3 situations, the range of potential outcomes cannot be identified, let alone scenarios within that range. It might not even be possible to identify, much less predict, all the relevant variables that will define the future.

Level 4 situations are quite rare, and they tend to migrate toward one of the other levels over time. Nevertheless, they do exist. Consider a telecommunications company deciding where and how to compete in the emerging consumer-multimedia market. It is confronting multiple uncertainties concerning technology, demand, and relationships between hardware and content providers, all of which may interact in ways so unpredictable that no plausible range of scenarios can be identified.

Companies considering making major entry investments in post-Communist Russia in 1992 faced level 4 uncertainty. They could not outline the potential laws or regulations that would govern property rights and transactions. That central uncertainty was compounded by additional uncertainty over the viability of supply chains and the demand for previously unavailable consumer goods and services. And shocks such as a political assassination or a currency default could have spun the whole system toward completely unforeseen outcomes.

Those examples illustrate how difficult strategic decisions can be at level 4, but they also underscore their transitory nature. Greater political and regulatory stability has turned decisions about whether to enter Russian markets into level 3 problems for the majority of industries today. Similarly, uncertainty about strategic decisions in the consumer multimedia market will migrate to level 3 or to level 2 as the industry begins to take shape over the next several years.

Tailoring Strategic Analysis to the Four Levels of Uncertainty

Our experience suggests that at least half of all strategy problems fall into levels 2 or 3, while most of the rest are level 1 problems. But executives who think about uncertainty in a binary way tend to treat all strategy problems as if they fell into either level 1 or level 4. And when those executives base their strategies on rigorous analysis, they are most likely to apply the same set of analytic tools regardless of the level of residual uncertainty they face. For example, they might attempt to use standard, quantitative market-research techniques to forecast demand for data traffic over wireless communications networks as far out as ten years from now.

But, in fact, a different kind of analysis should be done to identify and evaluate strategy options at each level of uncertainty. All strategy making begins with some form of situation analysis—that is, a picture of what the world will look like today and what is likely to happen in the future. Identifying the levels of uncertainty thus helps define the best such an analysis can do to describe each possible future an industry faces.

To help generate level 1's usefully precise prediction of the future, managers can use the standard strategy tool kit—market research, analyses of competitors' costs and capacity, value chain analysis, Michael Porter's five-forces framework, and so on. A discounted-cash-flow model that incorporates those predictions can then be used to determine the value of various alternative strategies. It's not surprising that most managers feel extremely comfortable in level 1 situations—these are the tools and frameworks taught in every leading business program in the United States.

Level 2 situations are a bit more complex. First, managers must develop a set of discrete scenarios based on their understanding of how the key residual uncertainties might play out—for example, whether deregulation occurs or not, a competitor builds a new plant or not. Each scenario may require a different valuation model—general industry structure and conduct will often be fundamentally different depending on which scenario occurs, so alternative valuations can't be handled by performing sensitivity analyses around a single baseline model. Getting information that helps establish the relative probabilities of the alternative outcomes should be a high priority.

After establishing an appropriate valuation model for each possible outcome and determining how probable each is likely to be, a classic decision-analysis framework can be used to evaluate the risks and returns inherent in alternative strategies. This process will identify the likely winners and losers in alternative scenarios, and perhaps more important, it will help quantify what's at stake for companies that follow status quo strategies. Such an analysis is often the key to making the case for strategic change.

In level 2 situations, it is important not only to identify the different possible future outcomes but also to think through the likely paths the industry might take to reach those alternative futures. Will change occur in major steps at some particular point in time, following, for example, a regulatory ruling or a competitor's decision to enter the market? Or will change occur in a more evolutionary fashion, as often happens after a resolution of competing technology standards? This is vital information because it determines which market signals or trigger variables should be monitored closely. As events unfold and the relative probabilities of alternative scenarios change, it is likely that one's strategy will also need to be adapted to these changes.

At one level, the analysis in level 3 is very similar to that in level 2. A set of scenarios needs to be identified that describes alternative future outcomes, and analysis should focus on the trigger events signaling that the market is moving toward one or another scenario. Developing a meaningful set of scenarios, however, is less straightforward in level 3. Scenarios that describe the extreme points in the range of possible outcomes are often relatively easy to develop, but these rarely provide much concrete guidance for current strategic decisions. Since there are no other natural discrete scenarios in level 3, deciding which possible outcomes should be fully developed into alternative scenarios is a real art. But there are a few general rules. First, develop only a limited number of alternative scenarios—the complexity of juggling more than four or five tends to hinder decision making. Second, avoid developing redundant scenarios that have no unique implications for strategic decision making; make sure each scenario offers a distinct picture of the industry's structure, conduct, and performance. Third, develop a set of scenarios that collectively account for the *probable* range of future outcomes and not necessarily the entire *possible* range.

Because it is impossible in level 3 to define a complete list of scenarios and related probabilities, it is impossible to calculate the expected value of different strategies. However, establishing the range of scenarios should allow managers to determine how robust their strategy is, identify likely winners and losers, and determine roughly the risk of following status quo strategies.

Situation analysis at level 4 is even more qualitative. Still, it is critical to avoid the urge to throw one's hands up and act purely on gut instinct. Instead, managers need to catalog systematically what they know and what is possible to know. Even if it is impossible to develop a meaningful set of probable, or even possible, outcomes in level 4 situations, managers can gain valuable strategic perspective. Usually, they can identify at least a subset of the variables that will determine how the market will evolve over time—for example, customer penetration rates or technology performance attributes. And they can identify favorable and unfavorable indicators of these variables that will let them track the market's evolution over time and adapt their strategy as new information becomes available.

Managers can also identify patterns indicating possible ways the market may evolve by studying how analogous markets developed in other level 4 situations, determining the key attributes of the winners and losers in those situations and identifying the strategies they employed. Finally, although it will be impossible to quantify the risks and returns of different strategies, managers should be able to identify what information they would have to believe about the future to justify the investments they are considering. Early market indicators and analogies from similar markets will help sort out whether such beliefs are realistic or not.

Uncertainty demands a more flexible approach to situation analysis. The old one-size-fits-all approach is simply inadequate. Over time, companies in most industries will face strategy problems that have varying levels of residual uncertainty, and it is vitally important that the strategic analysis be tailored to the level of uncertainty.

Postures and Moves

Before we can talk about the dynamics of formulating strategy at each level of uncertainty, we need to introduce a basic vocabulary for talking about strategy. First, there are three *strategic postures* a company can choose to take vis-à-vis uncertainty: shaping, adapting, or reserving the right to play. Second, there are three types of moves in *the portfolio of actions* that can be used to implement that strategy: big bets, options, and no-regrets moves.

STRATEGIC POSTURE

Any good strategy requires a choice about strategic posture. Fundamentally, *posture* defines the intent of a strategy relative to the current and future state of an industry. (See Exhibit 4-2 "The Three Strategic Postures.") *Shapers* aim to drive their industries toward a new structure of their own devising. Their strategies are about creating new opportunities in a market—either by shaking up relatively stable level 1 industries or by trying to control the direction of the market in industries with higher levels of uncertainty. Kodak, for example, through its investment in digital photography, is pursuing a shaping strategy in an effort to maintain its leadership position, as a new technology supersedes the one currently generating most of its earnings. Although its product technology is new, Kodak's strategy is still based on a traditional model in which the company provides digital cameras and film while photo-processing stores provide many of the photo-printing and storage functions for the consumer. Hewlett-Packard also seeks to be a shaper in this market, but it is pursuing a radically different model in which high-quality, low-cost photo printers shift photo processing from stores to the home.

In contrast, *adapters* take the current industry structure and its future evolution as givens, and they react to the opportunities the market offers. In environments with little uncertainty, adapters choose a strategic positioning—that is, where and how to compete—in the current industry. At higher levels of uncertainty, their strategies are predicated on the ability to recognize and respond quickly to market developments. In the highly volatile telecommunications-service industry, for example, service resellers are adapters. They buy and resell the latest products and services offered by the major telecom providers,

Exhibit 4-2   The Three Strategic Postures

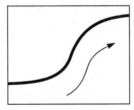

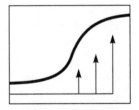

Shape the future

Play a leadership role in
establishing how the industry
operates, for example:
 —setting standards
 —creating demand

Adapt to the future

Win through speed, agility, and
flexibility in recognizing and
capturing opportunities in
existing markets

Reserve the right to play

Invest sufficiently to stay in
the game but avoid
premature commitments

relying on pricing and effective execution rather than on product innovation as their source of competitive advantage.

The third strategic posture, *reserving the right to play*, is a special form
of adapting. This posture is relevant only in levels 2 through 4; it involves making incremental investments today that put a company in a
privileged position, through either superior information, cost structures, or relationships between customers and suppliers. That allows
the company to wait until the environment becomes less uncertain
before formulating a strategy. Many pharmaceutical companies are reserving the right to play in the market for gene therapy applications by
acquiring or allying with small biotech firms that have relevant expertise. Providing privileged access to the latest industry developments,
these are low-cost investments compared with building a proprietary,
internal gene-therapy R&D program.

A PORTFOLIO OF ACTIONS

A posture is not a complete strategy. It clarifies strategic intent but
not the actions required to fulfill that intent. Three types of moves are
especially relevant to implementing strategy under conditions of uncertainty: big bets, options, and no-regrets moves. (See Exhibit 4-3
"What's in a Portfolio of Actions?")

Big bets are large commitments, such as major capital investments or
acquisitions, that will result in large payoffs in some scenarios and

Exhibit 4-3   What's in a Portfolio of Actions?

These building blocks are distinguished by three payoff profiles—that is, the amount of investment required up front and the conditions under which the investment will yield a positive return.

Scenario	Value
I.	+
2.	+
3.	+
4.	+

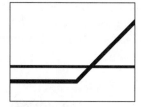

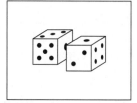

No-regrets moves
Strategic decisions that have positive payoffs in any scenario

Options
Decisions that yield a significant positive payoff in some outcomes and a (small) negative effect in others

Big bets
Focused strategies with positive payoffs in one or more scenarios but a negative effect in others

large losses in others. Not surprisingly, shaping strategies usually involve big bets, whereas adapting and reserving the right to play do not.

Options are designed to secure the big payoffs of the best-case scenarios while minimizing losses in the worst-case scenarios. This asymmetric payoff structure makes them resemble financial options. Most options involve making modest initial investments that will allow companies to ramp up or scale back the investment later as the market evolves. Classic examples include conducting pilot trials before the full-scale introduction of a new product, entering into limited joint ventures for distribution to minimize the risk of breaking into new markets, and licensing an alternative technology in case it proves to be superior to a current technology. Those reserving the right to play rely heavily on options, but shapers use them as well, either to shape an emerging but uncertain market as an early mover or to hedge their big bets.

Finally, *no-regrets moves* are just that—moves that will pay off no matter what happens. Managers often focus on obvious no-regrets moves like initiatives aimed at reducing costs, gathering competitive intelligence, or building skills. However, even in highly uncertain environments, strategic decisions like investing in capacity and entering certain markets can be no-regrets moves. Whether or not they put a name to them, most managers understand intuitively that no-regrets moves are an essential element of any strategy.

The choice of a strategic posture and an accompanying portfolio of actions sounds straightforward. But in practice, these decisions are highly dependent on the level of uncertainty facing a given business. Thus the four-level framework can help clarify the practical implications implicit in any choice of strategic posture and actions. The discussion that follows will demonstrate the different strategic challenges that each level of uncertainty poses and how the portfolio of actions may be applied.

STRATEGY IN LEVEL 1'S CLEAR-ENOUGH FUTURE

In predictable business environments, most companies are adapters. Analysis is designed to predict an industry's future landscape, and strategy involves making positioning choices about where and how to compete. When the underlying analysis is sound, such strategies are by definition made up of a series of no-regrets moves.

Adapter strategies in level 1 situations are not necessarily incremental or boring. For example, Southwest Airlines Company's no-frills, point-to-point service is a highly innovative, value-creating adapter strategy, as was Gateway 2000's low-cost assembly and direct-mail distribution strategy when it entered the personal computer market in the late 1980s. In both cases, managers were able to identify unexploited opportunities in relatively low-uncertainty environments within the existing market structure. The best level 1 adapters create value through innovations in their products or services or through improvements in their business systems without otherwise fundamentally changing the industry.

It is also possible to be a shaper in level 1 situations, but that is risky and rare, since level 1 shapers increase the amount of residual uncertainty in an otherwise predictable market—for themselves and their competitors—in an attempt to fundamentally alter long-standing industry structures and conduct. Consider Federal Express Corporation's overnight-delivery strategy. When it entered the mail-and-package delivery industry, a stable level 1 situation, FedEx's strategy in effect created level 3 uncertainty for itself. That is, even though CEO Frederick W. Smith commissioned detailed consulting reports that confirmed the feasibility of his business concept, only a broad range of potential demand for overnight services could be identified at the time. For the industry incumbents like United Parcel Service, FedEx created level 2 uncertainty. FedEx's move raised two questions for UPS: Will the overnight-delivery strategy succeed or not? and Will UPS have to offer a similar service to remain a viable competitor in the market?

Over time, the industry returned to level 1 stability, but with a fundamentally new structure. FedEx's bet paid off, forcing the rest of the industry to adapt to the new demand for overnight services.

What portfolio of actions did it take to realize that strategy? Like most shaper strategies, even in level 1 situations, this one required some big bets. That said, it often makes sense to build options into a shaper strategy to hedge against bad bets. Smith might have hedged his bets by leasing existing cargo airplanes instead of purchasing and retrofitting his original fleet of Falcon "minifreighters," or he could have outsourced ground pickup and delivery services. Such moves would have limited the amount of capital he would have needed to sink into his new strategy and facilitated a graceful exit had his concept failed. However, that kind of insurance doesn't always come cheap. In FedEx's case, had Smith leased standard-size cargo planes, he would have come under the restrictive regulations of the Civil Aeronautics Board. And outsourcing local pickups and deliveries would have diluted FedEx's unique door-to-door value to customers. Thus Smith stuck mainly to big bets in implementing his strategy, which drove him to the brink of bankruptcy in his first two years of operation but ultimately reshaped an entire industry.

STRATEGY IN LEVEL 2'S ALTERNATE FUTURES

If shapers in level 1 try to raise uncertainty, in levels 2 through 4 they try to lower uncertainty and create order out of chaos. In level 2, a shaping strategy is designed to increase the probability that a favored industry scenario will occur. A shaper in a capital-intensive industry like pulp and paper, for example, wants to prevent competitors from creating excess capacity that would destroy the industry's profitability. Consequently, shapers in such cases might commit their companies to building new capacity far in advance of an upturn in demand to preempt the competition, or they might consolidate the industry through mergers and acquisitions.

Consider the Microsoft Network (MSN). A few years ago, one could identify a discrete set of possible ways in which transactions would be conducted between networked computers. Either proprietary networks such as MSN would become the standard, or open networks like the Internet would prevail. Uncertainty in this situation was thus at level 2, even though other related strategy issues—such as determining the level of consumer demand for networked applications—were level 3 problems.

Microsoft could reasonably expect to shape the way markets for electronic commerce evolved if it created the proprietary MSN network. It would, in effect, be building a commerce hub that would link both suppliers and consumers through the MSN gateway. The strategy was a big bet: the development costs were significant and, more important, involved an enormously high level of industry exposure and attention. In effect, for Microsoft, it constituted a big credibility bet. Microsoft's activities in other areas—such as including one-button access to MSN from Windows95—were designed to increase the probability that this shaping bet would pay off.

But even the best shapers must be prepared to adapt. In the battle between proprietary and open networks, certain trigger variables—growth in the number of Internet and MSN subscribers, for example, or the activity profiles of early MSN subscribers—could provide valuable insight into how the market was evolving. When it became clear that open networks would prevail, Microsoft refocused the MSN concept around the Internet. Microsoft's shift illustrates that choices of strategic posture are not carved in stone, and it underscores the value of maintaining strategic flexibility under uncertainty. Shaping strategies can fail, so the best companies supplement their shaping bets with options that allow them to change course quickly if necessary. Microsoft was able to do just that because it remained flexible by being willing to cut its losses, by building a cadre of engineers who had a wide range of general-programming and product-development skills, and by closely monitoring key trigger variables. In uncertain environments, it is a mistake to let strategies run on autopilot, remaining content to update them only through standard year-end strategy reviews.

Because trigger variables are often relatively simple to monitor in level 2, it can be easy to adapt or reserve the right to play. For instance, companies that generate electricity—and others whose business depends on energy-intensive production processes—often face level 2 uncertainty in determining the relative cost of different fuel alternatives. Discrete scenarios can often be identified—for example, either natural gas or oil will be the low-cost fuel. Many companies thus choose an adapter strategy when building new plants: they construct flexible manufacturing processes that can switch easily between different fuels.

Chemical companies often choose to reserve the right to play when facing level 2 uncertainty in predicting the performance of a new technology. If the technology performs well, companies will have to employ it to remain competitive in the market. But if it does not fulfill its promise, incumbents can compete effectively with existing technologies. Most companies are reluctant to bet several hundred million dollars on building new capacity and retrofitting old plants around a new technology until it is proven. But if they don't make at least incremental investments in the short run, they risk falling too far behind competitors should the technology succeed. Thus many will purchase options to license the new technology within a specified time frame or begin retrofitting a proportion of existing capacity around the new technology. In either case, small, up-front commitments give the companies privileged positions, but not obligations, to ramp up or discontinue development of the new technology as its performance attributes become clearer over time.

STRATEGY IN LEVEL 3'S RANGE OF FUTURES

Shaping takes a different form in level 3. If at level 2, shapers are trying to make a discrete outcome occur, at level 3, they are trying to move the market in a general direction because they can identify only a range of possible outcomes. Consider the battle over standards for electronic cash transactions, currently a level 3 problem since one can define a range of potential products and services that fall between purely paper-based and purely electronic cash transactions, but it is unclear today whether there are any natural discrete scenarios within that range. Mondex International, a consortium of financial services providers and technology companies, is attempting to shape the future by establishing what it hopes will become universal electronic-cash standards. Its shaping posture is backed by big-bet investments in product development, infrastructure, and pilot experiments to speed customer acceptance.

In contrast, regional banks are mainly choosing adapter strategies. (See Exhibit 4-4 "How a Regional Bank Confronts the Uncertainties in Electronic Commerce.") An adapter posture at uncertainty levels 3 or 4 is often achieved primarily through investments in organizational capabilities designed to keep options open. Because they must make and implement strategy choices in real time, adapters need quick access to the best market information and the most flexible organizational structures. Many regional banks, for example, have put in place

Exhibit 4-4   How a Regional Bank Confronts the Uncertainties in Electronic Commerce

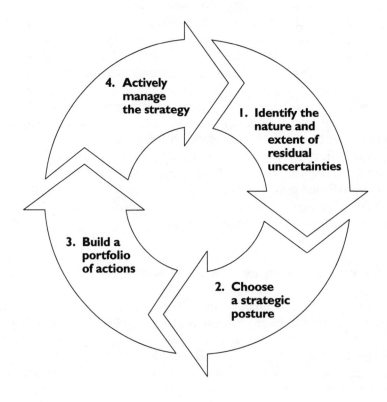

1. **Identify the nature and extent of residual uncertainties**

   Key areas of uncertainty include:
   - How much electronic commerce will occur on the Internet
   - How quickly consumers will switch from paper-based to electronic payments
   - Which specific instruments will become the primary payment vehicles (smart cards? E-cash?)
   - What structure will emerge for the electronic commerce industry
   - How vertically integrated most players will be
   - What roles banks and nonbanks will play

   The bank is facing level 3 uncertainty in some areas and level 4 in others

2. Choose a strategic posture

Objectives:
- Defend current customer franchise from attack by new technology-based competitors
- Capture new business opportunities in fast-growing markets

Overall posture: reserve the right to play

3. Build a portfolio of actions

Near-term opportunities to offer more innovative products in specific areas where the bank is strong (for example, procurement cards, industry-specific payment products) represent no-regrets moves.

Offering leading-edge payment products to high-value customer segments that are most vulnerable to attackers is another no-regrets move.

Forming a small new-business unit is a growth option to:
- Conduct R&D for new payment ideas
- Monitor industry developments in the broad area of retail electronic payments

4. Actively manage the strategy

Monitor key trigger events such as adoption rates for emerging products and the behavior of nontraditional competitors such as telephone companies.

Establish a short-cycle review of the portfolio of options.

Participate in a number of industry consortia to reduce uncertainty.

steering committees focused on electronic payments, R&D projects, and competitive-intelligence systems so that they can constantly monitor developments in electronic payment technology and markets. In addition, many regional banks are making small investments in industry consortia as another way to monitor events. This adapter approach makes sense for most regional banks—they don't have the deep pockets and skills necessary to set standards for the electronic payment market, yet it is essential that they be able to offer the latest electronic services to their customers as such services become available.

Reserving the right to play is a common posture in level 3. Consider a telecommunications company trying to decide whether to make a $1 billion investment in broadband cable networks in the early 1990s. The decision hinged on level 3 uncertainties such as demand for interactive TV service. No amount of solid market research could precisely forecast consumer demand for services that didn't even exist yet.

However, making incremental investments in broadband-network trials could provide useful information, and it would put the company in a privileged position to expand the business in the future should that prove attractive. By restructuring the broadband-investment decision from a big bet to a series of options, the company reserved the right to play in a potentially lucrative market without having to bet the farm or risk being preempted by a competitor.

STRATEGY IN LEVEL 4'S TRUE AMBIGUITY

Paradoxically, even though level 4 situations contain the greatest uncertainty, they may offer higher returns and involve lower risks for companies seeking to shape the market than situations in either level 2 or 3. Recall that level 4 situations are transitional by nature, often occurring after a major technological, macroeconomic, or legislative shock. Since no player necessarily knows the best strategy in these environments, the shaper's role is to provide a vision of an industry structure and standards that will coordinate the strategies of other players and drive the market toward a more stable and favorable outcome.

Mahathir bin Mohamad, Malaysia's prime minister, is trying to shape the future of the multimedia industry in the Asian Pacific Rim. This is truly a level 4 strategy problem at this point. Potential products are undefined, as are the players, the level of customer demand, and the technology standards, among other factors. The government is trying to create order out of this chaos by investing at least $15 billion to create a so-called Multimedia Super Corridor (MSC) in Malaysia. The MSC is a 750-square-kilometer zone south of Kuala Lumpur that will include state-of-the-art "smart" buildings for software companies, regional headquarters for multinational corporations, a "Multimedia University," a paperless government center called Putrajaya, and a new city called Cyberjaya. By leveraging incentives like a ten-year exemption from the tax on profits, the MSC has received commitments from more than 40 Malaysian and foreign companies so far, including such powerhouses as Intel, Microsoft, Nippon Telegraph and Telephone, Oracle, and Sun Microsystems. Mahathir's shaping strategy is predicated on the notion that the MSC will create a web of relationships between content and hardware providers that will result in clear industry standards and a set of complementary multimedia products and services. Intel's Malaysia managing director, David B. Marsing, recognized Mahathir's shaping aspirations when he noted, "If you're an evolutionist, it's strange. They're [the Malaysian government] trying to intervene instead of letting it evolve."

Shapers need not make enormous bets as the Malaysian government is doing to be successful in level 3 or 4 situations, however. All that is required is the credibility to coordinate the strategies of different players around the preferred outcome. Netscape Communications Corporation, for example, didn't rely on deep pockets to shape Internet browser standards. Instead, it leveraged the credibility of its leadership team in the industry so that other industry players thought, "If these guys think this is the way to go, they must be right."

Reserving the right to play is common, but potentially dangerous, in level 4 situations. Oil companies believed they were reserving the right to compete in China by buying options to establish various beachheads there some 20 years ago. However, in such level 4 situations, it is extremely difficult to determine whether incremental investments are truly reserving the right to play or simply the right to lose. A few general rules apply. First, look for a high degree of leverage. If the choice of beachhead in China comes down to maintaining a small, but expensive, local operation or developing a limited joint venture with a local distributor, all else being equal, go for the low-cost option. Higher-cost options must be justified with explicit arguments for why they would put the company in a better position to ramp up over time. Second, don't get locked into one position through neglect. Options should be rigorously reevaluated whenever important uncertainties are clarified—at least every six months. Remember, level 4 situations are transitional, and most will quickly move toward levels 3 and 2.

The difficulty of managing options in level 4 situations often drives players toward adapter postures. As in level 3, an adapter posture in level 4 is frequently implemented by making investments in organizational capabilities. Most potential players in the multimedia industry are adopting that posture today but will soon be making bigger bets as the industry moves into level 3 and 2 uncertainty over time.

A New Approach to Uncertainty

At the heart of the traditional approach to strategy lies the assumption that by applying a set of powerful analytic tools, executives can predict the future of any business accurately enough to allow them to choose a clear strategic direction. In relatively stable businesses, that approach continues to work well. But it tends to break down when the environment is so uncertain that no amount of good analysis will allow them to predict the future.

Levels of uncertainty regularly confronting managers today are so high that they need a new way to think about strategy. (See "Needed: A More Comprehensive Strategy Tool Kit.") The approach we've outlined will help executives avoid dangerous binary views of uncertainty. It offers a discipline for thinking rigorously and systematically about uncertainty. On one plane, it is a guide to judging which analytic tools can help in making decisions at various levels of uncertainty and which cannot. On a broader plane, our framework is a way to tackle the most challenging decisions that executives have to make, offering a more complete and sophisticated understanding of the uncertainty they face and its implications for strategy.

Needed: A More Comprehensive Strategy Tool Kit

In order to perform the kinds of analyses appropriate to high levels of uncertainty, many companies will need to supplement their standard strategy tool kit. Scenario-planning techniques are fundamental to determining strategy under conditions of uncertainty. Game theory will help managers understand uncertainties based on competitors' conduct. Systems dynamics and agent-based simulation models can help in understanding the complex interactions in the market. Real-options valuation models can help in correctly valuing investments in learning and flexibility. The following sources will help managers get started:

- **Scenario Planning.** Kees van der Heijden, *Scenarios: The Art of Strategic Conversation* (New York: John Wiley & Sons, 1996); Paul J.H. Schoemaker, "Scenario Planning: A New Tool for Strategic Thinking," *Sloan Management Review*, Winter 1995.

- **Game Theory.** Avinash K. Dixit and Barry J. Nalebuff, *Thinking Strategically: The Competitive Edge in Business, Politics, and Everyday Life* (New York: W.W. Norton, 1991); Adam M. Brandenburger and Barry J. Nalebuff, "The Right Game: Use Game Theory to Shape Strategy," *Harvard Business Review* July–August 1995.

- **System Dynamics.** Peter N. Senge, *Fifth Discipline: The Art and Practice of the Learning Organization* (New York: Doubleday, 1990); Arie de Geus, "Planning as Learning," *Harvard Business Review* March–April 1988.

- **Agent-Based Models.** John L. Casti, *Would-Be Worlds: How Simulation Is Changing the Frontiers of Science* (New York: John Wiley & Sons, 1997).
- **Real Options.** Avinash K. Dixit and Robert S. Pindyck, "The Options Approach to Capital Investment," *Harvard Business Review* May–June 1995; Timothy A. Luehrman, "What's It Worth?" *Harvard Business Review* May–June 1997.

5
Strategy as a Portfolio of Real Options

Timothy A. Luehrman

When executives create strategy, they project themselves and their organizations into the future, creating a path from where they are now to where they want to be some years down the road. In competitive markets, though, no one expects to formulate a detailed long-term plan and follow it mindlessly. As soon as we start down the path, we begin learning—about business conditions, competitors' actions, the quality of our preparations, and so forth—and we need to respond flexibly to what we learn. Unfortunately, the financial tool most widely relied on to estimate the value of strategy—discounted-cash-flow (DCF) valuation—assumes that we will follow a predetermined plan, regardless of how events unfold.

A better approach to valuation would incorporate both the uncertainty inherent in business and the active decision making required for a strategy to succeed. It would help executives think strategically on their feet by capturing the value of doing just that—of managing actively rather than passively. Options can deliver that extra insight. Advances in both computing power and our understanding of option pricing over the last 20 years make it feasible now to begin analyzing business strategies as chains of real options. As a result, the creative activity of strategy formulation can be informed by valuation analyses sooner rather than later. Financial insight may actually contribute to shaping strategy, rather than being relegated to an after-the-fact exercise of "checking the numbers."

In financial terms, a business strategy is much more like a series of options than a series of static cash flows. Executing a strategy almost always involves making a *sequence* of major decisions. Some actions are taken immediately, while others are deliberately deferred, so managers can optimize as circumstances evolve. The strategy sets the framework within which future decisions will be made, but at the same time it leaves room for learning from ongoing developments and for discretion to act based on what is learned.

To consider strategies as portfolios of related real options, this article exploits a framework presented in "Investment Opportunities as Real Options: Getting Started on the Numbers" (*Harvard Business Review* July–August 1998). That article explains how to get from conventional DCF value to option value for a typical project—in other words, it is about how to get a number. This article extends that framework, exploring how option pricing can be used to improve decision making about the sequence and timing of a portfolio of strategic investments.

A Gardening Metaphor: Options as Tomatoes

Managing a portfolio of strategic options is like growing a garden of tomatoes in an unpredictable climate. Walk into the garden on a given day in August, and you will find that some tomatoes are ripe and perfect. Any gardener would know to pick and eat those immediately. Other tomatoes are rotten; no gardener would ever bother to pick them. These cases at the extremes—now and never—are easy decisions for the gardener to make.

In between are tomatoes with varying prospects. Some are edible and could be picked now but would benefit from more time on the vine. The experienced gardener picks them early only if squirrels or other competitors are likely to get them. Other tomatoes are not yet edible, and there's no point in picking them now, even if the squirrels do get them. However, they are sufficiently far along, and there is enough time left in the season, that many will ripen unharmed and eventually be picked. Still others look less promising and may not ripen before the season ends. But with more sun or water, fewer weeds, or just good luck, even some of these tomatoes may make it. Finally, there are small green tomatoes and late blossoms that have little likelihood of growing and ripening before the season ends. There is no value in picking them, and they might just as well be left on the vine.

Most experienced gardeners are able to classify the tomatoes in their gardens at any given time. Beyond that, however, good gardeners also understand how the garden changes over time. Early in the season, none of the fruit falls into the "now" or "never" categories. By the last day, all of it falls into one or the other because time has run out. The interesting question is, What can the gardener do during the season, while things are changing week to week?

A purely passive gardener visits the garden on the last day of the season, picks the ripe tomatoes, and goes home. The weekend gardener visits frequently and picks ripe fruit before it rots or the squirrels get it. Active gardeners do much more. Not only do they watch the garden but, based on what they see, they also cultivate it: watering, fertilizing, and weeding, trying to get more of those in-between tomatoes to grow and ripen before time runs out. Of course, the weather is always a question, and not all the tomatoes will make it. Still, we'd expect the active gardener to enjoy a higher yield in most years than the passive gardener.

In option terminology, active gardeners are doing more than merely making exercise decisions (pick or don't pick). They are monitoring the options and looking for ways to influence the underlying variables that determine option value and, ultimately, outcomes.

Option pricing can help us become more effective, active gardeners in several ways. It allows us to estimate the value of the entire year's crop (or even the value of a single tomato) before the season actually ends. It also helps us assess each tomato's prospects as the season progresses and tells us along the way which to pick and which to leave on the vine. Finally, it can suggest what to do to help those in-between tomatoes ripen before the season ends.

A Tour of Option Space

Instead of a garden plot, visualize a rectangle we'll call *option space*. Option space is defined by two option-value metrics, each of which captures a different part of the value associated with being able to defer an investment. Option space can help address the issues an active gardener will care about: whether to invest or not (that is, whether to pick or not to pick), when to invest, and what to do in the meantime.

Let's briefly review the two metrics, which were developed in "Investment Opportunities as Real Options." The first metric contains all the usual data captured in net present value (NPV) but adds the time value of being able to defer the investment. We called that metric

NPVq and defined it as the value of the underlying assets we intend to build or acquire divided by the present value of the expenditure required to build or buy them. Put simply, this is a ratio of value to cost. For convenience, here, we'll call it our *value-to-cost* metric instead of NPVq, but bear in mind that *value* and *cost* refer to the project's assets, not to the option on those assets.

When the value-to-cost metric is between zero and one, we have a project worth less than it costs; when the metric is greater than one, the project is worth more than the present value of what it costs.

The second metric we'll call our *volatility* metric. It measures how much things can change before an investment decision must finally be made. That depends both on how uncertain, or risky, the future value of the assets in question is and on how long we can defer a decision. The former is captured by the *variance per period of asset returns*; the latter is the option's *time to expiration*. In the previous article, this second metric was called *cumulative volatility*.

Option space is defined by these two metrics, with value-to-cost on the horizontal axis and volatility on the vertical axis. (See Exhibit 5-1 "Option Space Is Defined by Two Option-Value Metrics.") The usual convention is to draw the space as a rectangle, with the value-to-cost metric increasing from left to right (its minimum value is zero), and the volatility metric increasing from top to bottom (its minimum value also is zero). Within the interior of the rectangle, option value increases as the value of either metric increases; that is, from any point in the space, if you move down, to the right, or in both directions simultaneously, option value rises.

How does option space help us with strategy? A business strategy is a series of related options: it is as though the condition of one tomato actually affected the size or ripeness of another one nearby. That obviously makes things more complicated. Before we analyze a strategy, let's first consider the simpler circumstance in which the tomatoes growing in the garden don't affect one another. To do that, we need to explore the option space further.

In a real garden, good, bad, and in-between tomatoes can turn up anywhere. Not so in option space, where there are six separate regions, each of which contains a distinct type of option and a corresponding managerial prescription. We carve up the space into distinct regions by using what we know about the value-to-cost and volatility metrics, along with conventional NPV.

What's the added value of dividing option space in this fashion? Traditional corporate finance gives us one metric—NPV—for evaluating

*Exhibit 5-1   Option Space Is Defined by Two
Option-Value Metrics*

We can use the two option-value metrics to locate projects in option space.
Moving to the right and/or downward corresponds to higher option value.

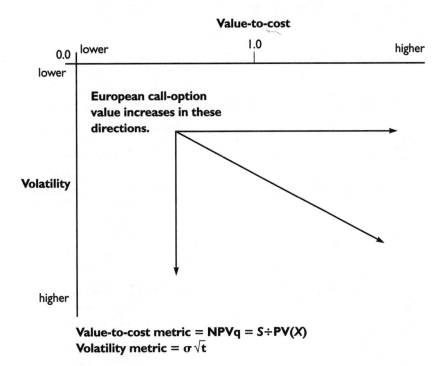

Value-to-cost metric = NPVq = S÷PV(X)
Volatility metric = σ √t

projects, and only two possible actions: invest or don't invest. In option space, we have NPV, two extra metrics, and six possible actions
that reflect not only where a project is now but also the likelihood of
it ending up somewhere better in the future. When we return to as-
sessing strategies, this forward looking judgment will be especially
useful.

TOP OF THE SPACE: *NOW AND NEVER*

At the very top of our option space, the volatility metric is zero. (See
Exhibit 5-2 "Dividing Option Space into Regions.") That's so either because all uncertainty has been resolved or because time has run

Exhibit 5-2   Dividing Option Space into Regions

The curve may be derived by holding the risk-free rate of return (r_f) and the standard deviation (σ) constant (from the Black-Scholes equation) as t varies and solving for the value of the value-to-cost metric that corresponds to NPV = 0. For example, in the extreme case of $r_f = 0$, the curve is a vertical line corresponding to points for which the value-to-cost metric = 1. As r_f increases, the slope of the curve decreases, bending to the right.

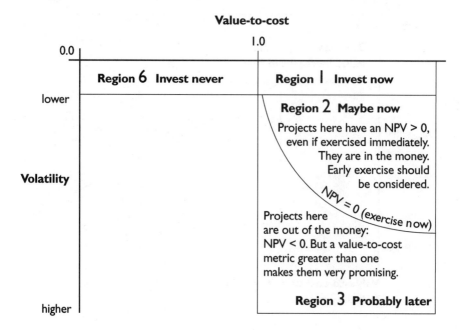

out. With business projects, the latter is far more likely. So projects that end up here differ from one another only according to their value-to-cost metrics, and it's easy to see what to do with them. If the value-to-cost metric is greater than one, we go ahead and invest now. If it's less than one, we invest never. Once time has run out, "now or never" completely describes our choices. It will be convenient to refer to regions by number, so let's number these extremes 1 and 6. Region 1 contains the perfectly ripe tomatoes; it is the *invest now* region. Region 6 contains the rotten ones; the prescription there is *invest never*.

RIGHT SIDE OF THE SPACE: *MAYBE NOW* AND *PROBABLY* LATER

What about projects whose value-to-cost metric is greater than one but whose time has not yet run out? All such projects fall somewhere in the right half of our option space but below the top. Projects here are very promising because the underlying assets are worth more than the present value of the required investment. Does that mean we should go ahead and invest right away? In some instances, the answer is clearly no, while in other cases, it's maybe. We want to be able to distinguish between those cases. The key to doing so is not option pricing but conventional NPV.

In terms of the tomato analogy, we are looking at a lot of promising tomatoes, none of which is perfectly ripe. We want to distinguish between those that, if picked right away, are edible (NPV > 0) and those that are inedible (NPV < 0). The distinction matters because there is no point in picking the inedible ones. Conventional NPV tells us the value of investing immediately despite the fact that time has not yet run out. If NPV is negative, immediate exercise is unambiguously suboptimal. In option terminology, we say that such an option is *out of the money*: it costs more to exercise it than the assets are worth. The exercise price *(X)* is greater than the underlying asset value *(S)*, therefore NPV = $S - X < 0$.

The curve in our diagram separates options that are out of the money (NPV < 0) from those that are *in the money* (NPV > 0). For points above the curve in the diagram, NPV is positive; for those below the curve, NPV is negative. For points actually on the curve itself, NPV = 0.

Projects below the curve, which we'll call region 3, are like the inedible tomatoes that we clearly don't want to pick right away. Even so, they are very promising because their value-to-cost metric is positive and time has not yet run out. I call this region *probably later* because, even though we should not invest yet, we expect to invest eventually for a relatively high fraction of these projects. In the meantime, they should be cultivated.

Projects that fall above the NPV = 0 curve are even more interesting. These options are in the money. They are like tomatoes that even though not perfectly ripe are nevertheless edible. We should be considering whether to pick them early.

It may seem contradictory to consider exercising an option early when all along I've argued in "Investment Opportunities as Real Options" that it is valuable to be able to defer the investment—to wait, see what happens, and then make an optimal choice at the last possible moment. If there is value associated with deferring, why would we ever do otherwise? Sometimes, especially with real options, value may be lost as well as gained by deferring, and the proper decision depends on which effect dominates.

The financial analog to such a real option is a call option on a share of stock. If the stock pays a large dividend, the shareholder receives value that the option holder does not. The option holder may wish to become a shareholder simply to participate in the dividend, which otherwise would be forgone. Think of the dividend as value lost by deferring the exercise decision.

In the case of real options, where the underlying asset is some set of business cash flows, any *predictable* loss of value associated with deferring the investment is like the dividend in our stock example. Phenomena like pending changes in regulations, a predictable loss of market share, or preemption by a competitor are all costs associated with investing later rather than sooner and might cause us to exercise an option early. Or, to use the tomato analogy, we might pick an edible tomato early if we can predict that squirrels will get it otherwise. *Unpredictable* gains and losses, however, would not lead us to exercise our options early.

Options that are in the money (that is, those for which NPV > 0) should be evaluated to see if they ought to be exercised early. Immediate investment will not always be the optimal course of action because by investing early the company loses the advantages of deferring, which also are real. Deciding whether to invest early requires a case-by-case comparison of the value of investing immediately with the value of waiting a bit longer—that is, of continuing to hold the project as an option. I refer to that part of the option space as *maybe now* because we might decide to invest right away. Let's label it region 2.

LEFT SIDE OF THE SPACE: *MAYBE LATER* AND *PROBABLY NEVER*

All options that fall in the left half of the space are less promising because the value-to-cost metric is everywhere less than one, and

Exhibit 5-3   The Tomato Garden

If we start on the right in region 1 and sweep through the space clockwise, projects become progressively less promising. In regions 1 through 3, the value-to-cost metric is greater than one, but only in regions 1 and 2 is conventional NPV positive, and only in region 1 is the exercise decision a foregone conclusion. In regions 4 through 6, the value-to-cost metric is less than one, but only in region 6 is the exercise decision a foregone conclusion.

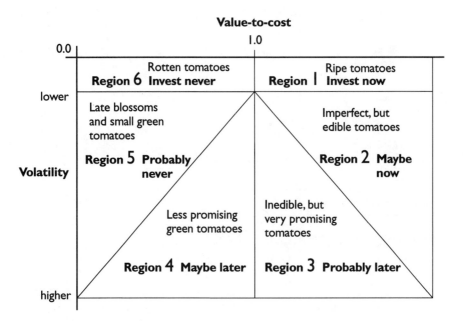

conventional NPV is everywhere less than zero. But even here we can separate the more valuable from the less valuable. The upper left is unpromising territory because both the value-to-cost and volatility metrics are low. These are the late blossoms and the small green tomatoes that are unlikely to ripen before the season ends. I call this part of the option space *probably never,* and we can label it region 5.

In contrast, the lower section (of this left half of the space) has better prospects because at least one of the two metrics is reasonably high. I call it *maybe later,* and we can label it region 4. Exhibit 5-3, "The Tomato Garden," dispenses with fancy curves and simply divides the option space roughly into the six regions.

Table 5-1   *Vital Statistics for Six Independent Projects*

Variable		A	B	C	D	E	F	Portfolio Value
S	Underlying asset value ($ millions)	$100.00	$100.00	$100.00	$100.00	$100.00	$100.00	
X	Exercise price ($ millions)	$90.00	$90.00	$110.00	$110.00	$110.00	$110.00	
t	Time to expiration (years)	0.00	2.00	0.00	0.50	1.00	2.00	
σ	Standard deviation (per year)	0.30	0.30	0.30	0.20	0.30	0.40	
r_f	Risk-free rate of return (% per year)	0.06	0.06	0.06	0.06	0.06	0.06	
NPVq	Value-to-cost metric	1.111	1.248	0.909	0.936	0.964	1.021	
$\sigma\sqrt{t}$	Volatility metric	0.000	0.424	0.000	0.141	0.300	0.566	
	Call value ($ millions)	$10.00	$27.23	$0.00	$3.06	$10.42	$23.24	$73.95
S-X	Conventional NPV ($ millions)	$10.00	$10.00	–$10.00	–$10.00	–$10.00	–$10.00	$20.00
	Region	1	2	6	5	4	3	
	Exercise decision	now	maybe now	never	probably never	maybe later	probably later	

When to Harvest

As an example of what we learn from the tomato garden, consider six hypothetical projects that are entirely unrelated to one another. Table 5-1, "Vital Statistics for Six Independent Projects," shows the relevant data for these projects, which have been labeled A through F. Note that each of them involves assets worth $100 million. Two of them (A and B) require capital expenditures of $90 million; the other four require expenditures of $110 million. So A and B each has a positive NPV of $10 million. Each of the other four has an NPV of negative $10 million. The NPV of the entire portfolio is negative $20 million or, more reasonably, positive $20 million, since the four projects with negative NPVs can be included at a value of zero. Conventional capital budgeting offers only two prescriptions—invest or don't invest. Following those rules, we'd accept projects A and B and reject all the others.

Although their NPVs are tightly clustered, the six projects have different time and volatility profiles, and hence different values for their value-to-cost and volatility metrics. Consequently, each is located in a different region of the option space. (See Exhibit 5-4 "Locating the Projects in the Tomato Garden.")

A is a *now* project that falls in region 1; C is a *never* project in region 6. For both of them, time has run out, so the volatility metric is zero. Project B is very promising: its NPV is positive, and its value-to-cost metric is greater than one. B plots in region 2, and we should consider whether we ought to exercise our option on this project early. However, unless there is some predictable loss in future value (either a rise in cost or a fall in value), then early exercise is not only unnecessary but also suboptimal. Project F's value-to-cost metric is greater than one, but its NPV is less than zero. It falls in region 3 and is very valuable as an option, despite its negative NPV. That's because it will not expire for two years and has the highest volatility of the whole group. Hence, project F's prognosis is *probably later.*

Project E has less going for it than project F. It is in region 4 and deserves some attention because, with a year to go and the moderate standard deviation of its underlying asset return ($\sigma = 0.3$ per year), it just might make it. That's why it is classified as *maybe later.* Project D is much less promising (a *probably never*) because a decision must be made in only six months and, with a low volatility, there's not much likelihood that D will pop into the money before time runs out.

Because it can account for flexibility and uncertainty, the options-based framework produces a different assessment of this portfolio

Exhibit 5-4   Locating the Projects in the Tomato Garden

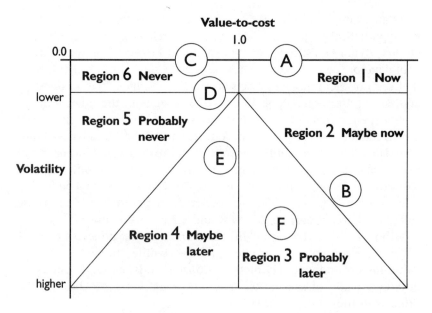

than the conventional DCF approach would. Most obviously, where DCF methods give the portfolio a value of $20 million, option pricing gives it a value of about $74 million, more than three times greater. Just as important, locating these projects in the tomato garden yields notably different exercise decisions. Instead of accepting two projects and rejecting four, our option analysis leads us to accept one, reject one, and wait and see about the other four. And as we wait, we know how each project's prospects differ. Moreover, we don't wait passively. Having only limited resources to devote to the portfolio, we realize that some wait-and-see projects are more likely to reward our active cultivation than others. In particular, we can see that projects E and F together are worth about $34 million (not negative $20 million or even $0) and should be actively cultivated rather than abandoned. At the very least, they could be sold to some other gardener.

A Dynamic Approach

Cultivation is intended to improve the crop, but it has to work within boundaries set by nature. In option space, as in nature, there are basic laws of time and motion. The most basic is that options tend to move upward and to the left in the option space as time passes. Upward, because the volatility metric decreases as time runs out. To the left, because, as a present-value calculation, the value-to-cost metric also decreases over time if its other constituent variables remain constant.

To illustrate, consider project F. Its volatility metric is 0.566, and its value-to-cost metric is 1.021. Now let a year pass, and suppose none of project F's variables changes except for t, which is now one year instead of two. Were we to recompute the metrics, we would discover that both have declined. The volatility metric falls from 0.566 to 0.400, which moves F upward in option space. And its value-to-cost metric declines from 1.021 to 0.964—that is, $100 \div [110 \div (1+0.06)^1]$—which moves F to the left. In fact, project F moves from region 3 (*probably later*) to the less promising region 4 (*maybe later*). Despite its initial promise, the only way project F is going to wind up in the money (that is, in region 1 or 2) and eventually get funded is if some force pushes it to the right, overcoming the natural tug to the left, before time runs out. Only two forces push in that direction: good luck and active management.

Neither force should be ignored. Sometimes we succeed by putting ourselves squarely in the way of good fortune. Other times we have to work at it. Managers actively cultivating a portfolio of opportunities are, in effect, working to push options as far as possible to the right in the space before they float all the way to the top. How is that done? By taking some action that increases either or both of our option-value metrics. Of the two, the value-to-cost metric is perhaps the more obvious one to work on first because managers are more accustomed to managing revenues, costs, and capital expenditures than volatility or time to expiration.

Anything managers can do to increase value or reduce cost will move the option to the right in our space. For example, price or volume increases, tax savings, or lower capital requirements, as well as any cost savings, will help. Such enhancements to value are obvious with or without a real-options framework. What the framework provides is a way to incorporate them visually and quantitatively into option value through the value-to-cost metric.

The real world seldom gives managers the luxury of isolating one variable and holding all others constant. Managers cannot simply declare, "Let's raise prices to increase the value of our project." More likely, they will invent and evaluate complex proposal modifications driven or constrained by technology, demographics, regulations, and so on. For example, one way to cultivate a market-entry option might be to add a new product feature. That may entail extra investment (raising X), but it will also help differentiate the product in the local market, permitting higher prices (raising S) but also adding extra manufacturing costs (lowering S), some of which are fixed. The net effect on the value-to-cost metric is what counts, and the net effect is unclear without further analysis.

Evaluating the project as an option means there is more, not less, to analyze, but the framework tells us what to analyze, gives us a way to organize the effects, and offers a visual interpretation. Observing the change in the option's location in our space tells us both whether its value has risen or fallen and whether it has migrated to a different region of the tomato garden.

There are still more considerations even in this simple example of adding a product feature. Extra fixed costs mean greater risk, which might lower the value of the project (due to the need to discount future cash flows at a higher risk-adjusted rate) and cause its value-to-cost metric to drop further. But the extra fixed costs also represent operating leverage that raises the volatility metric. That augments option value. We could hypothesize further that adding an extra feature will stimulate a competitor to match it. We, in turn, might be forced to introduce the next generation of our product (on which we hold a different option) earlier than we otherwise would have.

In general, actions taken by managers can affect not only the value-to-cost measure but also the volatility metric. In this example, both elements of the volatility metric—risk and time to expiration—are affected. And for more than one option. There is a spillover from one option to another: adding a feature reduces the length of time a subsequent decision can be deferred. For other situations, there are a myriad of possible spillover effects.

Nested Options in a Business Strategy

Once we allow options in a portfolio to directly influence other options, we are ready to consider strategies: series of options explicitly *designed* to affect one another. We can use "nests" of options upon options to represent the sequence of contingencies designed into a business, as in the following simplified and hypothetical example.

Three years ago, the WeatherIze Corporation bought an exclusive license to a technology for treating fabric to retard its breakdown in extreme weather conditions. The idea was to develop a new line of fabric especially suitable for outdoor commercial awnings, a market the company already serves with a less durable product. Now WeatherIze's engineers have developed their first treated fabric, and the company is considering making the expenditures required to roll it out commercially. If the product is well received by awning manufacturers, WeatherIze will have to expand capacity within three years of introduction just to serve awning producers.

The vice president for business development is ebullient. He anticipates that success in awnings will be followed within another two years by product extensions—similar treatment of different fabrics designed for such consumer goods as tents, umbrellas, and patio furniture. At that time, WeatherIze would expand capacity yet again. The company envisions trademarking its fabrics, expanding its sales force, and supporting the consumer products made from these fabrics with cooperative advertising.

WeatherIze's strategy for exploiting the treatment technology is pretty straightforward. It consists of a particular sequence of decision opportunities. The first step of the execution was to purchase the license. By doing so, the company acquired a sequence of nested options: to develop the product; to introduce the product; to expand capacity for manufacturing awning fabric; and to expand again to make related, branded fabrics. Just now, having developed the product, WeatherIze is part way through the strategy and is considering its next step: spending on the product introduction. That is, it's time to exercise (or not) the next real option in the chain.

WeatherIze's strategy, at this point in time, is depicted in option space in Exhibit 5-5 "WeatherIze's Strategy as Nested Call Options." Each circle represents an option whose location in space is determined by its value-to-cost and volatility metrics. The size of each solid circle is proportionate to the underlying asset value *(S)* for each option. The area within each dashed circle is proportionate to required expenditures *(X)*. Thus a dashed circle inside a solid one represents an option that is in the money *(S > X)*. A dashed circle outside a solid circle shows an option that is out of the money.

The line segments in the diagram indicate that the options are nested. The option to expand for awning production is acquired if and only if the option to introduce is exercised. As such, the underlying asset for the introduction option includes both the value of the operating cash flows associated with the product itself *and* the present value of the option to expand. Likewise, the option to expand a second time

Exhibit 5-5   *WeatherIze's Strategy as Nested Call Options*

The value of WeatherIze's strategy is:

$$PV \left\{ \begin{matrix} \text{product} \\ \text{introduction} \end{matrix} + \begin{matrix} \text{call} \\ \text{value} \end{matrix} \left[\begin{matrix} \text{(first} \\ \text{expansion} \\ \text{option)} \end{matrix} + \begin{matrix} \text{call} \\ \text{value} \end{matrix} \begin{matrix} \text{(second} \\ \text{expansion} \\ \text{option)} \end{matrix} \right] \right\}$$

The value of the innermost call option must be estimated first because its value is part of the underlying asset value (S) for the next option in the nest.

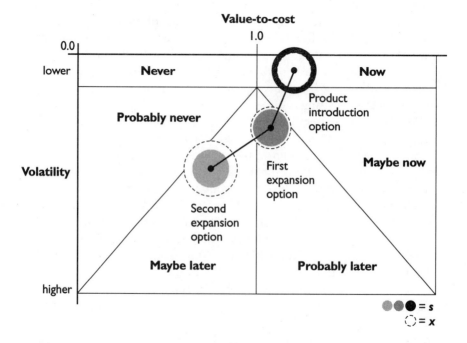

for commercial product production is acquired only if WeatherIze decides to exercise its first expansion option. The value of the whole strategy at this point is:

$$PV \left\{ \begin{matrix} \text{product} \\ \text{introduction} \end{matrix} + \begin{matrix} \text{call} \\ \text{value} \end{matrix} \left[\begin{matrix} \text{(first} \\ \text{expansion} \\ \text{option)} \end{matrix} + \begin{matrix} \text{call} \\ \text{value} \end{matrix} \begin{matrix} \text{(second} \\ \text{expansion} \\ \text{option)} \end{matrix} \right] \right\}$$

In effect, WeatherIze owns a call on a call.

The option to introduce the new awning fabric is in the money and about to expire. (WeatherIze will forfeit its license if it does not go ahead with the introduction.) As soon as this option is exercised, the

*Exhibit 5-6   What Happens If the Consumer Fabric
           Opportunity Becomes Riskier?*

If the volatility of returns on consumer-product fabrics increases, the second expansion option moves down. This causes the first expansion option to move to the right because the second option is part of the underlying assets for the first.

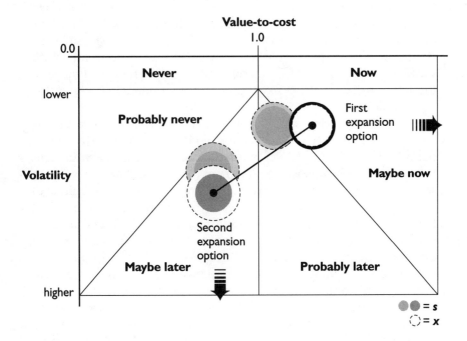

picture changes. The top circle goes away; the bottom two remain linked and begin drifting upward. One of the most important factors determining whether they move right or left on their way up is how well the awning fabric does in the marketplace. But there are other factors as well. Anything that enhances the value of the second expansion option enhances the value of the first, too, because the value of the second option forms part of the value of the underlying asset value for the first option.

Suppose, for example, the risks associated with the consumer-product fabric's assets increase. Let's trace the effects in Exhibit 5-6 "What Happens If the Consumer Fabric Opportunity Becomes Riskier?" The most direct effect is on the second expansion option, which moves down in the space because its volatility metric rises. The second expansion option becomes more valuable. But the increased risk also affects the first expansion option for awning fabric. Its value-to-cost metric rises because the second expansion option is part of the underlying assets *(S)* of the first. In fact, a change in either metric for the second option must also change the value-to-cost metric (at least) of the first.

As another example, suppose a competitor introduces a substitute fabric in the consumer goods markets that WeatherIze had planned to target. Try to visualize what will happen. Not only will the locations of the options change but so will the sizes of the circles. The solid circle, or asset value *(S)*, of WeatherIze's second expansion option will shrink, and both the first and second expansion options will move to the left. Further, the first expansion option's underlying asset value also should shrink.

Drawing simple circles in the option space also lets us compare strategies. For example, we have been assuming that WeatherIze would not introduce branded fabrics without first expanding its awning fabric capacity. Now suppose the company could do either first, or both simultaneously, but that a larger investment would be required to make branded fabrics if the awning expansion weren't accomplished first. We could also assume that profit margins on the branded goods would be higher if the company first gained more experience with awning fabric.

These options in WeatherIze's alternative strategy are not nested, and they are no longer in the same locations. Exhibit 5-7 "Call Options in WeatherIze's Alternative Strategy" depicts the new strategy. Note that the second option, the branded-fabric option, is now farther left, its solid circle, or asset value *(S)*, is smaller, and its dashed circle, or expenditures *(X)*, is larger than it was originally. It is further out of the money but is now linked directly to the product introduction option. Given that the branded-fabric option is farther left under this new strategy and its solid circle is smaller, could we possibly prefer it? Yes, actually, provided it also moves down in the space—that is, if its volatility metric has increased. The pricing table in the real-options framework can tell us how far down it would have to go to compensate for any given move to the left. Finally, note that for the nonnested strategy, the value of both options directly enhances the value of the underlying assets associated with the initial product introduction. But it is no longer the case that any change in the second expansion option must affect the location of the first expansion option: each could, in fact, move around independently.

Exhibit 5-7   Call Options in WeatherIze's Alternative Strategy

The expansion options are no longer nested under the alternative strategy, but the second option has moved down and to the left. In addition, its solid circle is smaller and its dashed circle larger than it was originally.

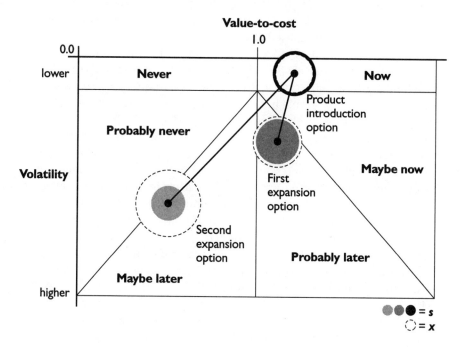

Although the options are not nested, they are very much related. Suppose, for example, that the awning expansion option pops into the money and is indeed exercised first, before the consumer fabric option. The value of the latter would be enhanced because the underlying assets associated with it would be expected to produce better margins—the value-to-cost metric for the consumer fabric option rises.

To compare WeatherIze's alternative strategies, we compute the value of each strategy's introduction option. We can do that quantitatively using the real-options framework. In visual terms, we prefer the introduction option to be farther to the right and to have a larger solid circle. Whichever strategy accomplishes that is more valuable.

Learning to Garden

I argued in "Investment Opportunities as Real Options" that companies should adopt option-pricing techniques as adjuncts to their existing system, not as replacements. If WeatherIze takes that approach, there is a good chance that the "tomato garden" will help the company create and execute a superior strategy.

Strategists at WeatherIze already were thinking several moves ahead when they purchased the license. They don't need a tomato garden to tell them merely to think ahead. But option pricing quantifies the value of the all-important follow-on opportunities much better than standard DCF-valuation techniques do. And the tomato garden adds a simple but versatile picture that reveals important insights into both the value and the timing of the exercise decisions. It gives managers a way to "draw" a strategy in terms that are neither wholly strategic nor wholly financial but some of both. Managers can play with the pictures much as they might with a physical model built of Legos or Tinker Toys. Some of us are most creative while at play.

As executives at WeatherIze experiment with circles in option space, it is important that they preserve the link between the pictures they draw and the disciplined financial projections required by the real-options framework. They need to remember that the circles occupy a certain part of the space because the numbers—the value-to-cost and volatility metrics—put them there. At the same time, they need to prevent the exercise from becoming just another variation on "valuation as usual." This is the well-worn rut in which valuation analysis is used primarily to check numbers and as due diligence documentation for investments. Instead, the purpose should be to incorporate financial insights at the stage when projects and strategies are actually being created.

How does one become a good gardener? Practice, practice. I recommend starting by drawing simple combinations of projects to learn some common forms. What are the different ways you can depict a pair of nested call options? How can the pair move in the space? What are the ways to transform their configuration by changing the variables? Then move on to simple generic strategies. What does a given strategy look like when drawn in the option space? How does the picture change over time? How does it change when an option is exercised?

Next, practice translating real business phenomena into visual effects to update pictures. For example, how will the picture change if you add a direct mail campaign to your product introduction? Or how will the picture change if your competitor cuts prices when you enter a market?

Finally, try drawing your strategy and your competitors' side by side: How does the value and location of your options affect the value and location of theirs? How will they all move over time?

In most companies, strategy formulation and business development are not located in the finance bailiwick. Nevertheless, both activities raise important financial questions almost right away. Although the questions arise early, answers typically do not. For finance to play an important creative role, it must be able to contribute insightful interpretive analyses of sequences of decisions that are purely hypothetical—that is, while they are still mere possibilities. By building option pricing into a framework designed to evaluate not only hard assets but also opportunities (and multiple, related opportunities at that), we can add financial insight earlier rather than later to the creative work of strategy.

PART

II

Leadership and Organization

6

Fair Process: Managing in the Knowledge Economy

W. Chan Kim and Renée Mauborgne

A London policeman gave a woman a ticket for making an illegal turn. When the woman protested that there was no sign prohibiting the turn, the policeman pointed to one that was bent out of shape and difficult to see from the road. Furious, the woman decided to appeal by going to court. Finally, the day of her hearing arrived, and she could hardly wait to speak her piece. But she had just begun to tell her side of the story when the magistrate stopped her and summarily ruled in her favor.

How did the woman feel? Vindicated? Victorious? Satisfied?

No, she was frustrated and deeply unhappy. "I came for justice," she complained, "but the magistrate never let me explain what happened." In other words, although she liked the outcome, she didn't like the process that had created it.

For the purposes of their theories, economists assume that people are maximizers of utility, driven principally by rational calculations of their own self-interest. That is, economists assume people focus solely on outcomes. That assumption has migrated into much of management theory and practice. It has, for instance, become embedded in the tools managers traditionally use to control and motivate employees' behavior—from incentive systems to organizational structures. But it is an assumption that managers should reexamine because we all know that in real life it doesn't always hold true. People do care about outcomes, but—like the woman in London—they also care about the processes that produce those outcomes. They want to know that they had their say—that their point of view was considered even if it was rejected. Outcomes matter, but no more than the fairness of the processes that produce them.

Never has the idea of fair process been more important for managers than it is today. Fair process turns out to be a powerful management tool for companies struggling to make the transition from a production-based to a knowledge-based economy, in which value creation depends increasingly on ideas and innovation. Fair process profoundly influences attitudes and behaviors critical to high performance. It builds trust and unlocks ideas. With it, managers can achieve even the most painful and difficult goals while gaining the voluntary cooperation of the employees affected. Without fair process, even outcomes that employees might favor can be difficult to achieve—as the experience of an elevator manufacturer we'll call Elco illustrates.

Good Outcome, Unfair Process

In the late 1980s, sales in the elevator industry headed south as overconstruction of office space left some large U.S. cities with vacancy rates as high as 20%. Faced with diminished domestic demand for its product, Elco knew it had to improve its operations. The company decided to replace its batch-manufacturing system with a cellular approach that would allow self-directed teams to achieve superior performance. Given the industry's collapse, top management felt the transformation had to be made in record time.

Lacking expertise in cellular manufacturing, Elco retained a consulting firm to design a master plan for the conversion. Elco asked the consultants to work quickly and with minimal disturbance to employees. The new manufacturing system would be installed first at Elco's Chester plant, where employee relations were so good that in 1983 workers had decertified their own union. Subsequently, Elco would roll the process out to its High Park plant, where a strong union would probably resist that, or any other, change.

Under the leadership of a much beloved plant manager, Chester was in all respects a model operation. Visiting customers were always impressed by the knowledge and enthusiasm of its employees, so much so that the vice president of marketing saw the plant as one of Elco's best marketing tools. "Just let customers talk with Chester employees," he observed, "and they walk away convinced that buying an Elco elevator is the smart choice."

But one day in January of 1991, Chester employees arrived at work to discover strangers at the plant. Who were these people wearing dark suits, white dress shirts, and ties? They weren't customers. They showed up daily and spoke in low tones to one another. They didn't interact with employees. They hovered behind people's backs, taking notes and drawing fancy diagrams. The rumor circulated that after employees went home in the afternoon, these people would swarm across the plant floor, snoop around people's workstations, and have heated discussions.

During this period, the plant manager was increasingly absent. He was spending more time at Elco's head office in meetings with the consultants—sessions deliberately scheduled away from the plant so as not to distract the employees. But the plant manager's absence produced the opposite effect. As people grew anxious, wondering why the captain of their ship seemed to be deserting them, the rumor mill moved into high gear. Everyone became convinced that the consultants would downsize the plant. They were sure they were about to lose their jobs. The fact that the plant manager was always gone—obviously, he was avoiding them—and that no explanation was given, could only mean that management was, they thought, "trying to pull one over on us." Trust and commitment at the Chester plant deteriorated quickly. Soon, people were bringing in newspaper clippings about other plants around the country that had been shut down with the help of consultants. Employees saw themselves as imminent victims of yet another management fad and resented it.

In fact, Elco managers had no intention of closing the plant. They wanted to cut out waste, freeing people to enhance quality and produce elevators for new international markets. But plant employees could not have known that.

THE MASTER PLAN

In March 1991, management gathered the Chester employees in a large room. Three months after the consultants had first appeared, they were formally introduced. At the same time, management unveiled to employees the master plan for change at the Chester plant. In a meeting that lasted only 30 minutes, employees heard how their time-honored way of working would be abolished and replaced by something called "cellular manufacturing." No one explained why the change was needed, nor did anyone say exactly what would be expected of employees under the new approach. The managers didn't mean to skirt the issues; they just didn't feel they had the time to go into details.

The employees sat in stunned silence, which the managers mistook for acceptance, forgetting how long it had taken them over the last few months to get comfortable with the idea of cellular manufacturing and the changes it entailed. The managers felt good when the meeting was over, believing the employees were on board. With such a terrific staff, they thought, implementation of the new system was bound to go well.

Master plan in hand, management quickly began rearranging the plant. When employees asked what the new layout aimed to achieve, the response was "efficiency gains." The managers didn't have time to explain why efficiency needed to be improved and didn't want to worry employees. But lacking an intellectual understanding of what was happening to them, some employees literally began feeling sick as they came to work.

Managers informed employees that they would no longer be judged on individual performance but rather on the performance of the cell. They said quicker or more experienced employees would have to pick up the slack for slower or less experienced colleagues. But they didn't elaborate. How the new system was supposed to work, management didn't make clear.

In fact, the new cell design offered tremendous benefits to employees, making vacations easier to schedule, for example, and giving them the opportunity to broaden their skills and engage in a greater variety of work. But lacking trust in the change process, employees could see only its negative side. They began taking out their fears and anger on one another. Fights erupted on the plant floor as employees refused to help those they called "lazy people who can't finish their own jobs" or interpreted offers of help as meddling, responding with, "This is my job. You keep to your own workstation."

Chester's model workforce was falling apart. For the first time in the plant manager's career, employees refused to do as they were asked, turning down assignments "even if you fire me." They felt they could no longer trust the once popular plant manager, so they began to go around him, taking their complaints directly to his boss at the head office.

The plant manager then announced that the new cell design would allow employees to act as self-directed teams and that the role of the supervisor would be abolished. He expected people to react with excitement to his vision of Chester as the epitome of the factory of the future, where employees are empowered as entrepreneurial agents. Instead, they were simply confused. They had no idea how to succeed in this new environment. Without supervisors, what would they do if stock ran short or machines broke down? Did empowerment mean that the teams could self-authorize overtime, address quality problems such as rework, or purchase new machine tools? Unclear about how to succeed, employees felt set up to fail.

TIME OUT

By the summer of 1991, both cost and quality performance were in free fall. Employees were talking about bringing the union back. Finally, in despair, the plant manager phoned Elco's industrial psychologist. "I need your help," he said. "I have lost control."

The psychologist conducted an employee opinion survey to learn what had gone wrong. Employees complained, "Management doesn't care about our ideas or about our input." They felt that the company had scant respect for them as individuals, treating them as if they were not worthy of knowing about business conditions: "They don't bother to tell us where we are going and what this means to us." And they were deeply confused and mistrustful: "We don't know what exactly management expects of us in this new cell."

What Is Fair Process?

The theme of justice has preoccupied writers and philosophers throughout the ages, but the systematic study of fair process emerged only in the mid-1970s, when two social scientists, John W. Thibaut and Laurens Walker, combined their interest in the psychology of justice with the study of process. Focusing their attention on legal settings, they sought to understand what makes people trust a legal system so that they will comply with laws without being coerced into doing so. Their research established that people care as much about the fairness of the process through which an outcome is produced as they do about the outcome itself. Subsequent researchers such as Tom R. Tyler and E. Allan Lind demonstrated the power of fair process across diverse cultures and social settings.

We discovered the managerial relevance of fair process more than a decade ago, during a study of strategic decision making in multinational corporations. Many top executives in those corporations were frustrated—and baffled—by the way the senior managers of their local subsidiaries behaved. Why did those managers so often fail to share information and ideas with the executives? Why did they sabotage the execution of plans they had agreed to carry out? In the 19 companies we studied, we found a direct link between processes, attitudes, and behavior. Managers who believed the company's processes were fair displayed a high level of trust and commitment, which, in turn, engendered active cooperation. Conversely, when managers felt fair process was absent, they hoarded ideas and dragged their feet.

In subsequent field research, we explored the relevance of fair process in other business contexts—for example, in companies in the midst of transformations, in teams engaged in product innovation, and in company-supplier partnerships. (See "Making Sense of Irrational Behavior at VW and Siemens-Nixdorf.") For companies seeking to harness the energy and creativity of committed managers and employees, the central idea that emerges from our fair-process research is this: individuals are most likely to trust and cooperate freely with systems—whether they themselves win or lose by those systems—when fair process is observed.

Making Sense of Irrational Behavior at VW and Siemens-Nixdorf

Economic theories do a good job of explaining the rational side of human behavior, but they fall short of explaining why people can act negatively in the face of positive outcomes. Fair process offers managers a theory of behavior that explains—or might help predict—what would otherwise appear to be bewilderingly noneconomic, or irrational, behavior.

Consider what happened to Volkswagen. In 1992, the German car maker was in the midst of expanding its manufacturing facility in Puebla, Mexico, its only production site in North America. The appreciation of the deutsche mark against the U.S. dollar was pricing Volkswagen out of the U.S. market. But after the North American Free Trade Agreement (NAFTA) became law in 1992, Volkswagen's cost-efficient Mexican facility was well positioned to reconquer the large North American market.

In the summer of 1992, a new labor agreement had to be hammered out. The accord VW signed with the union's secretary-general included a generous 20% pay raise for employees. VW thought the workers would be pleased.

But the union's leaders had not involved the employees in discussions about the contract's terms; they did a poor job of communicating what the new agreement would mean to employees and why a number of work-rule changes were necessary. Workers did not understand the basis for the decisions their leaders had taken. They felt betrayed.

VW's management was completely caught off guard when, on July 21, the employees started a massive walkout that cost the company as much as an estimated $10 million per day. On August 21, about 300 protesters were attacked by police dogs. The government was forced to step in to end the violence. Volkswagen's plans for the U.S. market were in disarray, and its performance was devastated.

In contrast, consider the turnaround of Siemens-Nixdorf Informationssysteme (SNI), the largest European supplier of information technology. Created in 1990 when Siemens acquired the troubled Nixdorf Computer Company, SNI had cut head count from 52,000 to 35,000 by 1994. Anxiety and fear were rampant at the company.

In 1994, Gerhard Schulmeyer, the newly appointed CEO, went out to talk to as many employees as he could. In a series of meetings large and small with a total of more than 11,000 people, Schulmeyer shared his crusading mission to engage everyone in turning the company around. He began by painting a bleakly honest picture of SNI's situation: The company was losing money despite recent efforts to slash costs. Deeper cuts were needed, and every business would have to demonstrate its viability or be eliminated. Schulmeyer set clear but tough rules about how decisions would be made. He then asked for volunteers to come up with ideas.

Within three months, the initial group of 30 volunteers grew to encompass an additional 75 SNI executives and 300 employees. These 405 change agents soon turned into 1,000, then 3,000, then 9,000, as they progressively recruited others to help save the company. Throughout the process, ideas were solicited from managers and employees alike concerning decisions that affected them, and they all understood how decisions would be made. Ideas would be auctioned off to executives willing to champion and finance them. If no executive bought a proposal on its merits, the idea would not be pursued. Although 20% to 30% of their proposals were rejected, employees thought the process was fair.

People voluntarily pitched in—mostly after business hours, often until midnight. In just over two years, SNI has achieved a transformation notable in European corporate history. Despite accumulated losses of DM 2

billion, by 1995 SNI was already operating in the black. In the same period, employee satisfaction has almost doubled, despite the radical and
difficult changes under way.

Why did employees of Volkswagen revolt, despite their upbeat economic circumstances? How, in the face of such demoralizing economic
conditions, could SNI turn around its performance? What is at issue is not
what the two companies did but *how* they did it. The cases illustrate the
tremendous power of fair process—fairness in the process of making and
executing decisions. Fair process profoundly influences attitudes and behavior critical to high performance.

Fair process responds to a basic human need. All of us, whatever
our role in a company, want to be valued as human beings and not as
"personnel" or "human assets." We want to be treated with respect for
our intelligence. We want our ideas to be taken seriously. And we
want to understand the rationale behind specific decisions. People are
sensitive to the signals conveyed through a company's decision-
making processes. Such processes can reveal a company's willingness
to trust people and to seek their ideas—or they can signal the
opposite.

THE THREE PRINCIPLES

In all the diverse management contexts we have studied, we have
asked people to identify the bedrock elements of fair process. And
whether we were working with senior executives or shop floor employees, the same three mutually reinforcing principles consistently
emerged: engagement, explanation, and expectation clarity.

Engagement means involving individuals in the decisions that affect
them by asking for their input and allowing them to refute the merits
of one another's ideas and assumptions. Engagement communicates
management's respect for individuals and their ideas. Encouraging ref-
utation sharpens everyone's thinking and builds better collective wisdom. Engagement results in better decisions by management and
greater commitment from all involved to executing those decisions.

Explanation means that everyone involved and affected should understand why final decisions are made as they are. An explanation of
the thinking that underlies decisions makes people confident that
managers have considered their opinions and have made those decisions impartially in the overall interests of the company. An

explanation allows employees to trust managers' intentions even if their own ideas have been rejected. It also serves as a powerful feedback loop that enhances learning.

Expectation clarity requires that once a decision is made managers state clearly the new rules of the game. Although the expectations may be demanding, employees should know up front by what standards they will be judged and the penalties for failure. What are the new targets and milestones? Who is responsible for what? To achieve fair process, it matters less what the new rules and policies are and more that they are clearly understood. When people clearly understand what is expected of them, political jockeying and favoritism are minimized, and they can focus on the job at hand.

Notice that fair process is not decision by consensus. Fair process does not set out to achieve harmony or to win people's support through compromises that accommodate every individual's opinions, needs, or interests. While fair process gives every idea a chance, it is the merit of the ideas—and not consensus—that drives the decision making.

Nor is fair process the same as democracy in the workplace. Achieving fair process does not mean that managers forfeit their prerogative to make decisions and establish policies and procedures. Fair process pursues the best ideas whether they are put forth by one or many.

"WE REALLY SCREWED UP"

Elco managers violated all three basic principles of fair process at the Chester plant. They failed to engage employees in decisions that directly affected them. They didn't explain why decisions were being made the way they were and what those decisions meant to employees' careers and work methods. And they neglected to make clear what would be expected of employees under cellular manufacturing. In the absence of fair process, the Chester plant's employees rejected the transformation.

A week after the psychologist's survey was completed, management invited employees to meetings in groups of 20. Employees surmised that managers were either going to pretend that the survey had never happened or accuse employees of disloyalty for having voiced their complaints. But to their amazement, managers kicked off the meeting by presenting the undiluted survey results and declaring, "We were wrong. We really screwed up. In our haste and ignorance, we did not go through the proper process." Employees couldn't believe their ears. There were whispers in the back of the room, "What the devil did they say?" At more than 20 meetings over the next few weeks, managers repeated their confession. "No one was prepared to believe us at first," one manager said. "We had screwed up too badly."

At subsequent meetings, management shared with employees the company's dismal business forecast and the limited options available. Without cost reduction, Elco would have to raise its prices, and higher prices would further depress sales. That would mean cutting production even more, perhaps even moving manufacturing offshore. Heads nodded. Employees saw the bind the company was in. The business problem was becoming theirs, not just management's.

But still there were concerns: "If we help to cut costs and learn to produce elevators that are twice as good in half the time, will we work ourselves out of a job?" In response, the managers described their strategy to increase sales outside the United States. They also announced a new policy called *proaction time:* No one would be laid off because of any improvements made by an employee. Instead, employees could use their newly free time to attend cross-training programs designed to give them the skills they would need to work in any area of operations. Or employees could act as consultants addressing quality issues. In addition, management agreed not to replace any departing employees with new hires until business conditions improved. At the same time, however, management made it clear that it retained the right to let people go if business conditions grew worse.

Employees may not have liked what they heard, but they understood it. They began to see that they shared responsibility with management for Elco's success. If they could improve quality and productivity, Elco could bring more value to the market and prevent further sales erosion. To give employees confidence that they were not being misled, management pledged to share data on sales, costs, and market trends regularly—a first step toward rebuilding trust and commitment.

Elco's managers could not undo past mistakes, but they could involve employees in making future decisions. Managers asked employees why they thought the new manufacturing cells weren't working and how to fix them. Employees suggested making changes in the location of materials, in the placement of machines, and in the way tasks were performed. They began to share their knowledge; as they did so, the cells were redesigned and performance steadily improved, often far exceeding the expectations originally set by the consultants.

As trust and commitment were restored, talk of bringing the union back died out.

HIGH PARK'S TURN

Meanwhile, management worried about introducing the new work methods at Elco's High Park plant, which, unlike the Chester plant, had a history of resisting change. The union was strong at High Park, and some employees there had as much as 25 years' seniority. Moreover, the plant manager, a young engineer new to High Park, had never run a plant before. The odds seemed to be against him. If change had created animosity at Chester, one could only imagine how much worse the situation could become at High Park.

But management's fears went unrealized. When the consultants came to the plant, the young manager introduced them to all employees. At a series of plant wide meetings, corporate executives openly discussed business conditions and the company's declining sales and profits. They explained that they had visited other companies' plants and had seen the productivity improvements that cellular manufacturing could bring. They announced the proaction-time policy to calm employees' justifiable fears of layoffs. At the High Park plant, managers encouraged employees to help the consultants design the new manufacturing cells, and they encouraged active debate. Then, as the old performance measures were discarded, managers worked with employees to develop new ones and to establish the cell teams' new responsibilities.

Every day, the High Park plant manager waited for the anticipated meltdown, but it never came. Of course, there were some gripes, but even when people didn't like the decisions, they felt they had been treated fairly and, so, willingly participated in the plant's eventual performance turnaround.

The Price of Unfairness

Historically, policies designed to establish fair process in organizations arise mainly in reaction to employees' complaints and uprisings. But by then it is too late. When individuals have been so angered by the violation of fair process that they have been driven to organized protest, their demands often stretch well beyond the reasonable to a desire for what theorists call *retributive justice*: not only do they want fair process restored, they also seek to visit punishment and vengeance upon those who have violated it in compensation for the disrespect the unfair process signals.

Lacking trust in management, employees push for policies that are laboriously detailed, inflexible, and often administratively constricting. They want to ensure that managers will never have the discretion to act unjustly again. In their indignation, they may try to roll back decisions imposed unfairly even when the decisions themselves were good ones—even when they were critical to the company's competitiveness or beneficial to the workers themselves. Such is the emotional power that unfair process can provoke.

Managers who view fair process as a nuisance or as a limit on their freedom to manage must understand that it is the violation of fair process that will wreak the most serious damage on corporate performance. Retribution can be very expensive.

Three years later, we revisited a popular local eatery to talk with people from both plants. Employees from both Chester and High Park now believe that the cellular approach is a better way to work. High Park employees spoke about their plant manager with admiration, and they commiserated with the difficulties Elco's managers had in making the changeover to cellular manufacturing. They concluded that it had been a necessary, worthwhile, and positive experience. But Chester employees spoke with anger and indignation as they described their treatment by Elco's managers. (See the insert "The Price of Unfairness.") For them, as for the London woman who had been unfairly ticketed, fair process was as important as—if not more important than—the outcome.

Fair Process in the Knowledge Economy

Fair process may sound like a soft issue, but understanding its value is crucial for managers trying to adapt their companies to the demands of the knowledge-based economy. Unlike the traditional factors of production—land, labor, and capital—knowledge is a resource locked in the human mind. Creating and sharing knowledge are intangible activities that can neither be supervised nor forced out of people. They happen only when people cooperate voluntarily. As the Nobel laureate economist Friedrich Hayek has argued, "Practically every individual . . . possesses unique information" that can be put to use only with "his active cooperation." Getting that active cooperation may well turn out to be one of the key managerial issues of the next few decades. (See "Fair Process Is Critical in Knowledge Work.")

Fair Process Is Critical in Knowledge Work

It is easy to see fair process at work on the plant floor, where its violation can produce such highly visible manifestations as strikes, slowdowns, and high defect rates. But fair process can have an even greater impact on the quality of professional and managerial work. That is because innovation is the key challenge of the knowledge-based economy, and innovation requires the exchange of ideas, which in turn depends on trust.

Executives and professionals rarely walk the picket line, but when their trust has not been won, they frequently withhold their full cooperation—and their ideas. In knowledge work, then, ignoring fair process creates high opportunity costs in the form of ideas that never see daylight and initiatives that are never seized. For example:

A multifunctional team is created to develop an important new product. Because it contains representatives from every major functional area of the company, the team *should* produce more innovative products, with less internal fighting, shortened lead times, and lower costs. The team meets, but people drag their feet. Executives at a computer maker developing a new workstation, for example, thoughtfully deploy the traditional management levers. They hammer out a good incentive scheme. They define the project scope and structure. And they allocate the right resources. Yet the trust, idea sharing, and commitment that everyone wants never materialize. Why? Early in the project, manufacturing and marketing representatives on the team propose building a prototype, but the strong design-engineering group driving the project ignores them. Subsequently, problems surface because the design is difficult to manufacture and the application software is inadequate. The team members from manufacturing and marketing are aware of these issues all along but remain passive in sharing their concerns with the powerful design engineers. Instead, they wait until the problems reveal themselves—at which time they are very expensive to fix.

Two companies create a joint venture that offers clear benefits to both parties. But they then hold their cards so close to their chests that they ensure the alliance will create limited value for either partner. The Chinese joint-venture partner of a European engineering group, for example, withholds critical information from the field, failing to report that customers are having problems installing the partner's products and sitting on requests for new product features. Why do the Chinese fail to cooperate fully, even if it means hurting their own business?

Early in the partnership, the Chinese felt they had been shut out of key product and operating decisions. To make matters worse, the Europeans never explained the logic guiding their decisions. As the Chinese withhold critical information, the increasingly frustrated European partner responds in kind by slowing the transfer of managerial know-how, which the Chinese need badly.

Two companies create a supplier partnership to achieve improved value at lower cost. They agree to act in a seamless fashion, as one company. But the supplier seems to spend more energy on developing other customers than on deepening the partnership. One consumer goods manufacturer, for example, keeps delaying the installation of a joint electronic consumer-response data system with a major food retailer. The system will substantially improve inventory management for both partners. But the supplier remains too wary to invest. Why? The retailer has a history of dropping some of the supplier's products without explanation. And the consumer company can't understand the retailer's ambiguous criteria for designating "preferred suppliers."

Voluntary cooperation was not what Frederick Winslow Taylor had in mind when at the turn of the century he began to develop an arsenal of tools to promote efficiency and consistency by controlling individuals' behavior and compelling employees to comply with management dictates. Thus, traditional management science, which is rooted in Taylor's time-and-motion studies, encouraged a managerial preoccupation with allocating resources, creating economic incentives and rewards, monitoring and measuring performance, and manipulating organizational structures to set lines of authority. These conventional management levers still have their role to play, but they have little to do with encouraging active cooperation. Instead, they operate in the realm of outcome fairness or what social scientists call *distributive justice*, where the psychology works like this: When people get the compensation (or the resources, or the place in the organizational hierarchy) they deserve, they feel satisfied with that outcome. They will reciprocate by fulfilling to the letter their obligation to the company. The psychology of fair process, or *procedural justice*, is quite different. Fair process builds trust and commitment, trust and commitment produce voluntary cooperation, and voluntary cooperation drives performance, leading people to go beyond the call of duty by sharing their knowledge and applying their creativity. In all the management contexts we've studied, whatever the task, we have consistently observed this dynamic at work. (See Exhibit 6-1 "Two Complementary Paths to Performance.")

Consider the transformation of Bethlehem Steel Corporation's Sparrows Point, Maryland, division, a business unit responsible for marketing, sales, production, and financial performance. Until 1993, the 106-year-old division was managed in the classic command-and-control style. People were expected to do what they were told to do— no more and no less—and management and employees saw themselves as adversaries.

That year, Bethlehem Steel introduced a management model so different at Sparrows Point that Taylor—who was, in fact, the company's consulting engineer about 100 years ago—wouldn't have recognized it. The new model was designed to invoke in employees an active sense of responsibility for sharing their knowledge and ideas with one another and with management. It was also meant to encourage them to take the initiative for getting things done. In the words of Joe Rosel, the president of one of the division's five unions, "It's all about involvement, justification for decisions, and a clear set of expectations."

At Sparrows Point, employees are involved in making and executing decisions at three levels. At the top is a joint-leadership team, composed of senior managers and five employee representatives, that deals with companywide issues when they arise. At the department level are area teams, consisting of managers like superintendents and of employees from the different areas of the plant, such as zone committee men. Those teams deal with day-to-day operational issues such as customer service, quality, and logistics. Ad hoc problem-solving teams of employees address opportunities and obstacles as they arise on the shop floor. At each level, teammates share and debate their ideas. Thus, employees are assured of a fair hearing for their point of view on decisions likely to affect them. With the exception of decisions involving major changes or substantial resource commitments, the teams make and execute the decisions themselves.

Sparrows Point uses numerous processes and devices to ensure that all employees can understand why decisions have been made and how such decisions need to be executed. There is, for example, a bulletin board where decisions are posted and explained, allowing employees who haven't been directly involved in those decisions to understand what's going on and why. In addition, in more than 70 four-hour seminars, groups ranging in size from 50 to 250 employees have

Exhibit 6-1   Two Complementary Paths to Performance

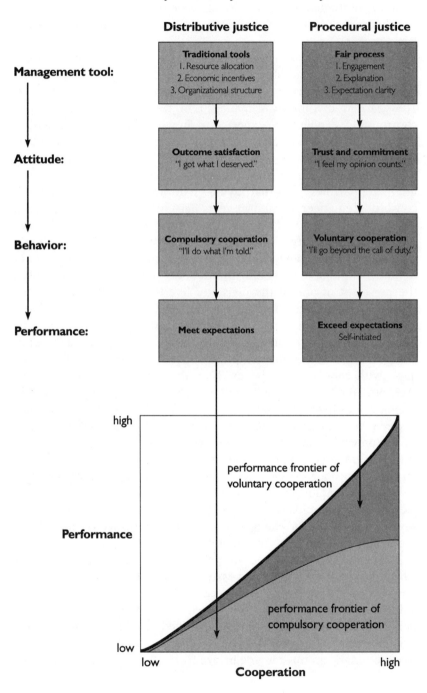

met to discuss changes occurring at the division, learn about new ideas under consideration, and find out how changes might affect employees' roles and responsibilities. A quarterly newsletter and a monthly "report card" of the division's strategic, marketing, operational, and financial performance keeps each of the unit's 5,300 employees informed. And the teams report back to their colleagues about the changes they are making, seeking help in making the ideas work.

Fair process has produced significant changes in people's attitudes and behavior. Consider, for example, the tin mill unit at Sparrows Point. In 1992, the unit's performance was among the worst in the industry. But then, as one employee explains, "People started coming forward and sharing their ideas. They started caring about doing great work, not just getting by. Take the success we've had in light-gauge cable sheathing. We had let this high value-added product slip because the long throughput time required for production held up the other mills in the unit. But after we started getting everyone involved and explained why we needed to improve throughput, ideas started to flow. At first, the company was doubtful: If the product had created a bottleneck before, why should it be different now? But people came up with the idea of using two sequential mills instead of one to eliminate the bottleneck. Did people suddenly get smarter? No. I'd say they started to care."

The object in creating this new way of working at Sparrows Point was to improve the intellectual buy-in and emotional commitment of the employees to their work. It has apparently been successful. Since 1993, Sparrows Point has turned a profit three years in a row, the first time that has happened since the late 1970s. The division is becoming a showcase demonstrating how a declining industry can be revitalized in today's knowledge economy. In the words of one Sparrows Point employee, "Since we know now everything that's going on in the company, we have more trust in management and are more committed to making things happen. People have started doing things beyond the normal call of duty."

Overcoming Mental Barriers

If fair process is such a simple idea and yet so powerful, why do so few companies practice it? Most people think of themselves as fair, and managers are no exception. But if you ask them what it means to be a fair manager, most will describe how they give people the authority they deserve, or the resources they need, or the rewards they've earned. In other words, they will confuse fair process with fair outcomes. The few managers who focus on process might identify only one of the three fair-process principles (the most widely understood is engagement), and they would stop there.

But there are two more fundamental reasons, beyond this simple lack of understanding, that explain why fair process is so rare. The first involves power. Some managers continue to believe that knowledge is power and that they retain power only by keeping what they know to themselves. Their implicit strategy is to preserve their managerial discretion by deliberately leaving the rules for success and failure vague. Other managers maintain control by keeping employees at arm's length, substituting memos and forms for direct, two-way communication, thus avoiding challenges to their ideas or authority. Such styles can reflect deeply ingrained patterns of behavior, and rarely are managers conscious of how they exercise power. For them, fair process would represent a threat.

The second reason is also largely unconscious because it resides in that economic assumption that most of us have grown up taking at face value: the belief that people are concerned only with what's best for themselves. But, as we have seen, there is ample evidence to show that when the process is perceived to be fair, most people will accept outcomes that are not wholly in their favor. People realize that compromises and sacrifices are necessary on the job. They accept the need for short-term personal sacrifices in order to advance the long-term interests of the corporation. Acceptance is conditional, however, hinged as it is on fair process.

Fair process reaches into a dimension of human psychology underexplored in conventional management practice. Yet every company can tap into the voluntary cooperation of its people by building trust through fair processes.

7
Covert Leadership: Notes on Managing Professionals

Henry Mintzberg

Bramwell Tovey, artistic director and conductor of the Winnipeg Symphony Orchestra, may not seem like your typical manager. Indeed, in comparison with, say, the usual *New Yorker* cartoon of the nicely manicured executive surrounded by performance charts sitting in a corner office, orchestra conducting may seem like a rather quirky form of management. Yet as knowledge work has grown in importance—and as more and more work is done by trained and trusted professionals—the way Bramwell leads his orchestra may illustrate a good deal of what today's managing is all about.

I have been studying the work of managers on and off throughout my career, more recently spending days with a wide variety of managers. Because the metaphor of the orchestra leader is so often used to represent what business leaders do, I thought that spending time with a conductor might prove instructive. The day with Bramwell was intended to explore, and perhaps explode, the myth of the manager as the great conductor at the podium—the leader in complete control.

When you reflect on it, the symphony orchestra is like many other professional organizations—for example, consulting firms and hospitals—in that it is structured around the work of highly trained individuals who know what they have to do and just do it. Such professionals hardly need in-house procedures or time-study analysts to tell them how to do their jobs. That fundamental reality challenges many preconceptions that we have about management and leadership. Indeed, in such environments, *covert leadership* may matter more than overt leadership.

Who Controls?

When the maestro walks up to the podium and raises his baton, the musicians respond in unison. Another motion, and they all stop. It's the image of absolute control—management captured perfectly in caricature. And yet it is all a great myth.

What does Bramwell Tovey really control? What choices does he really have? Bramwell says his job consists of selecting the program, determining how the pieces are played, choosing guest artists, staffing the orchestra, and managing some external relations. (Conductors apparently vary in their propensity to engage in external work. Bramwell enjoys it.) The administrative and finance side of the orchestra is handled by an executive director—at the time, Max Tapper, who comanaged the orchestra with Bramwell.

So much of the classic literature on management has been about the need for *controlling*, which is about designing systems, creating structures, and making choices. There are systems galore in symphony orchestras, all meant to control the work. But they are systems inherent to the profession, not to management. Bramwell inherited them all. The same can be said about structures; in fact, even more so. Just look at how everyone sits, in prearranged rows, according to a very strict and externally imposed pecking order; how they tune their instruments before playing and stomp their feet after a good solo rehearsal. These rituals imply a high degree of structure, and yet they all come with the job.

The profession itself, not the manager, supplies much of the structure and coordination. While the work of some experts takes place in small teams and task forces with a great deal of informal communication, professional work here consists of applying standard operating routines: the composer started work with a blank sheet of paper, but the musicians start with the composer's score. The object is to play it well—interpreting it but hardly inventing something new. Indeed, the work, the workers, their tools—almost everything in a symphony is highly standardized. One person I met on my visit with the Winnipeg Symphony Orchestra told me about how he had conducted a university orchestra, where the players tended to show up sporadically for rehearsals. At times, he said, he found himself meeting the whole orchestra for the first time at the performance!

In organizations where standard operating routines are applied, the experts work largely on their own, free of the need to coordinate with their colleagues. This happens almost automatically. A doctoral student of mine, for example, once sat in on a five-hour open-heart surgical operation during which the surgeon and anesthesiologist exchanged hardly a word. They were able to coordinate their efforts because of the standardization of their skills and by what they were trained to expect from each other. Similarly, in the orchestra, even though the musicians play together, each and every one of them plays alone. They each follow a score and know precisely when to contribute. The instrument not only identifies each player but also distinguishes him or her from the other musicians.

Most professional workers require little direct supervision from managers. Indeed, many hospital physicians and university professors like to describe their structures as upside down, with themselves in charge at the top and with the managers on the bottom to serve them. This description is overstated, but hardly more so than the ubiquitous one of "top" management. I have been teaching at a university for three decades, yet I can remember no dean ever coming into my classroom. Surgeons, likewise, hardly expect a medical chief or a hospital director to appear, let alone set the pace for one of their operations. That observation may not seem to hold for a symphony orchestra, where the conductor certainly sets the pace. But it is a lot more relevant than it might at first appear.

Along with *controlling* and *coordinating, directing* is one of the oldest and most common words used to describe managerial work. Among other things, directing means issuing directives, delegating tasks, and authorizing decisions. Yet despite his designation as orchestra director, Bramwell's actual "directing" is highly circumscribed. The day I was with him, he hardly ran around giving orders. Indeed, he explained that even comments made during rehearsals have to be aimed at sections rather than at individuals. In fact, Bramwell says that singling out individuals is forbidden in certain union contracts (although not in Winnipeg). In his case, Bramwell makes such comments maybe "two or three times a year—if someone doesn't get the overall message." But conducting has changed considerably, Bramwell points out, since the days of the great autocrats like Toscanini.

A great deal of the conventional manager's control is exercised through formal information. Such information plays a rather limited role for the orchestra conductor. When Bramwell reads or processes information on the job, it is more about scores than about budgets. For him, musical information provides a much more relevant and direct way of judging performance. Just by listening with a trained ear, the conductor knows immediately how well the orchestra has done. Nothing needs to be measured. How could it be? One is led to wonder how much of the music of more conventional managing gets drowned out by the numbers. Of course, there is a need to count here, too—for example, the number of seats occupied in the hall. But by making that the job of the executive director, Bramwell is left free to focus his attention on the real music of managing.

What, then, do conductors control? Although they choose the program and decide how the score should be played, they are constrained by the music that has been written, by the degree to which it can be interpreted, by the sounds the audience will be receptive to, and by the ability and willingness of the orchestra to produce the music. I mentioned to Bramwell a passage I had read about musicians being trained as soloists only to find themselves subordinated to the demands of an orchestra. He added, "You have to subordinate yourself to the composer, too." Being part of an orchestra is "just another kind of subordination." On this particular day, Hindemith and Stravinsky were pulling the strings—of the conductor no less than of the violinists.

Leonard Sayles, who has written extensively on middle management, once reversed the myth of manager as magisterial conductor. In his book *Managerial Behavior: Administration in Complex Organizations* (McGraw-Hill, 1964), Sayles wrote, "[The manager] is like a symphony orchestra conductor, endeavoring to maintain a melodious performance . . . while the orchestra members are having various personal difficulties, stage hands are moving music stands, alternating excessive heat and cold are creating audience and instrument problems, and the sponsor of the concert is insisting on irrational changes in the program." When I read this to Bramwell, he laughed. All of this had happened to him. In fact, there was currently a rift between two of the symphony's key players. If one preferred that a note be played long and the other short, then a simple suggestion made by Bramwell to play the note one way could be seen as "awarding points." In a similar vein, Bramwell said he cannot socialize with the musicians outside of work. There are too many agendas.

Taken together, the various constraints within which the orchestra conductor works describe a very common condition among managers—not being in absolute control of others nor being completely powerless, but functioning somewhere in between.

Leading Is Covert

When someone asked Indian-born Zubin Mehta about the difficulties of conducting the Israel Philharmonic, where everyone is said to consider him or herself a soloist, he reportedly replied, "I'm the only Indian; they're all the chiefs!" Leadership is clearly a tricky business in professional organizations. It was very much on Bramwell's mind in our discussions. He pointed out the qualifications of many of the players—some trained at Juilliard and Curtis, many of them with doctorates in music—and he expressed his discomfort in having to be a leader among ostensible equals. "I think of myself as a soccer coach who plays," he said, adding that "there are moments when I have to exert my authority in a fairly robust fashion . . . although it always puzzles me why I have to."

Watching Bramwell in a day of rehearsals, I saw a lot more *doing* than what we conventionally think of as *leading*. (See "A Model of Managerial Work.") More like a first-line supervisor than a hands-off executive, Bramwell was taking direct and personal charge of what was getting done. Rehearsals themselves are about results—about pace, pattern, tempo, and about smoothing, harmonizing, perfecting. The preparation for a concert could itself be described as a project, with the conductor as a hands-on project manager. This, if you like, is orchestra *operating*, not orchestra *leading*, let alone *directing*.

A Model of Managerial Work

Over the years, I have grown increasingly dissatisfied with managerial roles as they are discussed in almost all the classic literature on management. In such literature, roles are almost always presented as a disconnected list rather than an integrated model. So a few years ago, I returned to the study of managerial work that I had begun 30 years ago. Based on my own and other published descriptions, I developed a model in which managerial roles unfold on three successive levels, all of them both inside and outside the unit. There is an information level (closest to the managers), a people level, and an action level (closest to the unit and the world around it). The manager can intervene on any level but then must work through all the remaining levels.

Managerial behavior can be based on information, but it only has meaning if it influences people to take action. Or, managerial behavior can focus on people, but to be successful it must stimulate action. Managerial behavior can also influence action directly. All the roles discussed in this article—controlling and communicating, leading and linking, doing and dealing—are laid out in this framework.[1] (See the table below.) Although almost all well-known writers on the topic of management have suggested that managers focus on one of these roles to the exclusion of others, I believe that all managers must apply all six roles to their work.

INSIDE THE UNIT	OUTSIDE THE UNIT
Managing by Information	
Controlling and Communicating	Communicating
Managing through People	
Leading	Linking
Managing Action	
Doing	Dealing

After building the model, I undertook research to see how it looked in very different managerial situations. In particular, I wanted to see how managers differ in focus and style. I spent a day with each manager, not because I believed that a single day reveals all but because I believed that this approach would maximize my exposure to different managers. To date, I have observed 29 individuals, which might be thought of as a sample of 29 managerial days. The range has been vast: the head of the National Health Service of England (with almost a million employees), the heads of a small film company and of a retail chain, the CEO of the Royal Bank of Canada, the manager of a Red Cross delegation for a set of refugee camps in Tanzania, the front-country manager in Canada's Banff National Park, and others. Because the metaphor of the orchestra leader is so frequently used to describe what business leaders do, I found the idea of spending a day with an orchestra conductor irresistible.

Note

1. See Henry Mintzberg, "Rounding Out the Manager's Job," *Sloan Management Review*, Fall 1994.

In the course of my day with Bramwell, which involved many hours of rehearsal, I saw only one overt act of leadership. As the afternoon wore on, Bramwell was dissatisfied. "Come on guys—you're all asleep. You need to do this. It's not good enough." Later, he told me if he had to do that all the time, it would be intrusive. Fortunately, he does not. The fear of censure by the conductor is very powerful, he explained, because "instruments are the extensions of their souls!"

In conducting an orchestra, it seems that *covert leadership*—to use Bramwell's own phrase—may be far more important than overt leadership. Leadership infused everything Bramwell did, however invisibly. His "doing," in other words, was influenced by all the interpersonal concerns in the back of his mind: players' sensitivities, union contracts, and so on. Perhaps we need a greater appreciation in all managerial work of this kind of covert leadership: not leadership actions in and of themselves—motivating, coaching, and all that—but rather unobtrusive actions that infuse all the other things a manager does.

Bramwell, in fact, expressed discomfort with overt leadership. After all, the players are there because they are excellent performers—they all know the score, so to speak. Anyone who cannot play properly can be replaced. Rehearsals are not about enhancing skills but about coordinating the skills that are present.

Nevertheless, a symphony orchestra is not a jazz quartet any more than a racing scull is a canoe. With a large number of people, someone has to take the lead, set the pace, call the stroke. The Russians tried to achieve a leaderless orchestra in the heady days after the revolution, but all they succeeded in doing was relabelling the conductor. Given that all the musicians have to play in perfect harmony, the role of conductor emerges naturally. "I completely control the orchestra's timing—and timing is everything," Bramwell said, maybe because timing is one of the few things he can completely control.

Hence, a good symphony orchestra requires both highly trained professionals and clear personal leadership. And that has the potential to produce cleavage along the line where those two centers of power meet. If the players do not accept the conductor's authority or if the conductor does not accept the players' expertise, the whole system breaks down.

Bramwell's deepest concerns seem to focus precisely on this potential fault line. How can he remain true to his profession, which is music, while properly performing his job, which is management? He seems to find little comfort in that tension. Indeed, he appears most comfortable when he retreats back into the profession. Bramwell loves to play the piano by himself; he also composes music. Both of those activities, it should be noted, are pointedly free of the need to manage or be managed.

The Culture Is in the System

Leadership is generally exercised on three different levels. At the *individual* level, leaders mentor, coach, and motivate; at the *group* level, they build teams and resolve conflicts; at the *organizational* level, leaders build culture. In most organizations, these three levels are discrete and easily identifiable.

Not so in the symphony orchestra. Here we have a most curious phenomenon: one great big team with approximately 70 people and a single leader. (There are sections, but they have no levels of supervision.) The members of this team sit together, in one space, to be heard at one time. How often do customers see the whole product being delivered by the entire operating core of the organization?

As already noted, leadership at the individual level is highly circumscribed. Empowerment is a silly notion here. Musicians hardly need to be empowered by conductors. Inspired maybe—infused with feeling and energy—but not empowered. Leaders energize people by treating them not as detachable "human resources" (probably the most offensive term ever coined in management) but as respected members of a cohesive social system. When people are trusted, they do not have to be empowered.

Furthermore, in an orchestra, all these people come together for rehearsals and then disperse. How and where is the culture to be built up? The answers take us back to an earlier point: culture building, too, is covert, infused in everything the conductor does. Moreover, much of this culture is already built into the system. This is a culture of symphony orchestras—not just the Winnipeg Symphony Orchestra. A new player can to a large extent join days before a concert and still harmonize, socially as well as musically. This is not to deny the effects of the conductor's charisma or the effect that Bramwell Tovey can have on the culture of the Winnipeg Symphony Orchestra. It is only to argue that any conductor begins with several centuries of established cultural tradition.

This reality should make the job of leading at the cultural level that much easier. Culture does not have to be created so much as enhanced. People come together knowing what to expect and how they have to work. The leader has to use this culture to define the uniqueness of the group and its spirit in comparison with other orchestras. Indeed, maybe the culture, and not the personal chemistry, is the key to the ostensible "charisma" of all those famous conductors—and perhaps many other managers as well.

This point is reinforced by the fact that about half the time, symphony orchestras are not even led by their own conductors. An outsider comes in to perform the job—a so-called guest conductor. Imagine a "guest manager" almost anywhere else. Yet here it works—sometimes remarkably well—precisely because everything is so programmed by both the composer and the profession. That leaves the conductor free to inject his or her style and energy into the system.

Managing All Around

As noted above, Bramwell Tovey is a doer, right there on the floor. He doesn't read reports in some corner office. (Indeed, he took almost 18 months to give me feedback on my report.) He doesn't take his team off to some distant retreat to climb ropes so that they will come to trust one another. He simply ensures that a group of talented people come together to make beautiful music. In that sense, he is like a first-line supervisor, like a foreman in a factory or a head nurse of a hospital ward.

Yet at the end of our day together, Bramwell also turned around to maintain personal relationships with key stakeholders of the organization, the elite of the symphony's municipal society. In other words, the foreman acting on the factory floor by day becomes the statesman out networking in the Maestro's Circle—a group of the orchestra's most generous supporters—by night. The whole hierarchy gets compressed into the job of just one person.

Connecting to important outsiders—what is called *linking*—is an important aspect of all managerial work. There are always people to be convinced so that deals can be done. In Bramwell's case, this involves networking to represent the orchestra in the community to help it gain legitimacy and support. The other side of the linking role is serving as the conduit for social pressures on the organization. As we have seen, professionals require little direction and supervision. What they do require is protection and support. And so their managers have to pay a lot of attention to managing the boundary condition of the organization. In consulting firms, for example, it is top management that does the selling.

I have spent other days observing the executive director of a hospital and the head nurse of a surgical ward. The latter, like Bramwell, certainly kept her ward humming; she was the action-oriented front-line manager with a vengeance. She was on the floor most of the day. But unlike Bramwell, she expressed a dislike for what she called "the whole PR thing"—the linking role. The hospital director came out in quite the opposite way. He cherished what he called the "advocacy" role—dealing with government officials, negotiating with colleagues at other hospitals, working with prestigious board members, and so on. He put his greatest efforts into getting the most for his hospital from the outside world. The trouble was that when he turned around, he did not face professionals ready to harmonize but physicians and medical chiefs of staff demanding more resources.

This created a cleavage different from that noted before: between what could be called the managing *up* and *out* of the senior managers and the managing *down* and *in* of the operating managers. In hospitals, this is represented by a sort of *concrete floor* that blocks the downward exercise of authority. Beneath it, the clinicians work away, delivering their services, driven primarily by professional specializations, which are in turn driven by sophisticated technologies. Above it, senior managers advocate out, negotiate with one another, and manage the nonclinical operations when they are not, of course, engaged in one of their perpetual—and oftentimes fruitless—reorganizations.

The concrete floor, like the glass ceiling, is common in many of today's organizations, increasingly so as they grow bigger, as their hierarchies extend (despite so-called delayering), and as their management becomes more "professional," that is, more detached. Managing without an intimate understanding of what is being managed is an invitation to disharmony. External linking and dealing cannot be dissociated from internal leading and doing. Just consider how much money has been squandered on corporate acquisitions that have been managed in this way. You can't just "do the deal" and then drop it in the laps of others for implementation. Managing comes in a single pill; every manager, or well-coordinated management team, has to swallow all the roles we have been discussing—internal and external.

Bramwell Tovey does play all these roles—with a remarkable ability to turn from concerns on the inside to those on the outside. He directs the rehearsal and then turns to the Maestro's Circle, in effect, breaking through that concrete floor.

It should be noted here that the division of work between Bramwell and Max was not one of inside and outside but of artisan and administrator. The fact that they formed a harmonious comanagement team contrasts in an interesting way with a recommendation I once made as a consultant to a hospital. Since the executive director was more comfortable being an external advocate, while internally there was a great need for a mediator, I suggested that the hospital adopt a form of comanagement. A businessman who was a member of the board, horrified at any breach of the sanctified chain of command, insisted that the word be purged from my report. Too bad he had never spent a day with Bramwell and Max.

Coda

So what kind of organization is this in which one Indian has to put up with all those chiefs and someone like Bramwell Tovey can be so reticent about having to exercise leadership? More specifically, can we really call Bramwell a manager? Does he even want to be? Will the musicians let him be?

The answer has to be yes.

Uncomfortable as it may be to manage a group of such talented people, I believe Bramwell loves it. After all, he still gets to play often, and, when he does, no one is waving a baton at him. He is able to conduct the pieces he likes best, at least much of the time, and he experiences the extraordinary joy of seeing the work of the organization all come together at the wave of his hand—even if the composer is really pulling the strings. How many managers get this kind of satisfaction from their work?

And not only do the musicians let him do this, they actually encourage him, no matter how disagreeable some of them may find it. After all, they need him as much as he needs them. Bramwell commented, "I don't see myself as a manager. I consider myself more of a lion tamer." It is a good line, always likely to get a good laugh, and it echoes the popular description of managing professionals as "herding cats." But it hardly captures the image of 70 rather tame people sitting in neatly ordered rows ready to play together at the flick of a wand.

So even if he does not see his job as a manager, which I doubt, I certainly do. Get past the myth of the conductor in complete control and you may learn from this example what a good deal of today's managing is all about. Not obedience and harmony, but nuances and constraints. So maybe it is time for conventional managers to step down from their podiums, get rid of their budgeting batons, and see the conductor for who he or she really is. Only then can anyone appreciate the myth of the manager up there as well as the reality of the conductor down here. Perhaps that is how the manager and the organization can make beautiful music together.

8
The Dawn of the E-Lance Economy

Thomas W. Malone and Robert J. Laubacher

In October of 1991, Linus Torvalds, a 21-year-old computer-science student at the University of Helsinki, made available on the Internet a kernel of a computer operating system he had written. Called Linux, it was a rudimentary version of the ubiquitous UNIX operating system, which for more than a decade had been a mainstay of corporate and academic computing. Torvalds encouraged other programmers to download his software—for free—and use it, test it, and modify it as they saw fit. A few took him up on the offer. They fixed bugs, tinkered with the original code, and added new features, and they too posted their work on the Internet.

As the Linux kernel grew, it attracted the attention of more and more programmers, who contributed their own ideas and improvements. The Linux community grew steadily, soon coming to encompass thousands of people around the world, all sharing their work freely with one another. Within three years, this loose, informal group, working without managers and connected mainly through the Internet, had turned Linux into one of the best versions of UNIX ever created.

Imagine, now, how such a software development project would have been organized at a company like IBM or Microsoft. Decisions and funds would have been filtered through layers of managers. Formal teams of programmers, quality assurance testers, and technical writers would have been established and assigned tasks. Customer surveys and focus groups would have been conducted, their findings documented in thick reports. There would have been budgets, milestones, deadlines, status meetings, performance reviews, approvals.

There would have been turf wars, burnouts, overruns, delays. The project would have cost an enormous amount of money, taken longer to complete, and quite possibly produced a system less valuable to users than Linux.

For many executives, the development of Linux is most easily understood (and most easily dismissed) as an arcane story of hackers and cyberspace—a neat *Wired* magazine kind of story, but one that bears little relevance to the serious world of big business. This interpretation, while understandable, is shortsighted. What the Linux story really shows us is the power of a new technology—in this case, electronic networks—to fundamentally change the way work is done. The Linux community, a temporary, self-managed gathering of diverse individuals engaged in a common task, is a model for a new kind of business organization that could form the basis for a new kind of economy.

The fundamental unit of such an economy is not the corporation but the individual. Tasks aren't assigned and controlled through a stable chain of management but rather are carried out autonomously by independent contractors. These electronically connected freelancers— e-lancers—join together into fluid and temporary networks to produce and sell goods and services. When the job is done—after a day, a month, a year—the network dissolves, and its members become independent agents again, circulating through the economy, seeking the next assignment.

Far from being a wild hypothesis, the e-lance economy is, in many ways, already upon us. We see it not only in the development of Linux but also in the evolution of the Internet itself. We see it in the emergence of virtual companies, in the rise of outsourcing and telecommuting, and in the proliferation of freelance and temporary workers. Even within large organizations, we see it in the increasing importance of ad-hoc project teams, in the rise of "intrapreneurs," and in the formation of independent business units.[1]

All these trends point to the devolution of large, permanent corporations into flexible, temporary networks of individuals. No one can yet say exactly how important or widespread this new form of business organization will become, but judging from current signs, it is not inconceivable that it could define work in the twenty-first century as the industrial organization defined it in the twentieth. If it does, business and society will be changed forever.

Businesses of One

Business organizations are, in essence, mechanisms for coordination. They exist to guide the flow of work, materials, ideas, and money, and the form they take is strongly affected by the coordination technologies available. Until a hundred or so years ago, coordination technologies were primitive. Goods and messages were transported primarily by foot, horse, or boat, and the process was slow, unreliable, and often dangerous. Because there was no efficient way to coordinate disparate activities, most people worked near their homes, often by themselves, producing products or services for their neighbors. The business organizations that did exist—farms, shops, foundries—were usually small, comprising a few owners and employees. When their products had to reach distant consumers, they did so through a long series of transactions with various independent wholesalers, jobbers, shippers, storekeepers, and itinerant peddlers.

It was not until the second half of the nineteenth century, after railroad tracks had been laid and telegraph lines strung, that large, complex organizations became possible. With faster, more dependable communication and transportation, businesses could reach national and even international markets, and their owners had the means to coordinate the activities of large and dispersed groups of people. The hierarchical, industrial corporation was born, subsuming a broad array of functions and, often, a broad array of businesses, and it quickly matured to become the dominant organizational model of the twentieth century.

Despite all the recent talk of decentralized management, empowered employees, and horizontal processes, the large, industrial organization continues to dominate the economy today. We remain in the age of multinational megacompanies, and those companies appear to be rushing to meld into ever larger forms. The headlines of the business press tell the story: Compaq buys Digital. WorldCom buys MCI. Citibank merges with Travelers. Daimler-Benz acquires Chrysler. British Airways allies with American Airlines (which in turn allies with US Airways). Some observers, projecting this wave of consolidation into the future, foresee a world in which giant global corporations replace nations as the organizing units of humanity. We will be citizens of Sony or Shell or Wal-Mart, marching out every day to do battle with the citizens of Philips or Exxon or Sears.

Such a scenario certainly seems plausible. Yet when we look beneath the surface of all the M&A activity, we see signs of a counterphenomenon: the disintegration of the large corporation. People are leaving big companies and either joining much smaller companies or going into business for themselves as contract workers, freelancers, or temps. Twenty-five years ago, one in five U.S. workers was employed by a *Fortune* 500 company. Today the ratio has dropped to less than one in ten. The largest private employer in the United States is not General Motors or IBM or UPS. It's the temporary-employment agency Manpower Incorporated, which in 1997 employed 2 million people. While big companies control ever larger flows of cash, they are exerting less and less direct control over actual business activity. They are, you might say, growing hollow.

Even within large corporations, traditional command-and-control management is becoming less common. Decisions are increasingly being pushed lower down in organizations. Workers are being rewarded not for efficiently carrying out orders but for figuring out what needs to be done and then doing it. Some large industrial companies like Asea Brown Boveri and British Petroleum have broken themselves up into scores of independent units that transact business with one another almost as if they were separate companies. And in some industries, like investment banking and consulting, it is often easier to understand the existing organizations not as traditional hierarchies but as confederations of entrepreneurs, united only by a common brand name.

What underlies this trend? Why is the traditional industrial organization showing evidence of disintegration? Why are e-lancers proliferating? The answers lie in the basic economics of organizations. Economists, organizational theorists, and business historians have long wrestled with the question of why businesses grow large or stay small. Their research suggests that when it is cheaper to conduct transactions internally, within the bounds of a corporation, organizations grow larger, but when it is cheaper to conduct them externally, with independent entities in the open market, organizations stay small or shrink. If, for example, the owners of an iron smelter find it less expensive to establish a sales force than to contract with outside agencies to sell their products, they will hire salespeople, and their organization will grow. If they find that outside agencies cost less, they will not hire the salespeople, and their organization will not grow.

The coordination technologies of the industrial era—the train and the telegraph, the automobile and the telephone, the mainframe computer—made internal transactions not only possible but also advantageous. Companies were able to manage large organizations centrally, which provided them with economies of scale in manufacturing, marketing, distribution, and other activities. It made economic sense to directly control many different functions and businesses and to hire the legions of administrators and supervisors needed to manage them. Big was good.

But with the introduction of powerful personal computers and broad electronic networks—the coordination technologies of the twenty-first century—the economic equation changes. Because information can be shared instantly and inexpensively among many people in many locations, the value of centralized decision making and expensive bureaucracies decreases. Individuals can manage themselves, coordinating their efforts through electronic links with other independent parties. Small becomes good.

In one sense, the new coordination technologies enable us to return to the preindustrial organizational model of tiny, autonomous businesses—businesses of one or of a few—conducting transactions with one another in a market. But there's one crucial difference: electronic networks enable these microbusinesses to tap into the global reservoirs of information, expertise, and financing that used to be available only to large companies. The small companies enjoy many of the benefits of the big without sacrificing the leanness, flexibility, and creativity of the small.

In the future, as communications technologies advance and networks become more efficient, the shift to e-lancers promises to accelerate. Should that indeed take place, the dominant business organization of the future may not be a stable, permanent corporation but rather an elastic network that may sometimes exist for no more than a day or two. When a project needs to be undertaken, requests for proposals will be transmitted or electronic want ads posted, individuals or small teams will respond, a network will be formed, and new workers will be brought on as their particular skills are needed. Once the project is done, the network will disband. Following in the footsteps of young Linus Torvalds, we will enter the age of the temporary company.

The Temporary Company

From the 1920s through the 1940s, the movie business was controlled by big studios like MGM and Columbia. The studios employed

actors, directors, screenwriters, photographers, publicists, even projec-
tionists—all the people needed to produce a movie, get it into theaters,
and fill the seats. Central managers determined which films to make
and who would work on them. The film industry was a model of big-
company, industrial organization.

By the 1950s, however, the studio system had disintegrated. The
power had shifted from the studio to the individual. Actors, directors,
and screenwriters became freelancers, and they made their own
choices about which projects to work on. For a movie to be made,
these freelancers would join together into a temporary company,
which would employ different specialists as needed from day to day.
As soon as the film was completed, the temporary company would go
out of existence, but the various players would, in time, join together
in new combinations to work on new projects.

The shift in the film business from permanent companies to temporary companies shows how entire industries can evolve, quite rapidly,
from centralized structures to network structures. And such transformations are by no means limited to the idiosyncratic world of Hollywood. Consider the way many manufacturers are today pursuing radical outsourcing strategies, letting external agents perform more of
their traditional activities. The U.S. computer-display division of the
Finnish company Nokia, for example, chose to enter the U.S. display
market with only five employees. Technical support, logistics, sales,
and marketing were all subcontracted to specialists around the country. The fashion accessories company Topsy Tail, which has revenues of $80 million but only three employees, never even touches
its products through the entire supply chain. It contracts with various
injection-molding companies to manufacture its goods; uses design
agencies to create its packaging; and distributes and sells its products
through a network of independent fulfillment houses, distributors,
and sales reps. Nokia's and Topsy Tail's highly decentralized operations
bear more resemblance to the network model of organization than to
the traditional industrial model.

For another, broader example, look at what's happened to the textile industry in the Prato region of Italy. In the early 1970s, Massimo
Menichetti inherited his family's business, a failing textile mill.
Menichetti quickly broke up the firm into eight separate companies.
He sold a major portion of equity—between one-third and one-half—
to key employees, and he required that at least 50% of the new companies' sales come from customers that had not been served by the old
company. Within three years, the eight new businesses had achieved a

complete turnaround, attaining significant increases in machine utilization and productivity.

Following the Menichetti model, many other big mills in Prato broke themselves up into much smaller pieces. By 1990, more than 15,000 small textile firms, averaging fewer than five employees, were active in the region. The tiny firms built state-of-the-art factories and warehouses, and they developed cooperative ventures in such areas as purchasing, logistics, and R&D, where scale economies could be exploited. Textile production in the area tripled during this time, despite the fact that the textile industry was in decline throughout the rest of Europe. And the quality of the products produced in the Prato region rose as innovation flourished. Textiles from Prato have now become the preferred material for fashion designers around the world.

Playing a key role in the Prato textile industry are brokers, known as *impannatori,* who act as conduits between the small manufacturing concerns and the textile buyers. The impannatori help coordinate the design and manufacturing process by bringing together appropriate groups of businesses to meet the particular needs of a customer. They have even created an electronic market, which serves as a clearinghouse for information about projected factory utilization and upcoming requirements, allowing textile production capacity to be traded like a commodity.

The Prato experience shows that an economy can be built on the network model, but Prato, it could be argued, is a small and homogeneous region. How would a complex, diverse industry operate under the network model? The answer is: far more easily than one might expect. As a thought experiment, let's take a journey forward in time, into the midst of the twenty-first century, and see how automobiles, the archetypal industrial product, are being designed.

General Motors, we find, has split apart into several dozen separate divisions, and these divisions have outsourced most of their traditional activities. They are now small companies concerned mainly with managing their brands and funding the development of new types and models of cars. A number of independent manufacturers perform fabrication and assembly on a contract basis for anyone who wants to pay for it. Vehicles are devised by freelance engineers and designers, who join together into small, ever shifting coalitions to work on particular projects. A coalition may, for example, focus on engineering an electrical system or on designing a chassis, or it may concentrate on managing the integration of all of the subsystems into complete automobiles.

These design coalitions take many forms. Some are organized as joint ventures; some share equity among their members; some are built around electronic markets that set prices and wages. All are autonomous and self-organizing, and all depend on a universal, high-speed computer network—the descendant of the Internet—to connect them to one another and exchange electronic cash. A highly developed venture-capital infrastructure monitors and assesses the various teams and provides financing to the most promising ones.

In addition to being highly efficient, with little managerial or administrative overhead, this market-based structure has spurred innovation throughout the automotive industry. While much of the venture capital goes to support traditional design concepts, some is allocated to more speculative, even wild-eyed, ideas, which if successful could create enormous financial rewards. A small coalition of engineers may, for example, receive funds to design a factory for making individualized lighting systems for car grilles. If their idea pans out, they could all become multimillionaires overnight. And the next day, they might dissolve their coalition and head off to seek new colleagues and new challenges.

Over the past few years, under the auspices of the Massachusetts Institute of Technology's initiative on Inventing the Organizations of the 21st Century, we have worked with a group of business professors and executives to consider the different ways business might be organized in the next century.[2] The automotive design scenario we've just laid out was discussed and refined by this group, and we subsequently shared it with managers and engineers from big car companies. They not only agreed that it was a plausible model for car design but also pointed out that the auto industry was in some ways already moving toward such a model. Many automakers have been outsourcing more and more of their basic design work, granting ever greater autonomy to external design agencies.

A shift to an e-lance economy would bring about fundamental changes in virtually every business function, not just in product design. Supply chains would become ad hoc structures, assembled to fit the needs of a particular project and disassembled when the project ended. Manufacturing capacity would be bought and sold in an open market, and independent, specialized manufacturing concerns would undertake small batch orders for a variety of brokers, design shops, and even consumers. Marketing would be performed in some cases by brokers, in other cases by small companies that would own brands and certify the quality of the merchandise sold under them. In still other cases, the ability of consumers to share product information on the Internet would render marketing obsolete; consumers would simply "swarm" around the best offerings. Financing would come less from retained earnings and big equity markets and more from venture capitalists and interested individuals. Small investors might trade shares in ad hoc, project-based enterprises over the Internet.

Business would be transformed fundamentally. But nowhere would the changes be as great as in the function of management itself.

The Transformation of Management

In the mid-1990s, when the Internet was just entering the consciousness of most business executives, the press was filled with disaster stories. The Internet, the pundits proclaimed, was about to fall into disarray. Traffic on the World Wide Web was growing too fast. There were too many Web sites, too many people on-line. Demand was outstripping capacity, and it was only a matter of months before the entire network crashed or froze.

It never happened. The Internet has continued to expand at an astonishing rate. Its capacity has doubled every year since 1988, and today more than 90 million people are connected to it. They use it to order books and flowers, to check on weather conditions in distant cities, to trade stocks and commodities, to send messages and spread propaganda, and to join discussion groups on everything from soap operas to particle physics.

So who's responsible for this great and unprecedented achievement? Who oversaw what is arguably the most important business development of the last 50 years? No one. No one controls the Internet. No one's in charge. No one's the leader. The Internet grew out of the combined efforts of all its users, with no central management. In fact, when we ask people whether they think the Internet could have grown this fast for this long if it had been managed by a single company—AT&T, for example—most say no. Managing such a massive and unpredictable explosion of capacity and creativity would have been beyond the skills of even the most astute and capable executives. The Internet *had* to be self-managed.

The Internet is the greatest model of a network organization that has yet emerged, and it reveals a startling truth: in an e-lance economy, the role of the traditional business manager changes dramatically and sometimes disappears completely. The work of the temporary company is coordinated by the individuals who compose it, with little or no centralized direction or control. Brokers, venture capitalists, and general contractors all play key roles—initiating projects, allocating resources, and coordinating work—but there need not be any single point of oversight. Instead, the overall results *emerge* from the individual actions and interactions of all the different players in the system.

Of course, this kind of coordination occurs all the time in a free market, where products ranging from cars to copying machines to soft drinks all get produced and consumed without any centralized authority deciding how many or what kinds of these products to make. More than two hundred years ago, Adam Smith called this kind of decentralized coordination the invisible hand of the market, and we usually take for granted that it is the most effective way for companies to interact with one another.

But what if this kind of decentralized coordination were used to organize all the different kinds of activities that today go on *inside* companies? One of the things that allow a free market to work is the establishment and acceptance of a set of standards—the "rules of the game"—that governs all the transactions. The rules of the game can take many forms, including contracts, systems of ownership, and procedures for dispute resolution. Similarly, for an e-lance economy to work, whole new classes of agreements, specifications, and common architectures will need to evolve.

We see this already in the Internet, which works because everyone involved with it conforms to certain technical specifications. You don't have to ask anyone for permission to become a network provider or a service provider or a user; you just have to obey the communication protocols that govern the Internet. Standards are the glue that holds the Internet together, and they will be the glue that binds temporary companies together and helps them operate efficiently.

To return to our auto industry scenario, car designers would be able to work independently because they would have on-line access to highly detailed engineering protocols. These standards would ensure that individual component designs are compatible with the overall design of the vehicle. Headlight designers, for example, would know the exact space allocated for the light assembly as well as the nature of any connections that need to be made with the electrical and control systems.

Standards don't have to take the form of technical specifications. They may take the form of routinized processes, such as we see today in the medical community. When doctors, nurses, and technicians gather to perform emergency surgery, they usually all know what process to follow, what role each will play, and how they'll interact with one another. Even if they've never worked together before, they can collaborate effectively without delay. In other cases, the standards may simply be patterns of behavior that come to be accepted as norms—what might today be referred to as the culture of a company or "the way things are done" in an industry.

One of the primary roles for the large companies that remain in the future may be to establish rules, standards, and cultures for network organizations operating partly within and partly outside their own boundaries. Some global consulting firms already operate in more or less this way. For example, McKinsey & Company has established a strong organizational culture with well-understood norms for how people are selected and promoted and how they are expected to work with others in the company. But the top managers do not tell individual partners what kind of work to do, which clients to work for, or which people to select for their consulting teams. Instead, the partners make largely autonomous decisions about what they will do and how they will do it. In other words, the value the firm provides to its members comes mainly from the standards—the rules of the game—it has established, not from the strategic or operational skills of its top managers.

As more large companies establish decentralized, market-based organizational structures, the boundaries between companies will become much less important. Transactions within organizations will become indistinguishable from transactions between organizations, and business processes, once proprietary, will freely cross organizational boundaries. The key role for many individuals—whether they call themselves managers or not—will be to play their parts in shaping a network that neither they nor anyone else controls.

Thinking about the Future

Most of what you've just read is, of course, speculative. Some of it may happen; some of it may not. Big companies may split apart, or they may stay together but adopt much more decentralized structures. The future of business may turn out to be far less revolutionary than we've sketched out, or it may turn out to be far more revolutionary.

We're convinced, though, of one thing—an e-lance economy, though a radical concept, is by no means an impossible or even an implausible concept. Most of the necessary building blocks—high-bandwidth networks, data interchange standards, groupware, electronic currency, venture capital micromarkets—either are in place or are under development.

What is lagging behind technology is our imagination. Most people are not able to conceive of a completely new economy where much of what they know about doing business no longer applies. Mitch Resnick, a colleague of ours at MIT, says that most people are locked into a "centralized mind-set." When we look up into the sky and see a flock of birds flying in formation, we tend to assume that the bird in front is the leader and that the leader is somehow determining the organization of all the other birds. In fact, biologists tell us, each bird is following a simple set of rules—behavioral standards—that result in the emergence of the organization. The bird in the front is no more important than the bird in the back or the bird in the middle. They're all equally essential to the pattern that they're forming.

The reason it's so important for us to recognize and to challenge the biases of our existing mind-set is that the rise of an e-lance economy would have profound implications for business and society, and we should begin considering those implications sooner rather than later. An e-lance economy might well lead to a flowering of individual wealth, freedom, and creativity. Business might become much more flexible and efficient, and people might find themselves with much more time for leisure, for education, and for other pursuits. A Golden Age might dawn.

On the other hand, an e-lance economy might lead to disruption and dislocation. Loosed from its traditional moorings, the business world might become chaotic and cutthroat. The gap between society's haves and have-nots might widen, as those lacking special talents or access to electronic networks fall by the wayside. The safety net currently formed by corporate benefit programs, such as health and disability insurance, might unravel.[3] E-lance workers, separated from the communities that companies create today, may find themselves lonely and alienated. All of these potential problems could likely be avoided, but we won't be able to avoid them if we remain blind to them. Twenty-four years from now, in the year 2022, the *Harvard Business Review* will be celebrating its one hundredth year of publication. As part of its centennial celebration, it may well publish a series of articles that look back on recent business history and contemplate the massive changes that have taken place. The authors may write about the industrial organization of the twentieth century as merely a transitional structure that flourished for a relatively brief time. They may comment on the speed with which giant companies fragmented into the myriad microbusinesses that now dominate the economy. And they may wonder why, at the turn of the century, so few saw it coming.

Notes

1. For more about the influence of information technology on business organizations, see Thomas W. Malone, "Is 'Empowerment' Just a Fad? Control, Decision-Making, and Information Technology," *Sloan Management Review*, Winter 1997, p. 23; Thomas W. Malone, JoAnne Yates, and Robert I. Benjamin, "Electronic Markets and Electronic Hierarchies," *Communications of the ACM*, June 1987, p. 484; and Thomas W. Malone and John F. Rockart, "Computers, Networks, and the Corporation," *Scientific American*, September 1991, p. 128.

2. See Robert J. Laubacher, Thomas W. Malone, and the MIT Scenario Working Group, "Two Scenarios for 21st Century Organizations: Shifting Networks of Small Firms or All-Encompassing 'Virtual Countries'?" MIT Initiative on Inventing the Organizations of the 21st Century Working Paper No. 001 (Cambridge, Mass.: January 1997) available on the World Wide Web at http://ccs.mit.edu/21c/21CWP001.html.

3. Workers' guilds, common in the Middle Ages, may again rise to prominence, taking over many of the welfare functions currently provided by big companies. See Robert J. Laubacher and Thomas W. Malone, "Flexible Work Arrangements and 21st Century Worker's Guilds," MIT Initiative on Inventing the Organizations of the 21st Century Working Paper No. 004 (Cambridge, Mass.: October 1997) available on the World Wide Web at http://ccs.mit.edu/21c/21CWP004.html.

9

The Post-Capitalist Executive

An Interview with Peter F. Drucker

T George Harris

For half a century, Peter F. Drucker, 83, has been teacher and adviser to senior managers in business, human service organizations, and government. Sometimes called the godfather of modern management, he combines an acute understanding of socioeconomic forces with practical insights into how leaders can turn turbulence into opportunity. With a rare gift for synthesis, Drucker nourishes his insatiable mind on a full range of intellectual disciplines, from Japanese art to network theory in higher mathematics. Yet, he learns most from in-depth conversations with clients and students: a global network of men and women who draw their ideas from action and act on ideas.

Since 1946, when his book, *Concept of the Corporation*, redefined employees as a resource rather than a cost, Drucker's works have become an ever-growing resource for leaders in every major culture, particularly among Japan's top decision makers in the critical stages of their rise to world business leadership. A goodly share of productive organizations worldwide are led by men and women who consider Drucker their intellectual guide, if not their personal mentor.

Drucker's most productive insights have often appeared first in the *Harvard Business Review*. He has written 30 *Harvard Business Review* articles, more than any other contributor. In the September–October 1992 issue, he published core concepts from his major new work, *Post-Capitalist Society* (HarperCollins, 1993). *Harvard Business Review* editors sent T George Harris, a Drucker collaborator for 24 years, to the Drucker Management Center at the Claremont

Graduate School in California for two days of intensive conversation about the book's practical implications for today's executives.

Peter, you always bring ideas down to the gut level where people work and live. Now we need to know how managers can operate in the post-capitalist society.

You have to learn to manage in situations where you don't have command authority, where you are neither controlled nor controlling. That is the fundamental change. Management textbooks still talk mainly about managing subordinates. But you no longer evaluate an executive in terms of how many people report to him or her. That standard doesn't mean as much as the complexity of the job, the information it uses and generates, and the different kinds of relationships needed to do the work.

Similarly, business news still refers to managing subsidiaries. But this is the control approach of the 1950s or 1960s. The reality is that the multinational corporation is rapidly becoming an endangered species. Businesses used to grow in one of two ways: from grassroots up or by acquisition. In both cases, the manager had control. Today businesses grow through alliances, all kinds of dangerous liaisons and joint ventures, which, by the way, very few people understand. This new type of growth upsets the traditional manager who believes he or she must own or control sources and markets.

How will the manager operate in a work environment free of the old hierarchies?

Would you believe that you're going to work permanently with people who work for you but are not your employees? Increasingly, for instance, you outsource when possible. It is predictable, then, that ten years from now a company will outsource all work that does not have a career ladder up to senior management. To get productivity, you have to outsource activities that have their own senior management. Believe me, the trend toward outsourcing has very little to do with economizing and a great deal to do with quality.

Can you give an example?

Take a hospital. Everybody there knows how important cleanliness is, but doctors and nurses are never going to be very concerned with how you sweep in corners. That's not part of their value system. They need a hospital maintenance company. One company I got to know in Southern California had a cleaning woman who came in as an illiterate Latino immigrant. She is brilliant. She figured out how to split a bed sheet so that the bed of a very sick patient, no matter how heavy, could be changed. Using her method, you have to move the patient about only six inches, and she cut the bed-making time from 12 minutes to 2. Now she's in charge of the cleaning operations, but she is not an employee of the hospital. The hospital can't give her one single order. It can only say, "We don't like this; we'll work it out."

The point is, managers still talk about the people who "report" to them, but that word should be stricken from management vocabulary. Information is replacing authority. A company treasurer with outsourced information technology, IT, may have only two assistants and a receptionist, but his decisions in foreign exchange can lose—or make—more money in a day than the rest of the company makes all year. A scientist decides which research *not* to do in a big company lab. He doesn't even have a secretary or a title, but his track record means that he is not apt to be overruled. He may have more effect than the CEO. In the military, a lieutenant colonel used to command a battalion, but today he may have only a receptionist and be in charge of liaisons with a major foreign country.

Amidst these new circumstances, everybody is trying to build the ideal organization, generally flat with few layers of bosses and driven directly by consumer satisfaction. But how do managers gear up their lives for this new world?

More than anything else, the individual has to take more responsibility for himself or herself, rather than depend on the company. In this country, and beginning in Europe and even Japan, you can't expect that if you've worked for a company for 5 years you'll be there when you retire 40 years from now. Nor can you expect that you will be able to do what you want to do at the company in 40 years time. In fact, if you make a wager on any big company, the chances of it being split within the next 10 years are better than the chances of it remaining the way it is.

This is a new trend. Big corporations became stable factors before World War I and in the 1920s were almost frozen. Many survived the Depression without change. Then there were 30 or 40 years when additional stories were built onto skyscrapers or more wings added onto corporate centers. But now they're not going to build corporate skyscrapers. In fact, within the past ten years, the proportion of the work force employed by *Fortune* "500" companies has fallen from 30% to 13%.

Corporations once built to last like pyramids are now more like tents. Tomorrow they're gone or in turmoil. And this is true not only of companies in the headlines like Sears or GM or IBM. Technology is changing very quickly, as are markets and structures. You can't design your life around a temporary organization.

Let me give you a simple example of the way assumptions are changing. Most men and women in the executive program I teach are about 45 years old and just below senior management in a big organization or running a midsize one. When we began 15 or 20 years ago, people at this stage were asking, "How can we prepare ourselves for the next promotion?" Now they say, "What do I need to learn so that I can decide where to go next?"

If a young man in a gray flannel suit represented the lifelong corporate type, what's today's image?

Taking individual responsibility and not depending on any particular company. Equally important is managing your own career. The stepladder is gone, and there's not even the implied structure of an industry's rope ladder. It's more like vines, and you bring your own machete. You don't know what you'll be doing next, or whether you'll work in a private office or one big amphitheater or even out of your home. You have to take responsibility for knowing yourself, so you can find the right jobs as you develop and as your family becomes a factor in your values and choices.

That's a significant departure from what managers could expect in the past.

Well, the changes in the manager's work are appearing everywhere, though on different timetables. For instance, I see more career confusion among the many Japanese students I've had over the years. They're totally bewildered. Though they are more structured than we ever were, suddenly the Japanese are halfway between being totally managed and having to take responsibility for themselves. What frightens them is that titles don't mean what they used to mean. Whether you were in India or France, if you were an Assistant Director of Market Research, everybody used to know what you were doing. That's not true any more, as we found in one multinational. A woman who had just completed a management course told me not long ago that in five years she would be an assistant vice president of her bank. I'm afraid I had to tell her that she might indeed get the title, but it would no longer have the meaning she thought it did.

Another rung in the ladder?

Yes. The big-company mentality. Most people expect the personnel department to be Papa—or Ma Bell. When the AT&T personnel department was at its high point 30 years ago, it was the power behind the scenes. With all their testing and career planning, they'd know that a particular 27-year-old would be, by age 45, an Assistant Operating Manager and no more. They didn't know whether he'd be in Nebraska or Florida. But unless he did something quite extraordinary, his career path until retirement was set.

Times have certainly changed. And, in fact, the Bell people have done better than most, because they could see that change coming in the antitrust decision. They couldn't ignore it. But most people still have a big-company mentality buried in their assumptions. If they lose a job with Sears, they hunt for one with Kmart, unaware that small companies create most of the new jobs and are about as secure as big companies.

Even today, remarkably few Americans are prepared to select jobs for themselves. When you ask, "Do you know what you are good at? Do you know your limitations?" they look at you with a blank stare. Or they often respond in terms of subject knowledge, which is the wrong answer. When they prepare their resumes, they still try to list positions like steps up a ladder. It is time to give up thinking of jobs or career paths as we once did and think in terms of taking on assignments one after the other.

How does one prepare for this new kind of managerial career?

Being an educated person is no longer adequate, not even educated in management. One hears that the government is doing research on new job descriptions based on subject knowledge. But I think that we probably have to leap right over the search for objective criteria and get into the subjective—what I call *competencies*. Do you really like pressure? Can you be steady when things are rough and confused? Do you absorb information better by reading, talking, or looking at graphs and numbers? I asked one executive the other day, "When you sit down with a person, a subordinate, do you know what to say?" Empathy is a practical competence. I have been urging this kind of self-knowledge for years, but now it is essential for survival.

People, especially the young, think that they want all the freedom they can get, but it is very demanding, very difficult to think through who you are and what you do best. In helping people learn how to be responsible, our educational system is more and more counterproductive. The longer you stay in school, the fewer decisions you have to make. For instance, the decision whether to take French II or Art History is really based on whether one likes to get up early in the morning. And graduate school is much worse.

Do you know why most people start with big companies? Because most graduates have not figured out where to place themselves, and companies send in the recruiters. But as soon as the recruits get through training and into a job, they have to start making decisions about the future. Nobody's going to do it for them.

And once they start making decisions, many of the best move to midsize companies in three to five years, because there they can break through to top management. With less emphasis on seniority, a person can go upstairs and say, "I've been in accounting for three years, and I'm ready to go into marketing." Each year I phone a list of my old students to see what's happening with them. The second job used to be with another big company, often because people were beginning to have families and wanted security. But with two-career families, a different problem emerges. At a smaller organization, you can often work out arrangements for both the man and the woman to move to new jobs in the same city.

Some of the psychological tests being developed now are getting better at helping people figure out their competencies. But if the world economy is shifting from a command model to a knowledge model, why shouldn't education determine who gets each job?

Because of the enormous danger that we would not value the person in terms of performance, but in terms of credentials. Strange as it may seem, a knowledge economy's greatest pitfall is in becoming a Mandarin meritocracy. You see creeping credentialism all around. Why should people find it necessary to tell me so-and-so is really a good researcher even though he or she doesn't have a Ph.D.? It's easy to fall into the trap because degrees are black-and-white. But it takes judgment to weigh a person's contribution.

The problem is becoming more serious in information-based organizations. As Michael Hammer pointed out three years ago in the *Harvard Business Review*, when an organization reengineers itself around information, the majority of management layers becomes redundant. Most turn out to have been just information relays. Now, each layer has much more information responsibility. Most large companies have cut the number of layers by 50%, even in Japan. Toyota came down from 20-odd to 11. GM has streamlined from 28 to maybe 19, and even that number is decreasing rapidly. Organizations will become flatter and flatter.

As a result, there's real panic in Japan, because it's a vertical society based on subtle layers of status. Everybody wants to become a *kachō*, a supervisor or section manager. Still, the United States doesn't have the answer either. We don't know how to use rewards and recognition to move the competent people into the management positions that remain. I don't care for the popular theory that a generation of entrepreneurs can solve our problems. Entrepreneurs are monomaniacs. Managers are synthesizers who bring resources together and have that ability to "smell" opportunity and timing. Today perception is more important than analysis. In the new society of organizations, you need to be able to recognize patterns to see what is there rather than what you expect to see. You need the invaluable listener who says, "I hear us all trying to kill the new product to protect the old one."

How do you find these people?

One way is to use small companies as farm clubs, as in baseball. One of my ablest friends is buying minority stakes in small companies within his industry. When I said it didn't make sense, he said, "I'm buying farm teams. I'm putting my bright young people in these companies so they have their own commands. They have to do everything a CEO does in a big company."

And do you know the biggest thing these young executives have to learn in their new positions? My friend continued, "We have more Ph.D.'s in biology and chemistry than we have janitors, and they have to learn that their customers aren't Ph.D.'s, and the people who do the work aren't." In other words, they must learn to speak English instead of putting formulas on the blackboard. They must learn to listen to somebody who does not know what a regression analysis is. Basically, they have to learn the meaning and importance of respect.

A difficult thing to learn, let alone teach.

You have to focus on a person's performance. The individual must shoulder the burden of defining what his or her own contribution will be. We have to demand—and "demand" is the word, nothing permissive—that people think through what constitutes the greatest contribution that they can make to the company in the next 18 months or 2 years. Then they have to make sure that contribution is accepted and understood by the people they work with and for.

Most people don't ask themselves this question, however obvious and essential it seems. When I ask people what they contribute to an organization, they blossom and love to answer. And when I follow with, "Have you told other people about it?" the answer often is "No, that would be silly because they know." But of course "they" don't. We are 100 years past the simple economy in which most people knew what others did at work. Farmers knew what most farmers did, and industrial workers knew what other factory workers did. Domestic servants understood each other's work, as did the fourth major group in that economy: small tradesmen. No one needed to explain. But now nobody knows what others do, even within the same organization. Everybody you work with needs to know your priorities. If you don't ask and don't tell, your peers and subordinates will guess incorrectly.

What's the result of this lack of communication?

When you don't communicate, you don't get to do the things you are good at. Let me give you an example. The engineers in my class, without exception, say they spend more than half their time editing and polishing reports—in other words, what they are least qualified to do. They don't even know that you have to write and rewrite and rewrite again. But there are any number of English majors around for that assignment. People seldom pay attention to their strengths. For example, after thinking for a long time, an engineer told me he's really good at the first design, at the basic idea, but not at filling in the details for the final product. Until then, he'd never told anybody, not even himself.

You're not advocating self-analysis alone, are you?

No. You not only have to understand your own competencies, but you also have to learn the strengths of the men and women to whom you assign duties, as well as those of your peers and boss. Too many managers still go by averages. They still talk about "our engineers." And I say, "Brother, you don't have engineers. You have Joe and Mary and Jim and Bob, and each is different." You can no longer manage a work force. You manage individuals. You have to know them so well you can go and say, "Mary, you think you ought to move up to this next job. Well, then you have to learn not to have that chip on your shoulder. Forget you are a woman; you are an engineer. And you have to be a little considerate. Do not come in at 10 minutes to 5 on Friday afternoon to tell people they have to work overtime when you knew it at 9 A.M."

The key to the productivity of knowledge workers is to make them concentrate on the real assignment. Do you know why most promotions now fail? One-third are outright disasters, in my experience, while another third are a nagging backache. Not more than one in three works out. No fit. The standard case, of course, is the star salesman promoted to sales manager. That job can be any one of four things—a manager of salespeople, a market manager, a brand manager, or a super salesman who opens up an entire new area. But nobody figures out what it is, so the man or woman who got the promotion just tries to do more of whatever led to the promotion. That's the surest way to be wrong.

Expand on your idea of information responsibility and how it fits into post-capitalist society.

Far too many managers think computer specialists know what information they need to do their job and what information they owe to whom. Computer information tends to focus too much on inside information, not the outside sources and customers that count. In today's organization, you have to take responsibility for information because it is your main tool. But most don't know how to use it. Few are information literate. They can play "Mary Had a Little Lamb" but not Beethoven.

I heard today about a brand manager in a major OTC drug company who tried to get the scientific papers on the product he markets. But the corporate librarian complained to his superior. Under her rules, she gives hard science only to the company's scientists and lawyers. He had to get a consultant to go outside and use a computer database to pull up about 20 journal articles on his product, so he'd know how to develop honest advertising copy. The point of the story is that this brand manager is way ahead of the parade: 99 out of 100 brand managers don't know they need that kind of information for today's consumers and haven't a clue how to get it. The first step is to say, "I need it."

And many people don't recognize the importance of this step. I work with an information manager at a large financial institution that has invested $1.5 billion in information. He and I talked all morning with his department's eight women and ten men. Very intelligent, but not one began to think seriously about what information they need to serve their customers. When I pointed this out, they said, "Isn't the boss going to tell us?" We finally had to agree to meet a month later so that they could go through the hard work of figuring out what information they need and—more important—what they do not need.

So a manager begins the road to information responsibility first by identifying gaps in knowledge.

Exactly. To be information literate, you begin with learning what it is you need to know. Too much talk focuses on the technology, even worse on the speed of the gadget, always faster, faster. This kind of "techie" fixation causes us to lose track of the fundamental nature of information in today's organization. To organize the way work is done, you have to begin with the specific job, then the information input, and finally the human relationships needed to get the job done.

The current emphasis on reengineering essentially means changing an organization from the flow of things to the flow of information. The computer is merely a tool in the process. If you go to the hardware store to buy a hammer, you do not ask if you should do upholstery or fix the door. To put it in editorial terms, knowing how a typewriter works does not make you a writer. Now that knowledge is taking the place of capital as the driving force in organizations worldwide, it is all too easy to confuse data with knowledge and information technology with information.

What's the worst problem in managing knowledge specialists?

One of the most degenerative tendencies of the last 40 years is the belief that if you are understandable, you are vulgar. When I was growing up, it was taken for granted that economists, physicists, psychologists—leaders in any discipline—would make themselves understood. Einstein spent years with three different collaborators to make his theory of relativity accessible to the layman. Even John Maynard Keynes tried hard to make his economics accessible. But just the other day, I heard a senior scholar seriously reject a younger colleague's work because more than five people could understand what he's doing. Literally.

We cannot afford such arrogance. Knowledge is power, which is why people who had it in the past often tried to make a secret of it. In post-capitalism, power comes from transmitting information to make it productive, not from hiding it.

That means you have to be intolerant of intellectual arrogance. And I mean intolerant. At whatever level, knowledge people must make themselves understood, and whatever field the manager comes from, he or she must be eager to understand others. This may be the main job of the manager of technical people. He or she must not only be an interpreter but also work out a balance between specialization and exposure.

Exposure is an important technique. For an exotic example, look at weather forecasting, where meteorologists and mathematicians and other specialists now work with teams of experts on satellite data. Europeans, on the one hand, have tried to connect these different disciplines entirely through information managers. On the other hand, Americans rotate people at an early stage. Suppose you put a Ph.D. in meteorology on a team that is to work on the new mathematical model of hurricanes for three years. He isn't a mathematician, but he gets exposed to what mathematicians assume, what they eliminate, what their limitations are. With the combination of exposure and translation, the American approach yields forecasts that are about three times more accurate than the European, I'm told. And the exposure concept is useful in managing any group of specialists.

Is the fact that some teams provide exposure as well as interpreters a reason why the team has become such a hot topic?

There's a lot of nonsense in team talk, as if teams were something new. We have always worked in teams, and while sports give us hundreds of team styles there are only a few basic models to choose from. The critical decision is to select the right kind for the job. You can't mix soccer and doubles tennis. It's predictable that in a few years, the most traditional team will come back in fashion, the one that does research first, then passes the idea to engineering to develop, and then on to manufacturing to make. It's like a baseball team, and you may know I have done a little work with baseball-team management.

The great strength of baseball teams is that you can concentrate. You take Joe, who is a batter, and you work on batting. There is almost no interaction, nothing at all like the soccer team or the jazz combo, the implicit model of many teams today. The soccer team moves in unison but everyone holds the same relative position. The jazz combo has incredible flexibility because everyone knows each other so well that they all sense when the trumpet is about to solo. The combo model takes great discipline and may eventually fall out of favor, especially in Japanese car manufacturing, because we do not need to create new models as fast as we have been.

I know several German companies that follow the baseball-team model, whether they know it or not. Their strength is clear: they are fantastic at exploiting and developing old knowledge, and Germany's midsize companies may be better than their big ones simply because they concentrate better. On the other hand, when it comes to the new, from electronics to biotech, German scientists may do fine work, but their famous apprenticeship system discourages innovation.

So, beyond all the hype, teams can help the executive navigate a post-capitalist society?

Thinking about teams helps us highlight the more general problem of how to manage knowledge. In the production of fundamental new knowledge, the British groups I run into are way ahead of anybody. But they have never done much with their expertise, in part because many British companies don't value the technically oriented person enough. I don't know of a single engineer in top management there. My Japanese friends are just the opposite. While they still do not specialize in scientific advances, they take knowledge and make it productive very fast. In this country, on the other hand, we have not improved that much in existing industries. The automobile business, until recently, was perfectly satisfied doing what it did in 1939. But, as we are discovering in computers and in biotech, we may be at our very best when it comes to ground-breaking technology.

Where is the lesson in all this for the manager?

The lesson is that the productivity of knowledge has both a qualitative and a quantitative dimension. Though we know very little about it, we do realize executives must be both managers of specialists and synthesizers of different fields of knowledge—really of knowledges, plural. This situation is as threatening to the traditional manager, who worries about high-falutin' highbrows, as it is to the intellectual, who worries about being too commercial to earn respect in his or her discipline. But in the post-capitalist world, the highbrow and the lowbrow have to play on the same team.

That sounds pretty democratic. Does a post-capitalist society based more on knowledge than capital become egalitarian?

No. Both of these words miss the point. *Democratic* bespeaks a narrow political and legal organization. Nor do I use the buzzword *participative*. Worse yet is the *empowerment* concept. It is not a great step forward to take power out at the top and put it in at the bottom. It's still power. To build achieving organizations, you must replace power with responsibility.

And, while we're on the subject of words, I'm not comfortable with the word *manager* any more, because it implies subordinates. I find myself using *executive* more, because it implies responsibility for an area, not necessarily dominion over people. The word *boss*, which emerged in World War II, is helpful in that it can be used to suggest a mentor's role, someone who can back you up on a decision. The new organizations need to go beyond senior/junior polarities to a blend with sponsor and mentor relations. In the traditional organization—the organization of the last 100 years—the skeleton, or internal structure, was a combination of rank and power. In the emerging organization, it has to be mutual understanding and responsibility.

10
Values in Tension: Ethics Away from Home

Thomas Donaldson

When we leave home and cross our nation's boundaries, moral clarity often blurs. Without a backdrop of shared attitudes, and without familiar laws and judicial procedures that define standards of ethical conduct, certainty is elusive. Should a company invest in a foreign country where civil and political rights are violated? Should a company go along with a host country's discriminatory employment practices? If companies in developed countries shift facilities to developing nations that lack strict environmental and health regulations, or if those companies choose to fill management and other top-level positions in a host nation with people from the home country, whose standards should prevail?

Even the best-informed, best-intentioned executives must rethink their assumptions about business practice in foreign settings. What works in a company's home country can fail in a country with different standards of ethical conduct. Such difficulties are unavoidable for businesspeople who live and work abroad.

But how can managers resolve the problems? What are the principles that can help them work through the maze of cultural differences and establish codes of conduct for globally ethical business practice? How can companies answer the toughest question in global business ethics: What happens when a host country's ethical standards seem lower than the home country's?

Competing Answers

One answer is as old as philosophical discourse. According to cultural relativism, no culture's ethics are better than any other's; therefore there are no international rights and wrongs. If the people of Indonesia tolerate the bribery of their public officials, so what? Their attitude is no better or worse than that of people in Denmark or Singapore who refuse to offer or accept bribes. Likewise, if Belgians fail to find insider trading morally repugnant, who cares? Not enforcing insider-trading laws is no more or less ethical than enforcing such laws.

The cultural relativist's creed—When in Rome, do as the Romans do—is tempting, especially when failing to do as the locals do means forfeiting business opportunities. The inadequacy of cultural relativism, however, becomes apparent when the practices in question are more damaging than petty bribery or insider trading.

In the late 1980s, some European tanneries and pharmaceutical companies were looking for cheap waste-dumping sites. They approached virtually every country on Africa's west coast from Morocco to the Congo. Nigeria agreed to take highly toxic polychlorinated biphenyls. Unprotected local workers, wearing thongs and shorts, unloaded barrels of PCBs and placed them near a residential area. Neither the residents nor the workers knew that the barrels contained toxic waste.

We may denounce governments that permit such abuses, but many countries are unable to police transnational corporations adequately even if they want to. And in many countries, the combination of ineffective enforcement and inadequate regulations leads to behavior by unscrupulous companies that is clearly wrong. A few years ago, for example, a group of investors became interested in restoring the SS *United States,* once a luxurious ocean liner. Before the actual restoration could begin, the ship had to be stripped of its asbestos lining. A bid from a U.S. company, based on U.S. standards for asbestos removal, priced the job at more than $100 million. A company in the Ukranian city of Sevastopol offered to do the work for less than $2 million. In October 1993, the ship was towed to Sevastopol.

A cultural relativist would have no problem with that outcome, but I do. A country has the right to establish its own health and safety regulations, but in the case described above, the standards and the terms of the contract could not possibly have protected workers in Sevastopol from known health risks. Even if the contract met

Ukranian standards, ethical businesspeople must object. Cultural relativism is morally blind. There are fundamental values that cross cultures, and companies must uphold them. (For an economic argument against cultural relativism, see "The Culture and Ethics of Software Piracy.")

The Culture and Ethics of Software Piracy

Before jumping on the cultural relativism bandwagon, stop and consider the potential economic consequences of a when-in-Rome attitude toward business ethics. Take a look at the current statistics on software piracy: In the United States, pirated software is estimated to be 35% of the total software market, and industry losses are estimated at $2.3 billion per year. The piracy rate is 57% in Germany and 80% in Italy and Japan; the rates in most Asian countries are estimated to be nearly 100%.

There are similar laws against software piracy in those countries. What, then, accounts for the differences? Although a country's level of economic development plays a large part, culture, including ethical attitudes, may be a more crucial factor. The 1995 annual report of the Software Publishers Association connects software piracy directly to culture and attitude. It describes Italy and Hong Kong as having "'first world' per capita incomes, along with 'third world' rates of piracy." When asked whether one should use software without paying for it, most people, including people in Italy and Hong Kong, say no. But people in some countries regard the practice as *less* unethical than people in other countries do. Confucian culture, for example, stresses that individuals should share what they create with society. That may be, in part, what prompts the Chinese and other Asians to view the concept of intellectual property as a means for the West to monopolize its technological superiority.

What happens if ethical attitudes around the world permit large-scale software piracy? Software companies won't want to invest as much in developing new products, because they cannot expect any return on their investment in certain parts of the world. When ethics fail to support technological creativity, there are consequences that go beyond statistics—jobs are lost and livelihoods jeopardized.

Companies must do more than lobby foreign governments for tougher enforcement of piracy laws. They must cooperate with other companies and with local organizations to help citizens understand the consequences of piracy and to encourage the evolution of a different ethic toward the practice.

At the other end of the spectrum from cultural relativism is ethical imperialism, which directs people to do everywhere exactly as they do at home. Again, an understandably appealing approach but one that is clearly inadequate. Consider the large U.S. computer-products company that in 1993 introduced a course on sexual harassment in its Saudi Arabian facility. Under the banner of global consistency, instructors used the same approach to train Saudi Arabian managers that they had used with U.S. managers: the participants were asked to discuss a case in which a manager makes sexually explicit remarks to a new female employee over drinks in a bar. The instructors failed to consider how the exercise would work in a culture with strict conventions governing relationships between men and women. As a result, the training sessions were ludicrous. They baffled and offended the Saudi participants, and the message to avoid coercion and sexual discrimination was lost.

The theory behind ethical imperialism is absolutism, which is based on three problematic principles. Absolutists believe that there is a single list of truths, that they can be expressed only with one set of concepts, and that they call for exactly the same behavior around the world.

The first claim clashes with many people's belief that different cultural traditions must be respected. In some cultures, loyalty to a community—family, organization, or society—is the foundation of all ethical behavior. The Japanese, for example, define business ethics in terms of loyalty to their companies, their business networks, and their nation. Americans place a higher value on liberty than on loyalty; the U.S. tradition of rights emphasizes equality, fairness, and individual freedom. It is hard to conclude that truth lies on one side or the other, but an absolutist would have us select just one.

The second problem with absolutism is the presumption that people must express moral truth using only one set of concepts. For instance, some absolutists insist that the language of basic rights provide the framework for any discussion of ethics. That means, though, that entire cultural traditions must be ignored. The notion of a right evolved with the rise of democracy in post-Renaissance Europe and the United States, but the term is not found in either Confucian or Buddhist traditions. We all learn ethics in the context of our particular cultures, and the power in the principles is deeply tied to the way in which they are expressed. Internationally accepted lists of moral principles, such as the United Nations' Universal Declaration of Human Rights, draw on many cultural and religious traditions. As philosopher Michael Walzer has noted, "There is no Esperanto of global ethics."

The third problem with absolutism is the belief in a global standard of ethical behavior. Context must shape ethical practice. Very low wages, for example, may be considered unethical in rich, advanced countries, but developing nations may be acting ethically if they encourage investment and improve living standards by accepting low wages. Likewise, when people are malnourished or starving, a government may be wise to use more fertilizer in order to improve crop yields, even though that means settling for relatively high levels of thermal water pollution.

When cultures have different standards of ethical behavior—and different ways of handling unethical behavior—a company that takes an absolutist approach may find itself making a disastrous mistake. When a manager at a large U.S. specialty-products company in China caught an employee stealing, she followed the company's practice and turned the employee over to the provincial authorities, who executed him. Managers cannot operate in another culture without being aware of that culture's attitudes toward ethics.

If companies can neither adopt a host country's ethics nor extend the home country's standards, what is the answer? Even the traditional litmus test—What would people think of your actions if they were written up on the front page of the newspaper?—is an unreliable guide, for there is no international consensus on standards of business conduct.

Balancing the Extremes: Three Guiding Principles

Companies must help managers distinguish between practices that are merely different and those that are wrong. For relativists, nothing is sacred and nothing is wrong. For absolutists, many things that are different are wrong. Neither extreme illuminates the real world of business decision making. The answer lies somewhere in between.

When it comes to shaping ethical behavior, companies must be guided by three principles.

- Respect for core human values, which determine the absolute moral threshold for all business activities.

- Respect for local traditions.
- The belief that context matters when deciding what is right and what is wrong.

Consider those principles in action. In Japan, people doing business together often exchange gifts—sometimes expensive ones—in keeping with long-standing Japanese tradition. When U.S. and European companies started doing a lot of business in Japan, many Western businesspeople thought that the practice of gift giving might be wrong rather than simply different. To them, accepting a gift felt like accepting a bribe. As Western companies have become more familiar with Japanese traditions, however, most have come to tolerate the practice and to set different limits on gift giving in Japan than they do elsewhere.

Respecting differences is a crucial ethical practice. Research shows that management ethics differ among cultures; respecting those differences means recognizing that some cultures have obvious weaknesses—as well as hidden strengths. Managers in Hong Kong, for example, have a higher tolerance for some forms of bribery than their Western counterparts, but they have a much lower tolerance for the failure to acknowledge a subordinate's work. In some parts of the Far East, stealing credit from a subordinate is nearly an unpardonable sin.

People often equate respect for local traditions with cultural relativism. That is incorrect. Some practices are clearly wrong. Union Carbide's tragic experience in Bhopal, India, provides one example. The company's executives seriously underestimated how much on-site management involvement was needed at the Bhopal plant to compensate for the country's poor infrastructure and regulatory capabilities. In the aftermath of the disastrous gas leak, the lesson is clear: companies using sophisticated technology in a developing country must evaluate that country's ability to oversee its safe use. Since the incident at Bhopal, Union Carbide has become a leader in advising companies on using hazardous technologies safely in developing countries.

Some activities are wrong no matter where they take place. But some practices that are unethical in one setting may be acceptable in another. For instance, the chemical EDB, a soil fungicide, is banned for use in the United States. In hot climates, however, it quickly becomes harmless through exposure to intense solar radiation and high soil temperatures. As long as the chemical is monitored, companies may be able to use EDB ethically in certain parts of the world.

Defining the Ethical Threshold: Core Values

Few ethical questions are easy for managers to answer. But there are some hard truths that must guide managers' actions, a set of what I call *core human values,* which define minimum ethical standards for all companies.[1] The right to good health and the right to economic advancement and an improved standard of living are two core human values. Another is what Westerners call the Golden Rule, which is recognizable in every major religious and ethical tradition around the world. In Book 15 of his *Analects,* for instance, Confucius counsels people to maintain reciprocity, or not to do to others what they do not want done to themselves.

Although no single list would satisfy every scholar, I believe it is possible to articulate three core values that incorporate the work of scores of theologians and philosophers around the world. To be broadly relevant, these values must include elements found in both Western and non-Western cultural and religious traditions. Consider the examples of values in Table 10-1 "What Do These Values Have in Common?"

At first glance, the values expressed in the two lists seem quite different. Nonetheless, in the spirit of what philosopher John Rawls calls *overlapping consensus,* one can see that the seemingly divergent values converge at key points. Despite important differences between Western and non-Western cultural and religious traditions, both express shared attitudes about what it means to be human. First, individuals must not treat others simply as tools; in other words, they must recognize a person's value as a human being. Next, individuals and communities must treat people in ways that respect people's basic rights. Finally, members of a community must work together to support and improve the institutions on which the community depends. I call those three values *respect for human dignity, respect for basic rights,* and *good citizenship.*

Those values must be the starting point for all companies as they formulate and evaluate standards of ethical conduct at home and abroad. But they are only a starting point. Companies need much more specific guidelines, and the first step to developing those is to translate the core human values into core values for business. What does it mean, for example, for a company to respect human dignity? How can a company be a good citizen?

I believe that companies can respect human dignity by creating and sustaining a corporate culture in which employees, customers, and

Table 10-1   What Do These Values Have in Common?

Non-Western	Western
Kyosei (Japanese): Living and working together for the common good	Individual liberty
Dharma (Hindi): The fulfillment of inherited duty	Egalitarianism
Santutthi (Buddhist): The importance of limited desires	Political participation
Zakat (Muslim): The duty to give alms to the Muslim poor	Human rights

suppliers are treated not as means to an end but as people whose intrinsic value must be acknowledged, and by producing safe products and services in a safe workplace. Companies can respect basic rights by acting in ways that support and protect the individual rights of employees, customers, and surrounding communities, and by avoiding relationships that violate human beings' rights to health, education, safety, and an adequate standard of living. And companies can be good citizens by supporting essential social institutions, such as the economic system and the education system, and by working with host governments and other organizations to protect the environment.

The core values establish a moral compass for business practice. They can help companies identify practices that are acceptable and those that are intolerable—even if the practices are compatible with a host country's norms and laws. Dumping pollutants near people's homes and accepting inadequate standards for handling hazardous materials are two examples of actions that violate core values.

Similarly, if employing children prevents them from receiving a basic education, the practice is intolerable. Lying about product specifications in the act of selling may not affect human lives directly, but it too is intolerable because it violates the trust that is needed to sustain a corporate culture in which customers are respected.

Sometimes it is not a company's actions but those of a supplier or customer that pose problems. Take the case of the Tan family, a large supplier for Levi Strauss. The Tans were allegedly forcing 1,200

Chinese and Filipino women to work 74 hours per week in guarded compounds on the Mariana Islands. In 1992, after repeated warnings to the Tans, Levi Strauss broke off business relations with them.

Creating an Ethical Corporate Culture

The core values for business that I have enumerated can help companies begin to exercise ethical judgment and think about how to operate ethically in foreign cultures, but they are not specific enough to guide managers through actual ethical dilemmas. Levi Strauss relied on a written code of conduct when figuring out how to deal with the Tan family. The company's Global Sourcing and Operating Guidelines, formerly called the Business Partner Terms of Engagement, state that Levi Strauss will "seek to identify and utilize business partners who aspire as individuals and in the conduct of all their businesses to a set of ethical standards not incompatible with our own." Whenever intolerable business situations arise, managers should be guided by precise statements that spell out the behavior and operating practices that the company demands.

Ninety percent of all *Fortune* 500 companies have codes of conduct, and 70% have statements of vision and values. In Europe and the Far East, the percentages are lower but are increasing rapidly. Does that mean that most companies have what they need? Hardly. Even though most large U.S. companies have both statements of values and codes of conduct, many might be better off if they didn't. Too many companies don't do anything with the documents; they simply paste them on the wall to impress employees, customers, suppliers, and the public. As a result, the senior managers who drafted the statements lose credibility by proclaiming values and not living up to them. Companies such as Johnson & Johnson, Levi Strauss, Motorola, Texas Instruments, and Lockheed Martin, however, do a great deal to make the words meaningful. Johnson & Johnson, for example, has become well known for its Credo Challenge sessions, in which managers discuss ethics in the context of their current business problems and are invited to criticize the company's credo and make suggestions for changes. The participants' ideas are passed on to the company's senior managers. Lockheed Martin has created an innovative site on the World Wide Web and on its local network that gives employees, customers, and suppliers access to the company's ethical code and the chance to voice complaints.

Codes of conduct must provide clear direction about ethical behavior when the temptation to behave unethically is strongest. The pronouncement in a code of conduct that bribery is unacceptable is useless unless accompanied by guidelines for gift giving, payments to get goods through customs, and "requests" from intermediaries who are hired to ask for bribes.

Motorola's values are stated very simply as "How we will always act: [with] constant respect for people [and] uncompromising integrity." The company's code of conduct, however, is explicit about actual business practice. With respect to bribery, for example, the code states that the "funds and assets of Motorola shall not be used, directly or indirectly, for illegal payments of any kind." It is unambiguous about what sort of payment is illegal: "the payment of a bribe to a public official or the kickback of funds to an employee of a customer. . . ." The code goes on to prescribe specific procedures for handling commissions to intermediaries, issuing sales invoices, and disclosing confidential information in a sales transaction—all situations in which employees might have an opportunity to accept or offer bribes.

Codes of conduct must be explicit to be useful, but they must also leave room for a manager to use his or her judgment in situations requiring cultural sensitivity. Host-country employees shouldn't be forced to adopt all home-country values and renounce their own. Again, Motorola's code is exemplary. First, it gives clear direction: "Employees of Motorola will respect the laws, customs, and traditions of each country in which they operate, but will, at the same time, engage in no course of conduct which, even if legal, customary, and accepted in any such country, could be deemed to be in violation of the accepted business ethics of Motorola or the laws of the United States relating to business ethics." After laying down such absolutes, Motorola's code then makes clear when individual judgment will be necessary. For example, employees may sometimes accept certain kinds of small gifts "in rare circumstances, where the refusal to accept a gift" would injure Motorola's "legitimate business interests." Under certain circumstances, such gifts "may be accepted so long as the gift inures to the benefit of Motorola" and not "to the benefit of the Motorola employee."

Striking the appropriate balance between providing clear direction and leaving room for individual judgment makes crafting corporate values statements and ethics codes one of the hardest tasks that executives confront. The words are only a start. A company's leaders need to refer often to their organization's credo and code and must themselves be credible, committed, and consistent. If senior managers act as though ethics don't matter, the rest of the company's employees won't think they do, either.

Conflicts of Development and Conflicts of Tradition

Managers living and working abroad who are not prepared to grapple with moral ambiguity and tension should pack their bags and come home. The view that all business practices can be categorized as either ethical or unethical is too simple. As Einstein is reported to have said, "Things should be as simple as possible—but no simpler." Many business practices that are considered unethical in one setting may be ethical in another. Such activities are neither black nor white but exist in what Thomas Dunfee and I have called *moral free space*.[2] In this gray zone, there are no tight prescriptions for a company's behavior. Managers must chart their own courses—as long as they do not violate core human values.

Consider the following example. Some successful Indian companies offer employees the opportunity for one of their children to gain a job with the company once the child has completed a certain level in school. The companies honor this commitment even when other applicants are more qualified than an employee's child. The perk is extremely valuable in a country where jobs are hard to find, and it reflects the Indian culture's belief that the West has gone too far in allowing economic opportunities to break up families. Not surprisingly, the perk is among the most cherished by employees, but in most Western countries, it would be branded unacceptable nepotism. In the United States, for example, the ethical principle of equal opportunity holds that jobs should go to the applicants with the best qualifications. If a U.S. company made such promises to its employees, it would violate regulations established by the Equal Employment Opportunity Commission. Given this difference in ethical attitudes, how should U.S. managers react to Indian nepotism? Should they condemn the Indian companies, refusing to accept them as partners or suppliers until they agree to clean up their act?

Despite the obvious tension between nepotism and principles of equal opportunity, I cannot condemn the practice for Indians. In a country, such as India, that emphasizes clan and family relationships and has catastrophic levels of unemployment, the practice must be viewed in moral free space. The decision to allow a special perk for employees and their children is not necessarily wrong—at least for members of that country.

How can managers discover the limits of moral free space? That is, how can they learn to distinguish a value in tension with their own from one that is intolerable? Helping managers develop good ethical judgment requires companies to be clear about their core values and codes of conduct. But even the most explicit set of guidelines cannot always provide answers. That is especially true in the thorniest ethical dilemmas, in which the host country's ethical standards not only are different but also seem lower than the home country's. Managers must recognize that when countries have different ethical standards, there are two types of conflict that commonly arise. Each type requires its own line of reasoning.

In the first type of conflict, which I call a *conflict of relative development*, ethical standards conflict because of the countries' different levels of economic development. As mentioned before, developing countries may accept wage rates that seem inhumane to more advanced countries in order to attract investment. As economic conditions in a developing country improve, the incidence of that sort of conflict usually decreases. The second type of conflict is a *conflict of cultural tradition*. For example, Saudi Arabia, unlike most other countries, does not allow women to serve as corporate managers. Instead, women may work in only a few professions, such as education and health care. The prohibition stems from strongly held religious and cultural beliefs; any increase in the country's level of economic development, which is already quite high, is not likely to change the rules.

To resolve a conflict of relative development, a manager must ask the following question: Would the practice be acceptable at home if my country were in a similar stage of economic development? Consider the difference between wage and safety standards in the United States and in Angola, where citizens accept lower standards on both counts. If a U.S. oil company is hiring Angolans to work on an offshore Angolan oil rig, can the company pay them lower wages than it pays U.S. workers in the Gulf of Mexico? Reasonable people have to answer yes if the alternative for Angola is the loss of both the foreign investment and the jobs.

Consider, too, differences in regulatory environments. In the 1980s, the government of India fought hard to be able to import Ciba-Geigy's Entero Vioform, a drug known to be enormously effective in fighting dysentery but one that had been banned in the United States because some users experienced side effects. Although dysentery was not a big problem in the United States, in India, poor public sanitation was contributing to epidemic levels of the disease. Was it unethical to make the drug available in India after it had been banned in the United States? On the contrary, rational people should consider it unethical not to do so. Apply our test: Would the United States, at an earlier stage of development, have used this drug despite its side effects? The answer is clearly yes.

But there are many instances when the answer to similar questions is no. Sometimes a host country's standards are inadequate at any level of economic development. If a country's pollution standards are so low that working on an oil rig would considerably increase a person's risk of developing cancer, foreign oil companies must refuse to do business there. Likewise, if the dangerous side effects of a drug treatment outweigh its benefits, managers should not accept health standards that ignore the risks.

When relative economic conditions do not drive tensions, there is a more objective test for resolving ethical problems. Managers should deem a practice permissible only if they can answer no to both of the following questions: Is it possible to conduct business successfully in the host country without undertaking the practice? and Is the practice a violation of a core human value? Japanese gift giving is a perfect example of a conflict of cultural tradition. Most experienced businesspeople, Japanese and non-Japanese alike, would agree that doing business in Japan would be virtually impossible without adopting the practice. Does gift giving violate a core human value? I cannot identify one that it violates. As a result, gift giving may be permissible for foreign companies in Japan even if it conflicts with ethical attitudes at home. In fact, that conclusion is widely accepted, even by companies such as Texas Instruments and IBM, which are outspoken against bribery.

Does it follow that all nonmonetary gifts are acceptable or that bribes are generally acceptable in countries where they are common? Not at all. (See "The Problem with Bribery.") What makes the routine practice of gift giving acceptable in Japan are the limits in its scope and intention. When gift giving moves outside those limits, it soon collides with core human values. For example, when Carl Kotchian, president of Lockheed in the 1970s, carried suitcases full of cash to Japanese politicians, he went beyond the norms established by Japanese tradition. That incident galvanized opinion in the United States Congress and helped lead to passage of the Foreign Corrupt Practices Act. Likewise, Roh Tae Woo went beyond the norms established by Korean cultural tradition when he accepted $635.4 million in bribes as president of the Republic of Korea between 1988 and 1993.

The Problem with Bribery

Bribery is widespread and insidious. Managers in transnational companies routinely confront bribery even though most countries have laws against it. The fact is that officials in many developing countries wink at the practice, and the salaries of local bureaucrats are so low that many consider bribes a form of remuneration. The U.S. Foreign Corrupt Practices Act defines allowable limits on petty bribery in the form of routine payments required to move goods through customs. But demands for bribes often exceed those limits, and there is seldom a good solution.

Bribery disrupts distribution channels when goods languish on docks until local handlers are paid off, and it destroys incentives to compete on quality and cost when purchasing decisions are based on who pays what under the table. Refusing to acquiesce is often tantamount to giving business to unscrupulous companies.

I believe that even routine bribery is intolerable. Bribery undermines market efficiency and predictability, thus ultimately denying people their right to a minimal standard of living. Some degree of ethical commitment—some sense that everyone will play by the rules—is necessary for a sound economy. Without an ability to predict outcomes, who would be willing to invest?

There was a U.S. company whose shipping crates were regularly pilfered by handlers on the docks of Rio de Janeiro. The handlers would take about 10% of the contents of the crates, but the company was never sure which 10% it would be. In a partial solution, the company began sending two crates—the first with 90% of the merchandise, the second with 10%. The handlers learned to take the second crate and leave the first untouched. From the company's perspective, at least knowing which goods it would lose was an improvement.

Bribery does more than destroy predictability; it undermines essential social and economic systems. That truth is not lost on businesspeople in countries where the practice is woven into the social fabric. CEOs in India admit that their companies engage constantly in bribery, and they say that they have considerable disgust for the practice. They blame government policies in part, but Indian executives also know that their country's business practices perpetuate corrupt behavior. Anyone walking the streets of

Calcutta, where it is clear that even a dramatic redistribution of wealth would still leave most of India's inhabitants in dire poverty, comes face-to-face with the devastating effects of corruption.

Guidelines for Ethical Leadership

Learning to spot intolerable practices and to exercise good judgment when ethical conflicts arise requires practice. Creating a company culture that rewards ethical behavior is essential. The following guidelines for developing a global ethical perspective among managers can help.

TREAT CORPORATE VALUES AND FORMAL STANDARDS OF CONDUCT AS ABSOLUTES. Whatever ethical standards a company chooses, it cannot waver on its principles either at home or abroad. Consider what has become part of company lore at Motorola. Around 1950, a senior executive was negotiating with officials of a South American government on a $10 million sale that would have increased the company's annual net profits by nearly 25%. As the negotiations neared completion, however, the executive walked away from the deal because the officials were asking for $1 million for "fees." CEO Robert Galvin not only supported the executive's decision but also made it clear that Motorola would neither accept the sale on any terms nor do business with those government officials again. Retold over the decades, this story demonstrating Galvin's resolve has helped cement a culture of ethics for thousands of employees at Motorola.

DESIGN AND IMPLEMENT CONDITIONS OF ENGAGEMENT FOR SUPPLIERS AND CUSTOMERS. Will your company do business with any customer or supplier? What if a customer or supplier uses child labor? What if it has strong links with organized crime? What if it pressures your company to break a host country's laws? Such issues are best not left for spur-of-the-moment decisions. Some companies have realized that. Sears, for instance, has developed a policy of not contracting production to companies that use prison labor or infringe on workers' rights to health and safety. And BankAmerica has specified as a condition for many of its loans to developing countries that environmental standards and human rights must be observed.

ALLOW FOREIGN BUSINESS UNITS TO HELP FORMULATE ETHICAL STANDARDS AND INTERPRET ETHICAL ISSUES. The French pharmaceutical company Rhône-Poulenc Rorer has allowed foreign subsidiaries to augment lists of corporate ethical principles with their own suggestions. Texas Instruments has paid special attention to issues of international business ethics by creating the Global Business Practices Council, which is made up of managers from countries in which the company operates. With the overarching intent to create a "global ethics strategy, locally deployed," the council's mandate is to provide ethics education and create local processes that will help managers in the company's foreign business units resolve ethical conflicts.

IN HOST COUNTRIES, SUPPORT EFFORTS TO DECREASE INSTITUTIONAL CORRUPTION. Individual managers will not be able to wipe out corruption in a host country, no matter how many bribes they turn down. When a host country's tax system, import and export procedures, and procurement practices favor unethical players, companies must take action.

Many companies have begun to participate in reforming host-country institutions. General Electric, for example, has taken a strong stand in India, using the media to make repeated condemnations of bribery in business and government. General Electric and others have found, however, that a single company usually cannot drive out entrenched corruption. Transparency International, an organization based in Germany, has been effective in helping coalitions of companies, government officials, and others work to reform bribery-ridden bureaucracies in Russia, Bangladesh, and elsewhere.

EXERCISE MORAL IMAGINATION. Using moral imagination means resolving tensions responsibly and creatively. Coca-Cola, for instance, has consistently turned down requests for bribes from Egyptian officials but has managed to gain political support and public trust by sponsoring a project to plant fruit trees. And take the example of Levi Strauss, which discovered in the early 1990s that two of its suppliers in Bangladesh were employing children under the age of 14—a practice that violated the company's principles but was tolerated in Bangladesh. Forcing the suppliers to fire the children would not have ensured that the children received an education, and it would have caused serious hardship for the families depending on the children's wages. In a creative arrangement, the suppliers agreed to pay the children's regular wages while they attended school and to offer each child a job at age 14. Levi Strauss, in turn, agreed to pay the children's tuition and provide books and uniforms. That arrangement allowed Levi Strauss to uphold its principles and provide long-term benefits to its host country.

Many people think of values as soft; to some they are usually unspoken. A South Seas island society uses the word *mokita*, which means, "the truth that everybody knows but nobody speaks." However difficult they are to articulate, values affect how we all behave. In a global business environment, values in tension are the rule rather than the exception. Without a company's commitment, statements of values and codes of ethics end up as empty platitudes that provide managers with no foundation for behaving ethically. Employees need and deserve more, and responsible members of the global business community can set examples for others to follow. The dark consequences of incidents such as Union Carbide's disaster in Bhopal remind us how high the stakes can be.

Notes

1. In other writings, Thomas W. Dunfee and I have used the term *hypernorm* instead of *core human value*.
2. Thomas Donaldson and Thomas W. Dunfee, "Toward a Unified Conception of Business Ethics: Integrative Social Contracts Theory," *Academy of Management Review*, April 1994; and "Integrative Social Contracts Theory: A Communitarian Conception of Economic Ethics," *Economics and Philosophy*, spring 1995.

PART

III

Ideas at Work

11

The Power of Virtual Integration

An Interview with Dell Computer's Michael Dell

Joan Magretta

How do you create a $12 billion company in just 13 years? Michael Dell began in 1984 with a simple business insight: he could bypass the dealer channel through which personal computers were then being sold. Instead, he would sell directly to customers and build products to order. In one swoop, Dell eliminated the reseller's markup and the costs and risks associated with carrying large inventories of finished goods. The formula became known as the *direct business model,* and it gave Dell Computer Corporation a substantial cost advantage.

The direct model turned out to have other benefits that even Michael Dell couldn't have anticipated when he founded his company. "You actually get to have a relationship with the customer," he explains. "And that creates valuable information, which, in turn, allows us to leverage our relationships with both suppliers and customers. Couple that information with technology, and you have the infrastructure to revolutionize the fundamental business models of major global companies."

In this interview with *Harvard Business Review* editor-at-large Joan Magretta, Michael Dell describes how his company is using technology and information to blur the traditional boundaries in the value chain among suppliers, manufacturers, and end users. In so doing, Dell Computer is evolving in a direction that Michael Dell calls *virtual integration.* The individual pieces of the strategy—customer focus, supplier partnerships, mass customization, just-in-time manufacturing—may all be familiar. But Michael Dell's insight into how to combine them is highly innovative: technology is enabling coordination across company boundaries to achieve new levels of efficiency and productivity, as well as extraordinary returns to investors. Virtual integration harnesses the economic benefits of two very different business models. It offers the advantages of a tightly coordinated supply chain that have traditionally come through vertical integration. At the same time, it benefits from the focus and specialization that drive virtual corporations. Virtual integration, as Michael Dell envisions it, has the potential to achieve both coordination and focus. If it delivers on that promise, it may well become a new organizational model for the information age.

How has Dell pioneered a new business model within the computer industry?

If you look back to the industry's inception, the founding companies essentially had to create all the components themselves. They had to manufacture disk drives and memory chips and application software; all the various pieces of the industry had to be vertically integrated within one firm.

So the companies that were the stars ten years ago, the Digital Equipments of this world, had to build massive structures to produce everything a computer needed. They had no choice but to become expert in a wide array of components, some of which had nothing to do with creating value for the customer.

As the industry grew, more specialized companies developed to produce specific components. That opened up the opportunity to create a business that was far more focused and efficient. As a small start-up, Dell couldn't afford to create every piece of the value chain. But more to the point, why should we want to? We concluded we'd be better off leveraging the investments others have made and focusing on delivering solutions and systems to customers.

Consider a component like a graphics chip. Five or ten years ago, a whole bunch of companies in the personal computer industry were trying to create their own graphics chips. Now, if you've got a race with 20 players that are all vying to produce the fastest graphics chip in the world, do you want to be the twenty-first horse, or do you want to evaluate the field of 20 and pick the best one?

It's a pretty simple strategy, but at the time it went against the dominant, "engineering-centric" view of the industry. The IBMs and Compaqs and HPs subscribed to a "we-have-to-develop-everything" view of the world. If you weren't doing component assembly, you weren't a real computer company. It was like a rite of passage. You somehow proved your manhood by placing small semiconductor chips on printed circuit boards.

And Dell Computer came along and said, "Now wait a second. If I understand this correctly, the companies that do nothing but put chips on motherboards don't actually earn tremendous profit doing it. If we want to earn higher returns, shouldn't we be more selective and put our capital into activities where we can add value for our customers, not just into activities that need to get done?" I'm not saying those activities are unimportant. They need to get done very, very well. But they're not sources of value that Dell is going to create.

When the company started, I don't think we knew how far the direct model could take us. It has provided a consistent underlying strategy for Dell despite a lot of change in our industry. Along the way, we have learned a lot, and the model has evolved. Most important, the direct model has allowed us to leverage our relationships with both suppliers and customers to such an extent that I believe it's fair to think of our companies as being virtually integrated. That allows us to focus on where we add value and to build a much larger firm much more quickly. I don't think we could have created a $12 billion business in 13 years if we had tried to be vertically integrated.

Why can you grow so much faster without all those physical assets?

There are fewer things to manage, fewer things to go wrong. You don't have the drag effect of taking 50,000 people with you. Suppose we have two suppliers building monitors for us, and one of them loses its edge. It's a lot easier for us to get more capacity from the remaining supplier than to set up a new manufacturing plant ourselves. If we had to build our own factories for every single component of the system, growing at 57% per year just would not be possible. I would spend 500% of my time interviewing prospective vice presidents because the company would have not 15,000 employees but 80,000.

Indirectly, we employ something like that many people today. There are, for example, 10,000 service technicians in the field who service our products, but only a small number of them work for us. They're contracted with other firms. But ask the customer, "Who was that person who just fixed your computer?" The vast majority think that person works for us, which is just great. That's part of virtual integration.

Aren't you just outsourcing your after-sales service? Is what you're describing fundamentally different from outsourcing?

Outsourcing, at least in the IT world, is almost always a way to get rid of a problem a company hasn't been able to solve itself. The classic case is the company with 2,000 people in the IT department. Nobody knows what they do, and nobody knows why they do it. The solution—outsource IT to a service provider, and hopefully they'll fix it. But if you look at what happens five years later, it's not necessarily a pretty picture.

That's not what we're doing at all. We focus on how we can coordinate our activities to create the most value for customers.

With our service providers, we're working to set quality measures and, more important, to build data linkages that let us see in real time how we're doing—when parts are dispatched, for instance, or how long it takes to respond to a request for service. We look at our business and see, for example, that over the next ten years we are going to be making lots of notebook computers. Dell might need 20 million flat-panel displays, and some years there will be more demand than supply. Other years, there will be more supply than demand. A few companies are currently making multibillion-dollar investments in the manufacture of these displays.

So we cook up a little deal where the supplier agrees to meet 25% of our volume requirements for displays, and because of the long-term commitment we make to them, we'll get our displays year in and year out, even when there's more demand than supply. The supplier effectively becomes our partner. They assign their engineers to our design team, and we start to treat them as if they were part of the company. For example, when we launch a new product, their engineers are stationed right in our plants. If a customer calls in with a problem, we'll stop shipping product while they fix design flaws in real time.

Figuring out how many partners we need has been a process of trial and error. You learn when you operate on the cutting edge of technology that things don't always work as planned. The rule we follow is to have as few partners as possible. And they will last as long as they maintain their leadership in technology and quality. This isn't like the automobile business, where you find a tire supplier that you will probably stick with forever. Where the technology is fairly stable—in monitors, for example—we expect our partnerships to last a long time. Others will be more volatile. But regardless of how long these relationships last, virtual integration means you're basically stitching together a business with partners that are treated as if they're inside the company. You're sharing information in a real-time fashion.

We tell our suppliers exactly what our daily production requirements are. So it's not, "Well, every two weeks deliver 5,000 to this warehouse, and we'll put them on the shelf, and then we'll take them off the shelf." It's, "Tomorrow morning we need 8,562, and deliver them to door number seven by 7 A.M."

You would deal with an internal supplier that way, and you can do so because you share information and plans very freely. Why doesn't the same sharing of information take place across company boundaries? Buyers are often so busy trying to protect themselves that the seller can't really add a lot of value. Government purchasing is the extreme case, with its overly structured procurement system. Protecting the buyer usually ends up disabling the seller—and both lose.

The technology available today really boosts the value of information sharing. We can share design databases and methodologies with supplier-partners in ways that just weren't possible five to ten years ago. This speeds time to market—often dramatically—and creates a lot of value that can be shared between buyer and supplier. So technology enhances the economic incentives to collaborate.

What are the challenges involved in establishing these collaborations?

The key challenge—and the biggest change from business as usual—is changing the focus from how much inventory there is to how fast it's moving. All computer chips carry a four-digit date code. For example, "97-23" means it was built in the twenty-third week of 1997. You can take the cover off any computer and find out how old its parts are, how long it took to make its way through the system. In our industry, if you can get people to think about how fast inventory is moving, then you create real value. Why? Because if I've got 11 days of inventory and my competitor has 80, and Intel comes out with a new 450-megahertz chip, that means I'm going to get to market 69 days sooner.

I think about it this way: Assets collect risks around them in one form or another. Inventory is one risk, and accounts receivable is another risk. In our case—with 70% of our sales going to large corporate customers—accounts receivable isn't hard to manage because companies like Goldman Sachs and Microsoft and Oracle tend to be able to pay their bills. But in the computer industry, inventory can actually be a pretty massive risk because if the cost of materials goes down 50% a year and you have two or three months of inventory versus 11 days, you've got a big cost disadvantage. And you're vulnerable to product transitions, when you can get stuck with obsolete inventory.

Inventory velocity is one of a handful of key performance measures we watch very closely. It focuses us on working with our suppliers to keep reducing inventory and increasing speed. With a supplier like Sony, which makes very good, reliable monitors, we figure there's no need for us to have any inventory at all. We are confident in putting the Dell name on them, and they work fine. We don't even take these monitors out of the box to test them because we've gotten them to under 1,000 defects per million. So what's the point in having a monitor put on a truck to Austin, Texas, and then taken off the truck and sent on a little tour around the warehouse, only to be put back on another truck? That's just a big waste of time and money, unless we get our jollies from touching monitors, which we don't.

So we went to Sony and said, "Hey, we're going to buy two or three million of these monitors this year. Why don't we just pick them up every day as we need them?" At first, it's a little confusing to the suppliers because you're saying, "Now listen carefully. If you will help us get your product from the end of your line to our customer faster, we won't have any in our warehouse." And the suppliers look at you like you're crazy and not making any sense. They're used to delivering in larger quantities, so at first they think this means you're going to buy less from them. And then the lightbulb goes on, and they realize we'll be buying more because we'll be taking it faster.

So now you have Sony producing a level supply of monitors for you. What happens next?

We tell Airborne Express or UPS to come to Austin and pick up 10,000 computers a day and go over to the Sony factory in Mexico and pick up the corresponding number of monitors. Then while we're all sleeping, they match up the computers and the monitors, and deliver them to the customer.

Of course, this requires sophisticated data exchange. Most people are familiar with the way a company like Black & Decker uses information links with the thousands of retailers that sell its products. When a customer in Omaha buys a drill from his local hardware store, the system immediately tells Black & Decker to send another unit of that particular drill to that particular store. So their system has to replenish supply, unit by unit, to thousands of outlets. From the supplier's point of view, Dell is dramatically simpler. Our orders are typically for thousands of units, and they need to go to only one of three manufacturing centers: Austin, Ireland, and Malaysia. It's almost ideal from a supplier standpoint because we have real-time information on what the demand is, and all the supplier has to do is get the product to us.

And because we build to our customers' order, typically, with just five or six days of lead time, suppliers don't have to worry about sell-through. We only maintain a few days—in some cases a few hours—of raw materials on hand. We communicate inventory levels and replenishment needs regularly—with some vendors, hourly.

The typical case in our industry is the factory building 10,000 units a day, day in and day out. First the machines stack up in the warehouse, and then they stack up in the channel. And all of a sudden, the guy at the end of the chain hollers, "Whoa, hey, we've got too many of these. Everybody stop!" And the order to stop flows back through the chain until it reaches every component supplier. It's literally stop and start, because if you have a 90-day lag between the point of demand and the point of supply, you're going to have a lot of inefficiency in the process. And the more inventory and time you have, the more variability, and the more problems.

In our industry, there's a lot of what I call bad hygiene. Companies stuff the channel to get rid of old inventory and to meet short-term financial objectives. We think our approach is better. We substitute information for inventory and ship only when we have real demand from real end customers.

How does the direct model benefit your suppliers?

We can go to Sony and say, "We're going to be pulling monitors from you in a very consistent, predictable way because the distance between the demand and the source of supply is totally shrunk." The longer that distance, the more intermediary channels you add, the less likely it is you will have good information about demand—so you will end up with more variability, more inventory, higher costs, and more risk.

Another factor that helps keep our demand for computers level is the mix of customers we serve. We don't have any customer that represents more than 1% to 2% of our revenues. One week Exxon is buying, the next week Shell is buying, the next week Ford is buying. But all companies don't decide in unison, "Well, this week we're going to buy, next week we're not."

You mention your customer mix. Does the direct model imply a particular customer strategy?

If you'd asked me that question 12 years ago, I would have said that we didn't differentiate much between our largest and our smallest customer. Today we do. Our customer strategy is one area where our model has evolved. We've become good at developing what we call "scalable" businesses—that is, those in which we can grow revenues faster than expenses. We really look closely at financial measures like gross margins by customer segment—and we focus on segments we can serve profitably as we achieve scale. People are sometimes surprised to learn that 90% of our sales go to institutions—business or government—and 70% to very large customers that buy at least $1 million in PCs per year.

When you're trying to target profitable segments, averages obscure a lot, and aggregate financial statements are pretty meaningless. Our approach to segmentation is to take really big numbers and "de-average" them. Until you look inside and understand what's going on by business, by customer, by geography, you don't know anything. This is a lesson we learned the hard way. We incorrectly entered the retail business in 1989, thinking that our direct business wouldn't grow enough, and went into computer superstores and warehouse clubs. But when we really started to understand the segment's profitability, we realized we'd made a mistake, and so we exited.

For years, we didn't actively pursue the consumer market because we couldn't reach our profit objectives. So we let our competitors introduce machines with rock-bottom prices and zero margins. We figured they could be the ones to teach consumers about PCs while we focused our efforts on more profitable segments. And then, because we're direct and can see who is buying what, we noticed something interesting. The industry's average selling price to consumers was going down, but ours was going up. Consumers who were now buying their second or third machines—who wanted the most powerful machines and needed less hand-holding—were coming to us. And without focusing on it in a significant way, we had a billion-dollar consumer business that was profitable. So we decided in 1997 that it was time to dedicate a group to serving that segment.

So, over time, you cut the market into finer and finer segments?

Yes, for a lot of reasons. One is to identify unique opportunities and economics. The other is purely a managerial issue: you can't possibly manage something well if it's too big. Segmentation gives us better attention and focus. (See Exhibit 11-1 "Fast-Cycle Segmentation.")

Each segment has its own issues. In education, for instance, how do you get tech support to a classroom when the teacher doesn't have a telephone? You need a totally different approach. Segmenting lets you tailor your programs to the customers' needs. If you just lump diverse customers together, you can be sure that some of them will come last on some manager's list, and he may never get around to solving their problems. That's why we make serving one segment the manager's only job.

Do you get other benefits from segmenting your customers?

Segmentation gets us closer to them. It allows us to understand their needs in a really deep way. This closeness gives us access to information that's absolutely critical to our strategy. It helps us forecast what they're going to need and when. And good forecasts are the key to keeping our costs down.

We turn our inventory over 30 times per year. If you look at the complexity and the diversity of our product line, there's no way we could do that unless we had credible information about what the customer is actually buying. It's a key part of why rivals have had great difficulty competing with Dell. It's not just that we sell direct, it's also our ability to forecast demand—it's both the design of the product and the way the information from the customer flows all the way through manufacturing to our suppliers. If you don't have that tight linkage—the kind of coordination of information that used to be possible only in vertically integrated companies—then trying to manage to 11 days of inventory would be insane. We simply couldn't do it without customers who work with us as partners.

Could you describe how you forecast demand?

We see forecasting as a critical sales skill. We teach our sales-account managers to lead customers through a discussion of their future PC needs. We'll walk a customer through every department of his company, asking him to designate which needs are certain and which are contingent. And when they're contingent on some event, the salesperson will know what that event is so he can follow up. We can do this with our large accounts, which make up the bulk of our business. With smaller customers, we have real-time information about what they're buying from our direct telephone salespeople. And we can also

Exhibit 11-1   Fast-Cycle Segmentation

Dell's rapid growth in recent years has been accompanied by ever finer cuts at customer segmentation. This is an important element of Dell's virtual integration with customers. The finer the segmentation, the better able Dell is to forecast what its customers are going to need and when. Dell then coordinates the flow of that strategic information all the way back to its suppliers, effectively substituting information for inventory.

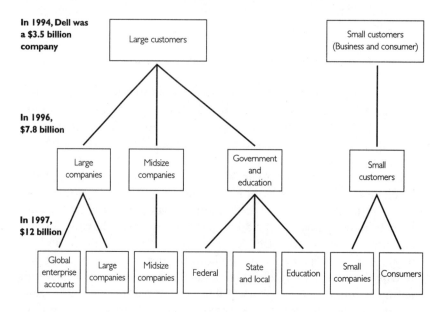

steer them in real time, on the phone, toward configurations that are available, so this is another way we can fine-tune the balance between supply and demand.

Is that what you mean by virtual integration with your customers?

It's part of it. There are so many information links between us and our customers. For example, we can help large global customers manage their total purchase of PCs by selling them a standard product. Then when the guy whose computer isn't working calls in from Singapore, the IT people don't have to spend the first 30 minutes just figuring out what configuration of hardware and software he's using. Selling direct allows us to keep track of the company's total PC purchases, country by country—and that's valuable information we can feed back to them. We sometimes know more about a customer's operations than they do themselves.

Close customer relationships have allowed us to dramatically extend the value we deliver to our customers. Today we routinely load the customer's software in our factory. Eastman Chemical, for example, has their own unique mix of software, some of it licensed from Microsoft, some of it they've written themselves, some of it having to do with the way their network works. Normally, they would get their PCs, take them out of the box, and then some guy carrying a walkie-talkie and diskettes and CD-ROMs would come to each employee's desk to hook the system up and load all that software. Typically, this takes an hour or two—and costs $200 to $300—and it's a nuisance.

Our solution was to create a massive network in our factory with high-speed, 100-megabit Ethernet. We'll load Eastman Chemical's software onto a huge Dell server. Then when a machine comes down the assembly line and says, "I'm an Eastman Chemical analyst workstation, configuration number 14," all of a sudden a few hundred megabytes of data come rushing through the network and onto the workstation's hard disk, just as part of the progressive build through our factory. If the customer wants, we can put an asset tag with the company's logo on the machine, and we can keep an electronic register of the customer's assets. That's a lot easier than the customer sending some guy around on a thankless mission, placing asset tags on computers when he can find them.

What happens to the money our customer is saving? They get to keep most of it. We could say, "Well, it costs you $300 to do it, so we'll charge you $250." But instead we charge $15 or $20, and we make our product and our service much more valuable. It also means we're not going to be just your PC vendor anymore. We're going to be your IT department for PCs.

Boeing, for example, has 100,000 Dell PCs, and we have 30 people that live at Boeing, and if you look at the things we're doing for them or for other customers, we don't look like a supplier, we look more like Boeing's PC department. We become intimately involved in planning their PC needs and the configuration of their network.

It's not that we make these decisions by ourselves. They're certainly using their own people to get the best answer for the company. But the people working on PCs together, both from Dell and Boeing, understand the needs in a very intimate way. They're right there living it and breathing it, as opposed to the typical vendor who says, "Here are your computers. See you later."

We've always visited clients, but now some of our accounts are large enough to justify a dedicated on-site team. Remember, a lot of companies have far more complex problems to deal with than PC purchasing and servicing. They can't wait to get somebody else to take care of that so they can worry about more strategic issues.

So some of your coordination with customers is made possible through technology, but there's still a good measure of old-fashioned, face-to-face human contact?

Yes, that's right. The idea is to use technology to free people up to solve more complicated problems. For example, a customer like MCI can access our internal support tools on-line in the same way our own technical-support teams do, saving time and money on both sides. They simply go to www.dell.com, enter some information about their system, and they have immediate access to the same information that we use at Dell to help customers. These tools are used by internal help-desk groups at large companies as well as by individuals.

We've developed customized intranet sites called Premier Pages for well over 200 of our largest global customers. These exist securely within the customers' firewalls, and they give them direct access to purchasing and technical information about the specific configurations they buy from us. One of our customers, for example, allows its 50,000 employees to view and select products on-line. They use the Premier Page as an interactive catalog of all the configurations the company authorizes; employees can then price and order the PC they want. They are happy to have some choice, and Dell and the customer are both happy to eliminate the paperwork and sales time normally associated with corporate purchasing. That frees our salespeople to play a more consultative role.

We also have developed tools to help customers set up their own customized versions of dell.com. There are about 7,000 of these to date.

How else do you stay close to your customers?

In a direct business like ours, you have, by definition, a relationship with customers. But beyond the mechanisms we have for sales and support, we have set up a number of forums to ensure the free flow of information with the customer on a constant basis. Our Platinum Councils, for example, are regional meetings—in Asia-Pacific, Japan, the United States, and Europe—of our largest customers. They meet every six to nine months; in the larger regions, there's one for the information executives—the CIO types—and then there's one for the technical types.

In these meetings, our senior technologists share their views on where the technology is heading and lay out road maps of product plans over the next two years. There are also breakout sessions and working groups in which our engineering teams focus on specific product areas and talk about how to solve problems that may not necessarily have anything to do with the commercial relationship with Dell. For example, Is leasing better than buying? or How do you manage the transition to Windows NT? or How do you manage a field force of notebook computers?

People in businesses as dissimilar as Unilever and ICI can learn from each other because, amazingly, they have very similar problems when it comes to PCs. And we send not only our top technologists and engineers but also the real engineers, the people who usually don't get out to talk to customers because they're too busy developing products. All of our senior executives from around the company participate, spending time with the customer, listening to how we're doing. The ratio is about one Dell person to one customer. At our last session, we had about 100 customers.

The councils are another way we're able to play more of an advisory role, trying to help our customers understand what the flow of new technology really means, how it will translate into specific products. We try to help the customer anticipate what's happening and be ready. And that helps us, as well, with our own demand forecasting. So we're helping each other in important ways. We hire a lot of people from other companies in the industry, and they tell us that these meetings are unique.

Do you spend a significant amount of your time at these meetings?

I spend three days at each of them. They're great events. In the normal course of our business, I have lots of opportunity to talk to customers one on one, but there is something much more powerful about this kind of forum. Customers tend to speak more openly when they're with their peers and they know we're there and we're listening.

At every Platinum Council, we review what they told us last time and what we did about it. We keep an ongoing record of the issues. Let me give you a concrete example: A few years ago, the engineers responsible for our desktops were operating on the theory that customers really wanted performance from these products—the faster the better. But what the customers actually said at the Platinum Councils was, "Yeah, performance, that's okay. But what I really want is a stable product that doesn't change. Because if I'm trying to run a bank or an airline, I don't care if it's 2% faster or 3% slower. What really matters is stability." So our engineers thought one thing, the customers thought another thing. It took the direct feedback from the Platinum Councils to spotlight this failure to communicate. We responded by building product with intergenerational consistency over many years. The same feedback has helped shape the creation of our brands. For both our desktop and notebook businesses, we created different brands designed to deliver greater stability to corporate customers, as opposed to the fast technology changes that consumers demand. (See "Using Information to Speed Execution.")

Using Information to Speed Execution

KEVIN ROLLINS *is vice chairman of Dell Computer Corporation.*

Most of the managerial challenges at Dell Computer have to do with what we call *velocity*—speeding the pace of every element of our business. Life cycles in our business are measured in months, not years, and if you don't move fast, you're out of the game. Managing velocity is about managing information—using a constant flow of information to drive operating practices, from the performance measures we track to how we work with our suppliers.

Performance Metrics. At Dell, we use the balance sheet and the fundamentals of the P&L on a monthly basis as tools to manage operations. From the balance sheet, we track three cash-flow measures very closely. We look at weekly updates of how many days of inventory we have, broken out by product component. We can then work closely with our suppliers so we end up with the right inventory. When it's not quite right, we can use our direct-sales model to steer customers toward comparable products that we do have. So we use inventory information to work both the front and back ends at the same time.

We also track and manage receivables and payables very tightly. This is basic blocking and tackling, but we give it a high priority. The payoff is that we have a negative cash-conversion cycle of five days—that is, we get paid before we have to pay our suppliers. Since our competitors usually have to support their resellers by offering them credit, the direct model gives us an inherent cost advantage. And the more we can shorten our cash-collection cycle, the greater our advantage.

The real-time performance measures in the P&L that we regard as the best indicators of the company's health are our margins, our average selling price, and the overhead associated with selling. We split the P&L into these core elements by customer segment, by product, and by country. These metrics can alert us instantly to problems, for example, with the mix of products being sold in any particular country.

Working with Suppliers. The greatest challenge in working with suppliers is getting them in sync with the fast pace we have to maintain. The key to making it work is information. The right information flows allow us to work with our partners in ways that enhance speed, either directly by improving logistics or indirectly by improving quality.

Take our service strategy, for example. Customers pay us for service and support, and we contract with third-party maintainers (TPMs) to make the service calls. Customers call us when they have problems, and that initial call will trigger two electronic dispatches—one to ship the needed parts directly from Dell to the customers' sites and one to dispatch the TPMs to the customers. Our role as information broker facilitates the TPMs' work by making sure the necessary parts will be on-site when they arrive.

But our role doesn't stop there. Because poor quality creates friction in the system, which slows us down, we want to capture information that can be used to fix problems so they won't happen again. So we take back the bad part to diagnose what went wrong, and we feed that information back to our suppliers so they can redesign the component. Clearly, we couldn't operate that way if we were dealing with hundreds of suppliers. So for us, working with a handful of partners is one of the keys to improving quality—and therefore speed—in our system.

As I think back to some of those council meetings, things that would seem fairly small at the time have often turned out three or four years later to become the basis for billions of dollars of revenue—notebooks with longer-life batteries, for example, or loading customers' software for them in our plants.

As your customer strategy has evolved, has the Dell brand changed as well?

A big piece of our brand is being the most efficient and effective way for customers to buy Intel or Microsoft technologies. But beyond that, we're evolving into a technology selector, or navigator. We often talk to customers about "relevant technology." Intel and Microsoft tend to launch into a massive variety of things, some of which are speculative and aimed at exploring new technologies. We think it's our job to help our customers sort out the technology relevant to today's needs from the bleeding edge.

How does that strategy affect your own R&D function? What role does R&D play in your company?

At Dell, we believe the customer is in control, and our job is to take all the technology that's out there and apply it in a useful way to meet the customer's needs. We're not trying to invent new architecture ourselves, but we'll spend a quarter of a billion dollars this year and employ some 1,500 people to improve the whole user experience— that means delivering the latest relevant technology, making it easy to use, and keeping costs down. And in addition to selecting appropriate technology, our R&D group focuses on process and quality improvements in manufacturing.

Before industry standards came into play, the proprietary computing environment bred a kind of technical arrogance that, fortunately, won't fly anymore. Once standards were established, the customer started to define what was going to be successful, and it didn't matter what you invented or how good it was or how fast it was. Increasingly, what matters is what the customers want and whether it works with all their other stuff.

That means we have to stay on top of our customers' needs, and we have to monitor and understand the innovations in the material science world—everything from semiconductors to polymers to liquid crystal displays. You need to track anything having to do with the flow of electrons, and you need to keep asking how these marvelous developments might be useful to customers. The customer doesn't come to you and say, "Boy, I really like lithium ion batteries. I can't wait to get my hands on some lithium ion." The customer says, "I want a notebook computer that lasts the whole day. I don't want it to run out when I'm on the plane."

I was about to leave a meeting at Sony in Tokyo in January of 1993 when someone ran up to me and said, "Oh, Mr. Dell, please wait one minute. I'm from Sony's power technology company. We have a new power-system technology we want to explain to you." And I remember thinking, Is this guy going to try to sell me a power plant? He starts showing me chart after chart about the performance of lithium ion batteries. This is wonderful, I tell him. And if it's true, we're going to put this in every notebook computer we make.

We then sent a team over to check it out, and a year and a half later we were the first computer company to have a notebook that lasted five-and-a-half, six hours. We tested it with American Airlines, handing out the notebooks to passengers at the start of flights from New York to Los Angeles. By the end, the notebooks were still running.

How are the challenges of leadership in a virtually integrated organization different from those you would encounter running a corporation with more traditional boundaries?

The whole idea behind virtual integration is that it lets you meet customers' needs faster and more efficiently than any other model. (See Exhibit 11-2 "The Evolution of a Faster Business Model.") With vertical integration, you can be an efficient producer—as long as the world isn't changing very much. But virtual integration lets you be efficient and responsive to change at the same time—at least, that's what we're trying to do. We think about Internet commerce as a logical extension of our direct model—and within our first year, we reached a run rate of $2 million a day. It's now about $3 million a day, and during the peak of the Christmas buying season we saw several $6 million days. I'm only half joking when I say that the only thing better than the Internet would be mental telepathy. Because what we're all about is shrinking the time and the resources it takes to meet customers' needs. And we're trying to do that in a world where those needs are changing.

To lead in that kind of environment, you have to be on the lookout for shifts in value, and if the customer decides, "Hey, I don't care about that anymore, now I care about this," we may have to develop new capabilities rather quickly. One of the biggest challenges we face today is finding managers who can sense and respond to rapid shifts, people who can process new information very quickly and make decisions in real time. It's a problem for the computer industry as a whole—and not just for Dell—that the industry's growth has outpaced its ability to

Exhibit 11-2   The Evolution of a Faster Business Model

The dominant model in the personal computer industry—a value chain with arm's-length transactions from one layer to the next:

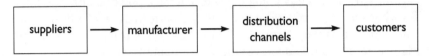

Dell's direct model eliminates the time and cost of third-party distribution:

Virtual integration works even faster by blurring the traditional boundaries and roles in the value chain:

create managers. We tell prospective hires, "If you want an environment that is never going to change, don't come here. This is not the place for you."

Our goal is to be one or two steps ahead of the change, and in fact to be creating or shaping it, to some extent. That's why we spend so much time with our customers. It's why I personally spend about 40% of my time with customers. Often it's a lead customer that says, "Hey, can you put an asset tag on my PC?" And the first reaction is, "Gee, we've never done that before, but why not? Let's give it a try." And then you do it for one customer, then for ten, then for a hundred, and eventually it becomes a standard offering. Putting asset tags on computers isn't by itself a major value shift, but what happens is that we get a series of seemingly small innovations that over time add up to a huge improvement. That's not a bad description of the way we get into businesses. We don't come at it the other way around, with a consulting study that says, "That's an attractive business. Let's go." Nor do we sit around and say, "What do we suppose our customers would like? If we were customers, what would we be thinking?"

So looking for value shifts is probably the most important dimension of leadership. Then there's the question of managing such a tightly coordinated value chain—and there it's all about execution. If you look at Dell's P&L structure, I think you'd be hard-pressed to find companies that deliver the kind of value-added we do with such a small markup. My theory is that if we can continue to keep our markup as low as it is today, we're going to be able to capture most of the opportunities available to us. But that means we cannot get complacent about our growth and get careless about execution.

Sometimes, I'm taken aback when I talk to people who've been in the company for six months or a year and who talk about "the model" as if it were an all-powerful being that will take care of everything. It's scary because I know that nothing is ever 100% constant, and the last thing we should do is assume that we're always going to be doing well. But for now, it's working. The direct system really delivers value to the customer all the way from distribution back through manufacturing and design. If you tried to divide Dell up into a manufacturer and a channel, you'd destroy the company's unique value. It's something completely new that nobody in our industry has ever done before.

12

Fast, Global, and Entrepreneurial: Supply Chain Management, Hong Kong Style

An Interview with Victor Fung

Joan Magretta

Supply chain management is working its way onto the strategic agendas of CEOs in an expanding list of industries, from autos to personal computers to fashion retailing. Propelling that change is the restructuring of global competition. As companies focus on their core activities and outsource the rest, their success increasingly depends on their ability to control what happens in the value chain outside their own boundaries. In the 1980s, the focus was on supplier partnerships to improve cost and quality. In today's faster-paced markets, the focus has shifted to innovation, flexibility, and speed.

Enter Li & Fung, Hong Kong's largest export trading company and an innovator in the development of supply chain management. On behalf of its customers, primarily American and European retailers, Li & Fung works with an ever-expanding network of thousands of suppliers around the globe, sourcing clothing and other consumer goods ranging from toys to fashion accessories to luggage. Chairman Victor Fung sees the company as part of a new breed of professionally managed, focused enterprises that draw on Hong Kong's expertise in distribution-process technology—a host of information-intensive service functions including product development, sourcing, financing, shipping, handling, and logistics.

Founded in 1906 in southern China by Victor Fung's grandfather, Li & Fung was the first Chinese-owned export company at a time when the China trade was controlled by foreign commercial houses.

In the early 1970s, Victor was teaching at the Harvard Business School, and his younger brother, William, was a newly minted Harvard M.B.A. The two young men were called home from the United States by their father to breathe new life into the company.

Since then, the brothers have led Li & Fung through a series of transformations. In this interview with *Harvard Business Review* editor-at-large Joan Magretta, Victor Fung describes how Li & Fung has made the transition from buying agent to supply chain manager, from the old economy to the new, from traditional Chinese family conglomerate to innovative public company. Victor and William Fung are creating a new kind of multinational, one that remains entrepreneurial despite its growing size and scope.

Victor Fung is also chairman of a privately held retailing arm of the company, which focuses on joint ventures with Toys "R" Us and the Circle K convenience-store chain in Hong Kong. He is also chairman of the Hong Kong Trade Development Council and of Prudential Asia.

How do you define the difference between what Li & Fung does today—supply chain management—and the trading business founded by your grandfather in 1906?

When my grandfather started the company in Canton, 90 years ago during the Ching dynasty, his "value-added" was that he spoke English. In those days, it took three months to get to China by boat from the West; a letter would take a month. No one at the Chinese factories spoke English, and the American merchants spoke no Chinese. As an interpreter, my grandfather's commission was 15%.

Continuing through my father's generation, Li & Fung was basically a broker, charging a fee to put buyers and sellers together. But as an intermediary, the company was squeezed between the growing power of the buyers and the factories. Our margins slipped to 10%, then 5%, then 3%. When I returned to Hong Kong in 1976 after teaching at Harvard Business School, my friends warned me that in ten years buying agents like Li & Fung would be extinct. "Trading is a sunset industry," they all said.

My brother and I felt we could turn the business into something different, and so we took it through several stages of development. In the first stage, we acted as what I would call a regional sourcing agent and extended our geographic reach by establishing offices in Taiwan, Korea, and Singapore. Our knowledge of the region had value for customers. Most big buyers could manage their own sourcing if they needed to deal only with Hong Kong—they'd know which ten factories to deal with and wouldn't need any help.

But dealing with the whole region was more complex. In textiles, quotas govern world trade. Knowing which quotas have been used up in Hong Kong, for example, tells you when you have to start buying from Taiwan.

Understanding products was also more complex. We knew that in Taiwan the synthetics were better, but that Hong Kong was the place to go for cottons. We could provide a package from the whole region rather than a single product from Hong Kong.

By working with a larger number of countries, we were able to assemble components; we call this "assortment packing." Say I sell a tool kit to a major discount chain. I could buy the spanners from one country and the screwdrivers from another and put together a product package. That has some value in it—not great value, but some.

In the second stage, we took the company's sourcing-agent strategy one step further and became a manager and deliverer of manufacturing programs. In the old model, the customer would say, "This is the item I want. Please go out and find the best place to buy it for me." The new model works this way. The Limited, one of our big customers, comes to us and says, "For next season, this is what we're thinking about—this type of look, these colors, these quantities. Can you come up with a production program?"

Starting with their designers' sketches, we research the market to find the right type of yarn and dye swatches to match the colors. We take product concepts and realize them in prototypes. Buyers can then look at the samples and say, "No, I don't really like that, I like this. Can you do more of this?" We then create an entire program for the season, specifying the product mix and the schedule. We contract for all the resources. We work with factories to plan and monitor production so we can ensure quality and on-time delivery.

This strategy of delivering manufacturing programs carried us through the 1980s, but that decade brought us a new challenge—and led to our third stage. As the Asian tigers emerged, Hong Kong became an increasingly expensive and uncompetitive place to manufacture. For example, we completely lost the low-end transistor-radio business to Taiwan and Korea. What saved us was that China began to open up to trade, allowing Hong Kong to fix its cost problem by moving the labor-intensive portion of production across the border into southern China.

So for transistor radios we created little kits—plastic bags filled with all the components needed to build a radio. Then we shipped the kits to China for assembly. After the labor-intensive work was completed, the finished goods came back to Hong Kong for final testing and inspection. If you missed a screw you were in trouble: the whole line stopped cold.

Breaking up the value chain as we did was a novel concept at the time. We call it "dispersed manufacturing." This method of manufacturing soon spread to other industries, giving Hong Kong a new lease on life and also transforming our economy. Between 1979 and 1997, Hong Kong's position as a trading entity moved from number 21 in the world to number 8. All our manufacturing moved into China, and Hong Kong became a huge service economy with 84% of its gross domestic product coming from services.

So dispersed manufacturing means breaking up the value chain and rationalizing where you do things?

That's right. Managing dispersed production was a real breakthrough. It forced us to get smart not only about logistics and transportation but also about dissecting the value chain.

Consider a popular children's doll—one similar to the Barbie doll. In the early 1980s, we designed the dolls in Hong Kong, and we also produced the molds because sophisticated machinery was needed to make them. We then shipped the molds to China, where they would shoot the plastic, assemble the doll, paint the figures, make the doll's clothing—all the labor-intensive work. But the doll had to come back to Hong Kong, not just for final testing and inspection but also for packaging. China at that time couldn't deliver the quality we needed for the printing on the boxes. Then we used Hong Kong's well-developed banking and transportation infrastructure to distribute the products around the world. You can see the model clearly: the labor-intensive middle portion of the value chain is still done in southern China, and Hong Kong does the front and back ends.

Managing dispersed manufacturing, where not everything is done under one roof, takes a real change of mind-set. But once we figured out how to do it, it became clear that our reach should extend beyond southern China. Our thinking was, for example, if wages are lower farther inland, let's go there. And so we began what has turned into a constant search for new and better sources of supply. Li & Fung made a quantum leap in 1995, nearly doubling our size and extending our geographic scope by acquiring Inchcape Buying Services. IBS was a large British *hong* with an established network of offices in India, Pakistan, Bangladesh, and Sri Lanka. The acquisition also brought with it a European customer base that complemented Li & Fung's predominantly American base.

This Hong Kong model of borderless manufacturing has become a new paradigm for the region. Today Asia consists of multiple networks of dispersed manufacturing—high-cost hubs that do the sophisticated planning for regional manufacturing. Bangkok works with the Indochinese peninsula, Taiwan with the Philippines, Seoul with northern China. Dispersed manufacturing is what's behind the boom in Asia's trade and investment statistics in the 1990s—companies moving raw materials and semifinished parts around Asia. But the region is still very dependent on the ultimate sources of demand, which are in North America and Western Europe. They start the whole cycle going.

What happens when you get a typical order?

Say we get an order from a European retailer to produce 10,000 garments. It's not a simple matter of our Korean office sourcing Korean products or our Indonesian office sourcing Indonesian products. For this customer we might decide to buy yarn from a Korean producer but have it woven and dyed in Taiwan. So we pick the yarn and ship it to Taiwan. The Japanese have the best zippers and buttons, but they manufacture them mostly in China. Okay, so we go to YKK, a big Japanese zipper manufacturer, and we order the right zippers from their Chinese plants. Then we determine that, because of quotas and labor conditions, the best place to make the garments is Thailand. So we ship everything there. And because the customer needs quick delivery, we may divide the order across five factories in Thailand. Effectively, we are customizing the value chain to best meet the customer's needs.

Five weeks after we have received the order, 10,000 garments arrive on the shelves in Europe, all looking like they came from one factory, with colors, for example, perfectly matched. Just think about the logistics and the coordination.

This is a new type of value added, a truly global product that has never been seen before. The label may say "made in Thailand," but it's not a Thai product. We dissect the manufacturing process and look for the best solution at each step. We're not asking which country can do

Exhibit 12-1   *Li & Fung's Global Reach*

Li & Fung produces a truly global product by pulling apart the manufacturing value chain and optimizing each step. Today it has 35 offices in 20 countries, but its global reach is expanding rapidly. In 1997, it had revenue of approximately $1.7 billion.

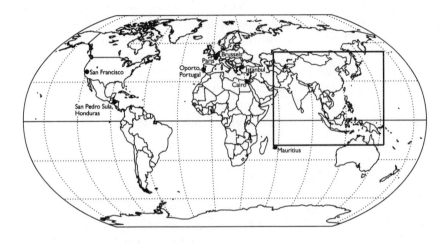

the best job overall. Instead, we're pulling apart the value chain and optimizing each step—and we're doing it globally. (See Exhibit 12-1 "Li & Fung's Global Reach.")

Not only do the benefits outweigh the costs of logistics and transportation, but the higher value added also lets us charge more for our services. We deliver a sophisticated product and we deliver it fast. If you talk to the big global consumer-products companies, they are all moving in this direction—toward being best on a global scale.

So the multinational is essentially its own supply-chain manager?

Yes, exactly. Large manufacturing companies are increasingly doing global supply-chain management, just as Li & Fung does for its retailing customers. That's certainly the case in the auto industry. Today assembly is the easy part. The hard part is managing your suppliers and the flow of parts. In retailing, these changes are producing a revolution. For the first time, retailers are really creating products, not just sitting in their offices with salesman after salesman showing them samples: "Do you want to buy this? Do you want to buy that?"

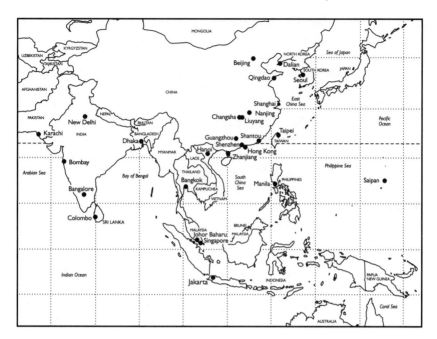

Instead, retailers are participating in the design process. They're now managing suppliers through us and are even reaching down to their suppliers' suppliers. Eventually that translates into much better management of inventories and lower markdowns in the stores.

Explain why that translates into lower markdowns for retailers?

Companies in consumer-driven, fast-moving markets face the problem of obsolete inventory with a vengeance. That means there is enormous value in being able to buy "closer to the market." If you can shorten your buying cycle from three months to five weeks, for example, what you are gaining is eight weeks to develop a better sense of where the market is heading. And so you will end up with substantial savings in inventory markdowns at the end of the selling season.

Good supply-chain management strips away time and cost from product delivery cycles. Our customers have become more fashion driven, working with six or seven seasons a year instead of just two or three. Once you move to shorter product cycles, the problem of obsolete inventory increases dramatically. Other businesses are facing the same kind of pressure. With customer tastes changing rapidly and markets segmenting into narrower niches, it's not just fashion products that are becoming increasingly time sensitive.

Several years ago, I had a conversation about ladies fashion garments with Stan Shih, CEO of Acer, the large Taiwan-based PC manufacturer. I jokingly said, "Stan, are you going to encroach on our territory?" He said, "No, no, but the PC business has the same basic problems you face. Things are changing so fast you don't want to wind up with inventory. You want to plan close to the market." He runs his business to cut down the delivery cycle and minimize inventory exposure by assembling PCs in local markets. So what I have to say about supply chain management for fashion products really applies to any product that's time sensitive.

Supply chain management is about buying the right things and shortening the delivery cycles. It requires "reaching into the suppliers" to ensure that certain things happen on time and at the right quality level. Fundamentally, you're not taking the suppliers as a given.

The classic supply-chain manager in retailing is Marks & Spencer. They don't own any factories, but they have a huge team that goes into the factories and works with the management. The Gap also is known for stretching into its suppliers.

Can you give me an example of how you reach into the supply chain to shorten the buying cycle?

Think about what happens when you outsource manufacturing. The easy approach is to place an order for finished goods and let the supplier worry about contracting for the raw materials like fabric and yarn. But a single factory is relatively small and doesn't have much buying power; that is, it is too small to demand faster deliveries from *its* suppliers.

We come in and look at the whole supply chain. We know the Limited is going to order 100,000 garments, but we don't know the style or the colors yet. The buyer will tell us that five weeks before delivery. The trust between us and our supply network means that we can reserve undyed yarn from the yarn supplier. I can lock up capacity at the mills for the weaving and dying with the promise that they'll get an order of a specified size; five weeks before delivery, we will let them know what colors we want. Then I say the same thing to the factories, "I don't know the product specs yet, but I have organized the colors and the fabric and the trim for you, and they'll be delivered to you on this date and you'll have three weeks to produce so many garments."

I've certainly made life harder for myself now. It would be easier to let the factories worry about securing their own fabric and trim. But then the order would take three months, not five weeks. So to shrink the delivery cycle, I go upstream to organize production. And the shorter production time lets the retailer hold off before having to commit to a fashion trend. It's all about flexibility, response time, small production runs, small minimum-order quantities, and the ability to shift direction as the trends move.

Is it also about cost?

Yes. At Li & Fung we think about supply chain management as "tackling the soft $3" in the cost structure. What do we mean by that? If a typical consumer product leaves the factory at a price of $1, it will invariably end up on retail shelves at $4. Now you can try to squeeze the cost of production down 10 cents or 20 cents per product, but today you have to be a genius to do that because everybody has been working on that for years and there's not a lot of fat left. It's better to look at the cost that is spread throughout the distribution channels— the soft $3. It offers a bigger target, and if you take 50 cents out, nobody will even know you are doing it. So it's a much easier place to effect savings for our customers.

Can you give me an example?

Sure. Shippers always want to fill a container to capacity. If you tell a manufacturer, "Don't fill up the container," he'll think you're crazy. And if all you care about is the cost of shipping, there's no question you should fill the containers. But if you think instead of the whole value chain as a system, and you're trying to lower the total cost and not just one piece of it, then it may be smarter not to fill the containers.

Let's say you want to distribute an assortment of ten products, each manufactured by a different factory, to ten distribution centers. The standard practice would be for each factory to ship full containers of its product. And so those ten containers would then have to go to a consolidator, who would unpack and repack all ten containers before shipping the assortment to the distribution centers.

Now suppose instead that you move one container from factory to factory and get each factory to fill just one-tenth of the container. Then you ship it with the assortment the customer needs directly to the distribution center. The shipping cost will be greater, and you will have to be careful about stacking the goods properly. But the total systems cost could be lower because you've eliminated the consolidator altogether. When someone is actively managing and organizing the whole supply chain, you can save costs like that.

So when you talk about organizing the value chain, what you do goes well beyond simply contracting for other people's services or inspecting their work. It sounds like the value you add extends almost to the point where you're providing management expertise to your supply network.

In a sense, we are a smokeless factory. We do design. We buy and inspect the raw materials. We have factory managers, people who set up and plan production and balance the lines. We inspect production. But we don't manage the workers, and we don't own the factories.

Think about the scope of what we do. We work with about 7,500 suppliers in more than 26 countries. If the average factory has 200 workers—that's probably a low estimate—then in effect there are more than a million workers engaged on behalf of our customers. That's why our policy is not to own any portion of the value chain that deals with running factories. Managing a million workers would be a colossal undertaking. We'd lose all flexibility; we'd lose our ability to fine-tune and coordinate. So we deliberately leave that management challenge to the individual entrepreneurs we contract with. (See Exhibit 12-2 "Supply Chain Management: How Li & Fung Adds Value.")

Our target in working with factories is to take anywhere from 30% to 70% of their production. We want to be important to them, and at 30% we're most likely their largest customer. On the other hand, we need flexibility—so we don't want the responsibility of having them completely dependent on us. And we also benefit from their exposure to their other customers.

If we don't own factories, can we say we are in manufacturing? Absolutely. Because, of the 15 steps in the manufacturing value chain, we probably do 10.

Exhibit 12-2   Supply Chain Management: How Li & Fung Adds Value

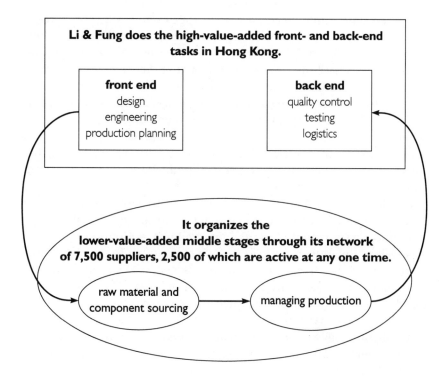

The way Li & Fung is organized is unusual in the industry. Can you describe the link between your organization and your strategy?

Just about every company I know says that they are customer focused. What, in fact, does that mean? Usually it means they design key systems that fit most of their customers, they hope, most of the time. Here we say—and do—something different: We organize for the customer. Almost all the large trading companies with extensive networks of suppliers are organized geographically, with the country units as their profit centers. As a result, it is hard for them to optimize the value chain. Their country units are competing against one another for business.

Our basic operating unit is the division. Whenever possible, we will focus an entire division on serving one customer. We may serve smaller customers through a division structured around a group of customers with similar needs. We have, for example, a theme-store division serving a handful of customers such as the Warner Brothers stores and Rainforest Cafe. This structuring of the organization around customers is very important—remember that what we do is close to creating a customized value chain for every customer order.

So customer-focused divisions are the building blocks of our organization, and we keep them small and entrepreneurial. They do anywhere from $20 million to $50 million of business. Each is run by a lead entrepreneur—we sometimes call them "little John Waynes" because the image of a guy standing in the middle of the wagon train, shooting at all the bad guys, seems to fit.

Consider our Gymboree division, one of our largest. The division manager, Ada Liu, and her headquarters team have their own separate office space within the Li & Fung building in Hong Kong. When you walk through their door, every one of the 40 or so people you see is focused solely on meeting Gymboree's needs. On every desk is a computer with direct software links to Gymboree. The staff is organized into specialized teams in such areas as technical support, merchandising, raw material purchasing, quality assurance, and shipping. And Ada has dedicated sourcing teams in our branch offices in China, the Philippines, and Indonesia because Gymboree buys in volume from all those countries. In maybe 5 of our 26 countries, she has her own team, people she hired herself. When she wants to source from, say, India, the branch office helps her get the job done.

In most multinational companies, fights between the geographic side of the organization and the product or customer side are legendary—and predictable. From the product side, it's "How can I get better service for my customer? It may be small for you in Bangladesh, but it's important for my product line globally." And from the country side, it's "Look, I can't let this product group take unfair advantage of this particular factory, because it produces for three other product groups and I'm responsible for our relationships in this country overall."

Here's our solution to this classic problem: Our primary alignment is around customers and their needs. But to balance the matrix, every product-group executive also has responsibility for one country. It makes them more sensitive to the problems facing a country director and less likely to make unreasonable demands.

Can you tell us more about the role of the little John Waynes?

The idea is to create small units dedicated to taking care of one customer, and to have one person running a unit like she would her own company. In fact, we hire people whose main alternative would be to run their own business. We provide them with the financial resources and the administrative support of a big organization, but we give them a great deal of autonomy. All the merchandising decisions that go into coordinating a production program for the customer—which factories to use, whether to stop a shipment or let it go forward—are made at the division-head level. For the creative parts of the business, we want entrepreneurial behavior, so we give people considerable operating freedom. To motivate the division leaders, we rely on substantial financial incentives by tying their compensation directly to the unit's bottom line. There's no cap on bonuses: we want entrepreneurs who are motivated to move heaven and earth for the customer.

Trading companies can be run effectively only when they are small. By making small units the heart of our company, we have been able to grow rapidly without becoming bureaucratic. Today we have about 60 divisions. We think of them as a portfolio we can create and collapse, almost at will. As the market changes, our organization can adjust immediately.

What role, then, does the corporate center play?

When it comes to financial controls and operating procedures, we don't want creativity or entrepreneurial behavior. In these areas, we centralize and manage tightly. Li & Fung has a standardized, fully computerized operating system for executing and tracking orders, and everyone in the company uses the system.

We also keep very tight control of working capital. As far as I'm concerned, inventory is the root of all evil. At a minimum, it increases the complexity of managing any business. So it's a word we don't tolerate around here. All cash flow is managed centrally through Hong Kong. All letters of credit, for example, come to Hong Kong for approval and are then reissued by the central office. That means we are guaranteed payment before we execute an order. I could expand the company by another 10% to 20% by giving customers credit. But while we are very aggressive in merchandising—in finding new sources, for example—when it comes to financial management, we are very conservative.

I understand, though, that Li & Fung is involved in venture capital. Can you explain how that fits in?

We've set up a small venture-capital arm, with offices in San Francisco, London, and Brussels, whose primary purpose is corporate development. If you look at a product market grid, Li & Fung has expertise in sourcing many types of products for many types of retailers, but there are also holes in our coverage. A big piece of our corporate development is plugging those holes—the phrase we use is "filling in the mosaic"—and we use venture capital to do it.

Let's say Li & Fung is not strong in ladies fashion shoes. We'll have our venture group look for opportunities to buy into relatively young entrepreneurial companies with people who can create designs and sell them but who do not have the ability to source or to finance. That's what we bring to the deal. More important, doing the sourcing for the company lets us build presence and know-how in the segment. At the same time, we think it's a good way to enhance our returns. All venture capitalists will tell you that they bring more than money to their investments. In our case, we are able to back the companies with our sourcing network.

One of our biggest successes is a company called Cyrk. We wanted to fill a hole in our mosaic in the promotional premiums business—clothing or gift items with company logos, for example. We bought a 30% stake in Cyrk for $200,000 in 1990. We ended up doing all the M&M gum ball dispensers with them, but the real coup was a full line of promotional clothing for Philip Morris. After five years, we sold our investment for about $65 million.

We're more than happy with our investment results, but our real interest is in corporate development, in filling in the mosaic. We're not looking to grow by taking over whole companies. We know we can't manage a U.S. domestic company very well because we're so far away, and the culture is different. By backing people on a minority basis, however, we improve our sourcing strength and enhance our ability to grow existing client relationships or to win new ones. That's real synergy.

You've grown substantially both in size and in geographic scope in the last five years. Does becoming more multinational bring any fundamental changes to the company?

Since 1993, we've changed from a Hong Kong-based Chinese company that was 99.5% Chinese and probably 80% Hong Kong Chinese into a truly regional multinational with a workforce from at least 30 countries. We used to call ourselves a Chinese trading company. (The Japanese trading companies are very big, and we wanted to be a big fish in a small pond, so we defined the pond as consisting of Chinese trading companies.) As we grow, and as our workforce becomes more nationally diverse, we wonder how Koreans or Indians or Turks will feel about working for a Chinese multinational.

We're torn. We know that if we call ourselves a multinational, we're very small compared to a Nestlé or a Unilever. And we don't want to be faceless. We are proud of our cultural heritage. But we don't want it to be an impediment to growth, and we want to make people comfortable that culturally we have a very open architecture. We position ourselves today as a Hong Kong-based multinational trading company. Hong Kong itself is both Chinese and very cosmopolitan. In five years, we've come a long way in rethinking our identity.

As we grow and become more multinational, the last thing we want to do is to run the company like the big multinationals. You know—where you have a corporate policy on medical leave or housing allowances or you name it.

How do you avoid setting policies, a path that would seem inevitable for most companies?

We stick to a simple entrepreneurial principle. For the senior ranks of the company, the mobile executives, we "encash"—that is, we translate the value of benefits into dollar figures—as much as we can. Cash gives individuals the most flexibility. I cannot design a policy to fit 1,000 people, so when in doubt we give people money instead. You want a car? You think you deserve a car? We'd rather give you the cash and let you manage the car. You buy it, you service it. The usual multinational solution is to hire experts to do a study. Then they write a manual on car ownership and hire ten people to administer the manual.

If you ask yourself whether you would rather have a package of benefits or its equivalent in cash, maybe you'll say, I don't want such a nice car, but I'd prefer to spend more money on my home leave. Cash gives individuals a lot more freedom. That's our simplifying principle.

Since you operate in so many countries, do you have to index cash equivalents to local economies?

Wherever we operate, we follow local rules and best practices. We do not want uniformity for lower-level managers. If they say in Korea,

"We don't want bonuses but everybody gets 16 months salary," that's the market. What we do would probably drive the HR department in a multinational crazy. But it works for us: for the top people, we figure out a cash equivalent for benefits, and for the local staff, we follow local best practices. It's fine if we do things differently from country to country. And remember, we are an incentive-driven company. We try to make the variable component of compensation as big as possible and to extend that principle as far down into the organization as possible. That's the entrepreneurial approach.

As you spread out geographically, how do you hold the organization together?

The company is managed on a day-to-day basis by the product group managers. Along with the top management, they form what we call the policy committee, which consists of about 30 people. We meet once every five to six weeks. People fly in from around the region to discuss and agree on policies. Consider, for example, the topic of compliance, or ethical sourcing. How do we make sure our suppliers are doing the right thing—by our customers' standards and our own—when it comes to issues such as child labor, environmental protection, and country-of-origin regulations?

Compliance is a very hot topic today—as well it should be. Because our inspectors are in and out of the factories all the time, we probably have a better window on the problem than most companies. If we find factories that don't comply, we won't work with them. However, because there is so much subcontracting, you can't assume that everyone is doing the right thing. That is, you have to make sure that a supplier that was operating properly last month is still doing so this month. The committee of 30 not only shapes our policies but also translates them into operating procedures we think will be effective in the field. And then they become a vehicle for implementing what we've agreed on when they return to their divisions.

There are few businesses as old as trading. Yet the essence of what you do at Li & Fung—managing information and relationships—sounds like a good description of the information economy. How do you reconcile the new economy with the old?

At one level, Li & Fung is an information node, flipping information between our 350 customers and our 7,500 suppliers. We manage all that today with a lot of phone calls and faxes and on-site visits. That's the guts of the company. Soon we will need a sophisticated information system with very open architecture to accommodate different protocols from suppliers and from customers, one robust enough to work in Hong Kong and New York—as well as in places like Bangladesh, where you can't always count on a good phone line.

I have a picture in my mind of the ideal trader for today's world. The trader is an executive wearing a pith helmet and a safari jacket. But in one hand is a machete and in the other a very high-tech personal-computer and communication device. From one side, you're getting reports from suppliers in newly emerging countries, where the quality of the information may be poor. From the other side, you might have highly accurate point-of-sale information from the United States that allows you to replenish automatically. In other words, you're maneuvering between areas that have a lot of catching up to do—you're fighting through the underbrush, so to speak—and areas that are already clearly focused on the twenty-first century.

As the sources of supply explode, managing information becomes increasingly complex. Of course, we have a lot of hard data about performance and about the work we do with each factory. But what we really want is difficult to pin down; a lot of the most valuable information resides in people's heads. What kind of attitude does the owner have? Do we work well together? How good is their internal management? That kind of organizational memory is a lot harder to retain and to share. We see the capturing of such information as the next frontier. You could look at us as a very sophisticated IT system. So that's the modern side of who we are.

What about the more traditional side?

In the information age, there is an impersonality that seems to say that all the old-world thoughts about relationships don't matter anymore. We're all taken with the notion that a bright young guy can bring his great idea to the Internet, and it's okay if no one knows him from Adam. Right?

Maybe. But at the same time, the old relationships, the old values, still matter. I think they matter in our dealings with suppliers, with customers, and with our own staff.

Right now we're so big, three of our divisions could be scheduling work with the same factory. We could be fighting ourselves for factory capacity. So I'm in the process of creating a database to track systematically all our supplier relationships. We need something that everyone in the company can use to review the performance history of all our suppliers. One of my colleagues said, "We'd better guard that with our lives, because if somebody ever got into our system, they could steal one of the company's greatest assets." I'm not so worried. Someone might steal our database, but when they call up a supplier, they don't have the long relationship with the supplier that Li & Fung has. It makes a difference to suppliers when they know that you are dedicated to the business, that you've been honoring your commitments for 90 years.

I think there is a similar traditional dimension to our customer relationships. In the old days, my father used to read every telex from customers. That made a huge difference in a business where a detail as small as the wrong zipper color could lead to disastrous delays for customers. Today William and I continue to read faxes from customers— certainly not every one, but enough to keep us in personal touch with our customers and our operations on a daily basis. Through close attention to detail, we try to maintain our heritage of customer service.

As we have transformed a family business into a modern one, we have tried to preserve the best of what my father and grandfather created. There is a family feeling in the company that's difficult to describe. We don't care much for titles and hierarchy. Family life and the company's business spill over into each other. When staff members are in Hong Kong to do business, my mother might have tea with their families. Of course, as we have grown we have had to change. My mother can't know everyone as she once did. But we hold on to our wish to preserve the intimacies that have been at the heart of our most successful relationships. If I had to capture it in one phrase, it would be this: Think like a big company, act like a small one.

Is the growing importance of information technology good or bad for your business?

Frankly, I am not unhappy that the business will be more dependent on information technology. The growing value of dispersed manufacturing makes us reach even further around the globe, and IT helps us accomplish that stretching of the company.

As Western companies work to remain competitive, supply chain management will become more important. Their need to serve smaller niche markets with more frequent changes in products is pushing us to establish new sources in less developed countries. (See "A Tradition of Innovation.")

We're forging into newly emerging centers of production, from Bangladesh to Sri Lanka to Madagascar. We're now landing in northern Africa—in Egypt, Tunisia, Morocco. We're starting down in South Africa and moving up to some of the equatorial countries. As the global supply network becomes larger and more far-flung, managing it will require scale. As a pure intermediary, our margins were squeezed. But as the number of supply chain options expands, we add value for our customers by using information and relationships to manage the network. We help companies navigate through a world of expanded choice. And the expanding power of IT helps us do that.

A Tradition of Innovation

In the company's early years, Li & Fung dealt in porcelain and other traditional Chinese products, including bamboo and rattan ware, jade and ivory handicrafts—and fireworks. Li & Fung's invention of paper-sealed firecrackers in 1907 to replace the traditional mud-sealed firecracker was a major breakthrough. At that time, the U.S. import duty on firecrackers was based on weight. The paper-sealed firecrackers not only incurred lower import duties by being lighter but also eliminated the problem of excessive dust produced by the discharge of the mud-sealed variety. Li & Fung's paper-sealed manufacturing process has become the industry's standard.

So the middle where we operate is broadening, making what we do more valuable and allowing us to deliver a better product, which translates into better prices and better margins for our customers. In fact, we think export trading is not a sunset industry but a growth business.

Was the professional management training you and William brought with you from the United States helpful in running an Asian family business?

It's an interesting question. For my first 20 years with the company, I had to put aside—unlearn, in fact—a lot of what I had learned in the West about management. It just wasn't relevant. The Li & Fung my grandfather founded was a typical patriarchal Chinese family conglomerate. Even today, most companies in Asia are built on that model. But a lot has changed in the last five years, and the current Asian financial crisis is going to transform the region even more.

Now, instead of managing a few relationships—the essence of the old model—we're managing large, complex systems. It used to be that one or two big decisions a year would determine your success. In the 1980s, for example, many of the Asian tycoons were in asset-intensive businesses like real estate and shipping. You would make a very small number of very big decisions—you would acquire a piece of land or decide to build a supertanker—and you were done. And access to the deals depended on your connections.

The Li & Fung of today is quite different from the company my grandfather founded in 1906. As it was in a lot of family companies, people had a sense over the years that the company's purpose was to serve as the family's livelihood. One of the first things William and I did was to persuade my father to separate ownership and management by taking the company public in 1973.

When our margins were squeezed during the 1980s, we felt we needed to make dramatic changes that could best be done if we went back to being a private company. So in 1988, we undertook Hong Kong's first management buyout, sold off assets, and refocused the company on its core trading business. Later we took our export trading business public again. I'm sure some of our thinking about governance structure and focus was influenced by our Western training.

But I'm more struck by the changes in the company's decision making. Right now in this building, we probably have 50 buyers making hundreds of individual transactions. We're making a large number of small decisions instead of a small number of big ones. I can't be involved in all of them. So today I depend on structure, on guiding principles, on managing a system.

Of course, I think relationships are still important, but I'm not managing a single key relationship and using it to leverage my entire enterprise. Instead, I'm running a very focused business using a systems approach. That's why I say that in the last five years, everything I learned in business school has come to matter.

Li & Fung is a good example of the new generation of companies coming out of Asia. As the currency crisis destroys the old model, stronger companies will emerge from the ashes, still bolstered by Asia's strong work ethic and high savings rates, but more narrowly focused and professionally run by what we can call the "M.B.A. sons."

What's driving Hong Kong is a large number—about 300,000—of small and midsize enterprises. About 40% of those companies are transnational; that is, they operate in two or more territories. Some may have 20 to 30 people in Hong Kong, plus a factory in mainland

China with 200 or 300 people. Hong Kong runs about 50,000 factories in southern China, employing about 5 million workers. Hong Kong is producing a new breed of company. I don't think there will be many the size of General Motors or AT&T. But there will be lots of very focused companies that will break into the *Fortune* 1,000. I hope Li & Fung is one of them.

13

Growth through Global Sustainability

An Interview with Monsanto's CEO, Robert B. Shapiro

Joan Magretta

Robert B. Shapiro, chairman and CEO of Monsanto Company, based in St. Louis, Missouri, sees the conundrum facing his company this way. On the one hand, if a business doesn't grow, it will die. And the world economy must grow to keep pace with the needs of population growth. On the other hand, how does a company face the prospect that growing and being profitable could require intolerable abuse of the natural world? In Shapiro's words, "It's the kind of question that people who choose to spend their lives working in business can't shrug off or avoid easily. And it has important implications for business strategy."

Sustainable development is the term for the dual imperative—economic growth and environmental sustainability—that has been gaining ground among business leaders since the 1992 United Nations Earth Summit in Rio de Janeiro. As Shapiro puts it, "We can't expect the rest of the world to abandon their economic aspirations just so we can continue to enjoy clean air and water. That is neither ethically correct nor likely to be permitted by the billions of people in the developing world who expect the quality of their lives to improve."

Monsanto—with its history in the chemicals industry—may seem an unlikely company to lead the way on an emerging environmental issue. But a number of resource- and energy-intensive companies criticized as environmental offenders in the 1980s have been the first to grasp the strategic implications of sustainability.

Monsanto, in fact, is seeking growth *through* sustainability, betting on a strategic discontinuity from which few businesses will be immune. To borrow Stuart L. Hart's phrase, Monsanto is moving "beyond greening." In the following interview with *Harvard Business Review* editor-at-large Joan Magretta, the 58-year-old Shapiro discusses how Monsanto has moved from a decade of progress in pollution prevention and clean-up to spotting opportunities for revenue growth in environmentally sustainable new products and technologies.

Why is sustainability becoming an important component of your strategic thinking?

Today there are about 5.8 billion people in the world. About 1.5 billion of them live in conditions of abject poverty—a subsistence life that simply can't be romanticized as some form of simpler, preindustrial lifestyle. These people spend their days trying to get food and firewood so that they can make it to the next day. As many as 800 million people are so severely malnourished that they can neither work nor participate in family life. That's where we are today. And, as far as I know, no demographer questions that the world population will just about double by sometime around 2030.

Without radical change, the kind of world implied by those numbers is unthinkable. It's a world of mass migrations and environmental degradation on an unimaginable scale. At best, it means the preservation of a few islands of privilege and prosperity in a sea of misery and violence.

Our nation's economic system evolved in an era of cheap energy and careless waste disposal, when limits seemed irrelevant. None of us today, whether we're managing a house or running a business, is living in a sustainable way. It's not a question of good guys and bad guys. There is no point in saying, If only those bad guys would go out of business, then the world would be fine. The whole system has to change; there's a huge opportunity for reinvention.

We're entering a time of perhaps unprecedented discontinuity. Businesses grounded in the old model will become obsolete and die. At Monsanto, we're trying to invent some new businesses around the concept of environmental sustainability. We may not yet know exactly what those businesses will look like, but we're willing to place some bets because the world cannot avoid needing sustainability in the long run.

Can you explain how what you're describing is a discontinuity?

Years ago, we would approach strategic planning by considering "the environment"—that is, the economic, technological, and competitive context of the business—and we'd forecast how it would change over the planning horizon. Forecasting usually meant extrapolating recent trends. So we almost never predicted the critical discontinuities in which the real money was made and lost—the changes that really determined the future of the business. Niels Bohr was right when he said it is difficult to make predictions—especially about the future. But every consumer marketer knows that you can rely on demographics. Many market discontinuities were predictable—and future ones can still be predicted—based on observable, incontrovertible facts such as baby booms and busts, life expectancies, and immigration patterns. Sustainable development is one of those discontinuities. Far from being a soft issue grounded in emotion or ethics, sustainable development involves cold, rational business logic.

This discontinuity is occurring because we are encountering physical limits. You can see it coming arithmetically. Sustainability involves the laws of nature—physics, chemistry, and biology—and the recognition that the world is a closed system. What we thought was boundless has limits, and we're beginning to hit them. That's going to change a lot of today's fundamental economics, it's going to change prices, and it's going to change what's socially acceptable.

Is sustainability an immediate issue today in any of Monsanto's businesses?

In some businesses, it's probably less apparent why sustainability is so critical. But in our agricultural business, we can't avoid it. In the twentieth century, we have been able to feed people by bringing more acreage into production and by increasing productivity through fertilizers, pesticides, and irrigation. But current agricultural practice isn't sustainable: we've lost something on the order of 15% of our topsoil over the last 20 years or so, irrigation is increasing the salinity of soil, and the petrochemicals we rely on aren't renewable.

Most arable land is already under cultivation. Attempts to open new farmland are causing severe ecological damage. So in the best case, we have the same amount of land to work with and twice as many people to feed. It comes down to resource productivity. You have to get twice the yield from every acre of land just to maintain current levels of poverty and malnutrition.

Now, even if you wanted to do it in an unsustainable way, no technology today would let you double productivity. With current best practices applied to all the acreage in the world, you'd get about a third of the way toward feeding the whole population. The conclusion is that new technology is the only alternative to one of two disasters: not feeding people—letting the Malthusian process work its magic on the population—or ecological catastrophe.

What new technology are you talking about?

We don't have 100 years to figure that out; at best, we have decades. In that time frame, I know of only two viable candidates: biotechnology and information technology. I'm treating them as though they're separate, but biotechnology is really a subset of information technology because it is about DNA-encoded information.

Using information is one of the ways to increase productivity without abusing nature. A closed system like the earth's can't withstand a systematic increase of material things, but it can support exponential increases of information and knowledge. If economic development means using more stuff, then those who argue that growth and environmental sustainability are incompatible are right. And if we grow by using more stuff, I'm afraid we'd better start looking for a new planet.

But sustainability and development might be compatible if you could create value and satisfy people's needs by increasing the information component of what's produced and diminishing the amount of stuff.

How does biotechnology replace stuff with information in agriculture?

We can genetically code a plant, for example, to repel or destroy harmful insects. That means we don't have to spray the plant with pesticides—with stuff. Up to 90% of what's sprayed on crops today is wasted. Most of it ends up on the soil. If we put the right information in the plant, we waste less stuff and increase productivity. With biotechnology, we can accomplish that. It's not that chemicals are inherently bad. But they are less efficient than biology because you have to manufacture and distribute and apply them.

I offer a prediction: the early twenty-first century is going to see a struggle between information technology and biotechnology on the one hand and environmental degradation on the other. Information technology is going to be our most powerful tool. It will let us miniaturize things, avoid waste, and produce more value without producing and processing more stuff. The substitution of information for stuff is essential to sustainability. (See "Monsanto's Smarter Products.") Substituting services for products is another.

Monsanto's Smarter Products

Scientists at Monsanto are designing products that use information at the genetic or molecular level to increase productivity. Here are three that are on the market today.

The NewLeaf Potato. The NewLeaf potato, bioengineered to defend itself against the destructive Colorado potato beetle, is already in use on farms. Monsanto also is working on the NewLeaf Plus potato with inherent resistance to leaf virus, another common scourge. Widespread

Why use all this to protect potatoes from insects and viruses when . . .

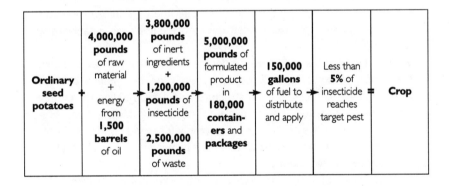

. . . built-in genetic information lets potatoes protect themselves?

adoption of the product could eliminate the manufacture, transportation, distribution, and aerial application of millions of pounds of chemicals and residues yearly.

B.t. Cotton. In ordinary soil, microbes known as B.t. microbes occur naturally and produce a special protein that, although toxic to certain pests, are harmless to other insects, wildlife, and people. If the destructive cotton budworm, for example, eats B.t. bacteria, it will die.

Some cotton farmers control budworms by applying to their cotton plants a powder containing B.t. But the powder often blows or washes away, and reapplying it is expensive. The alternative is for farmers to spray the field with a chemical insecticide as many as 10 or 12 times per season.

But Monsanto's scientists had an idea. They identified the gene that tells the B.t. bacteria to make the special protein. Then they inserted the gene in the cotton plant to enable it to produce the protein on its own while remaining unchanged in other respects. Now when budworms attack, they are either repelled or killed by the B.t.

With products like B.t. cotton, farmers avoid having to buy and apply insecticides. And the environment is spared chemicals that are persistent in the soil or that run off into the groundwater.

Roundup Herbicide and No-Till Farming. Sustainability has become an important design criterion in Monsanto's chemically based products as well as in its bioengineered products. Building the right information into molecules, for example, can render them more durable or enhance their recyclability.

Roundup herbicide is a molecule designed to address a major problem for farmers: topsoil erosion. Topsoil is necessary for root systems because of its organic matter, friability in structure, and water-holding capabilities. The subsoil underneath is incapable of supporting root systems. Historically, farmers have tilled their soil primarily for weed control and only to a minor extent for seed preparation. But plowing loosens soil structure and exposes soil to erosion.

By replacing plowing with application of herbicides like Roundup—a practice called *conservation tillage*—farmers end up with better soil quality and less topsoil erosion. When sprayed onto a field before crop planting, Roundup kills the weeds, eliminating the need for plowing. And because the Roundup molecule has been designed to kill only what is growing at the time of its initial application, the farmer can come back a few days after spraying and begin planting; the herbicide will have no effect on the emerging seeds.

The Roundup molecule has other smart features that contribute to sustainability. It is degraded by soil microbes into natural products such as nitrogen, carbon dioxide, and water. It is nontoxic to animals because its mode of action is specific to plants. Once sprayed, it sticks to soil particles; it doesn't move into the groundwater. Like a smart tool, it seeks out its work.

Explain what you mean by substituting services for products.

Bill McDonough, dean of the University of Virginia's School of Architecture in Charlottesville, made this come clear for me. He points out that we often buy things not because we want the things themselves but because we want what they can do. Television sets are an obvious example. No one says, "Gee, I'd love to put a cathode-ray tube and a lot of printed circuit boards in my living room." People *might* say, "I'd like to watch the ball game" or "Let's turn on the soaps." Another example: Monsanto makes nylon fiber, much of which goes into carpeting. Each year, nearly 2 million tons of old carpeting go into landfills, where they constitute about 1% of the entire U.S. municipal solid-waste load. Nobody really wants to own carpet; they just want to walk on it. What would happen if Monsanto or the carpet manufacturer owned that carpet and promised to come in and remove it when it required replacing? What would the economics of that look like? One of our customers is exploring that possibility today. It might be that if we got the carpet back, we could afford to put more cost into it in the first place in ways that would make it easier for us to recycle. Maybe then it wouldn't end up in a landfill.

We're starting to look at all our products and ask, What is it people really need to buy? Do they need the stuff or just its function? What would be the economic impact of our selling a carpet service instead of a carpet?

Can you cite other examples of how we can replace stuff with information?

Sure. Information technology, whether it's telecommunications or virtual reality—whatever that turns out to be—can eliminate the need to move people and things around. In the past, if you wanted to send a document from one place to another, it involved a lot of trains and planes and trucks. Sending a fax eliminates all that motion. Sending E-mail also eliminates the paper.

I have to add that any powerful new technology is going to create ethical problems—problems of privacy, fairness, ethics, power, or control. With any major change in the technological substrate, society has to solve those inherent issues.

You referred earlier to using information to miniaturize things. How does that work?

Miniaturization is another piece of sustainability because it reduces the amount of stuff we use. There are enormous potential savings in moving from very crude, massive designs to smaller and more elegant ones. Microelectronics is one example: the computing power you have in your PC would have required an enormous installation not many years ago.

We've designed things bigger than they need to be because it's easier and because we thought we had unlimited space and material. Now that we know we don't, there's going to be a premium on smaller, smarter design. I think of miniaturization as a way to buy time. Ultimately, we'd love to figure out how to replace chemical processing plants with fields of growing plants—literally, green plants capable of producing chemicals. We have some leads: we can already produce polymers in soybeans, for example. But I think a big commercial breakthrough is a long way off.

Today, by developing more efficient catalysts, for example, we can at least make chemical plants smaller. There will be a number of feasible alternatives if we can really learn to think differently and set design criteria other than reducing immediate capital costs. One way is to design chemical plants differently. If you looked at life-cycle costs such as energy consumption, for instance, you would design a plant so that processes needing heat were placed next to processes generating heat; you wouldn't install as many heaters and coolers that waste energy. We think that if you really dig into your costs, you can accomplish a lot by simplifying and shrinking.

Some people are talking about breakthroughs in mechanical devices comparable to what's being done with electronic devices. Maybe the next wave will come through nanotechnology, but probably in 10 or 20 years, not tomorrow.

The key to sustainability, then, lies in technology?

I am not one of those techno-utopians who just assume that technology is going to take care of everyone. But I don't see an alternative to giving it our best shot.

Business leaders tend to trust technology and markets and to be optimistic about the natural unfolding of events. But at a visceral level, people know we are headed for trouble and would love to find a way to do something about it. The market is going to want sustainable systems, and if Monsanto provides them, we will do quite well for ourselves and our shareowners. Sustainable development is going to be one of the organizing principles around which Monsanto and a lot of other institutions will probably define themselves in the years to come.

Describe how you go about infusing this way of thinking into the company?

It's not hard. You talk for three minutes, and people light up and say, "Where do we start?" And I say, "I don't know. And good luck."

Maybe some context would help. We've been grappling with sustainability issues here long before we had a term for the concept. Part of our history as a chemical company is that environmental issues have been in our face to a greater extent than they've been in many other industries.

My predecessor, Dick Mahoney, understood that the way we were doing things had to change. Dick grew up, as I did not, in the chemical industry, so he tended to look at what was coming out of our plants. The publication of our first toxic-release inventory in 1988 galvanized attention around the magnitude of plant emissions.

Dick got way out ahead of the traditional culture in Monsanto and in the rest of the chemical industry. He set incredibly aggressive quantitative targets and deadlines. The first reaction to them was, My God, he must be out of his mind. But it was an effective technique. In six years, we reduced our toxic air emissions by 90%.

Not having "grown up in the chemical industry," as you put it, do you think differently about environmental issues?

Somewhat. Dick put us on the right path. We have to reduce—and ultimately eliminate—the negative impacts we have on the world. There is no argument on that subject. But even if Monsanto reached its goal of zero impact next Tuesday, that wouldn't solve the world's problem. Several years ago, I sensed that there was something more required of us than doing no harm, but I couldn't articulate what that was.

So I did what you always do. I got some smart people together—a group of about 25 critical thinkers, some of the company's up-and-coming leaders—and sent them off to think about it. We selected a good cross-section—some business-unit leaders, a couple from the management board, and people from planning, manufacturing, policy, and safety and health. And we brought in some nontraditional outsiders to challenge our underlying assumptions about the world. My request to this group was, "Go off, think about what's happening to the world, and come back with some recommendations about what it means for Monsanto. Do we have a role to play? If so, what is it?"

That off-site meeting in 1994 led to an emerging insight that we couldn't ignore the changing global environmental conditions. The focus around sustainable development became obvious. I should have been able to come up with that in about 15 minutes. But it took a group of very good people quite a while to think it through, to determine what was real and what was just puff, to understand the data, and to convince themselves that this wasn't a fluffy issue—and that we ought to be engaged in it.

People came away from that meeting emotionally fired up. It wasn't just a matter of Okay, you threw me an interesting business problem, I have done the analysis, here is the answer, and now can I go back to work. People came away saying, "Damn it, we've got to get going on this. This is important." When some of your best people care intensely, their excitement is contagious.

So now we have a bunch of folks engaged, recognizing that we have no idea where we're going to end up. No one—not the most sophisticated thinker in the world—can describe a sustainable world with 10 billion to 12 billion people, living in conditions that aren't disgusting and morally impermissible. But we can't sit around waiting for the finished blueprint. We have to start moving in directions that make us less unsustainable.

How are you doing that?

There's a quote of Peter Drucker's—which I will mangle here—to the effect that at some point strategy has to degenerate into work. At Monsanto, there was a flurry of E-mail around the world, and in a matter of four months a group of about 80 coalesced. Some were chosen; many others just heard about the project and volunteered. They met for the first time in October 1995 and decided to organize into seven teams: three focused on developing tools to help us make better decisions, three focused externally on meeting world needs, and one focused on education and communication. (See "Monsanto's Seven Sustainability Teams.")

We realized that many of the things we were already doing were part of a sustainability strategy even if we didn't call it that. We'd been working on pollution prevention and investing in biotechnology for years before we thought about the concept of sustainability. As we made more progress in pollution prevention, it became easier for everyone to grasp how pollution—or waste—actually represents a resource that's lost. When you translate that understanding into how you run a business, it leads to cost reduction. You can ask, did we do it because it reduces our costs or because of sustainability? That would be hard to answer because optimizing resources has become part of the way we think. But having the sustainability framework has made a difference, especially in how we weigh new business opportunities.

Monsanto's Seven Sustainability Teams

Three of Monsanto's sustainability teams are working on tools and methodologies to assess, measure, and provide direction for internal management.

The Eco-efficiency Team. Because you can't manage what you don't measure, this team is mapping and measuring the ecological efficiency of Monsanto's processes. Team members must ask, In relation to the value produced, what inputs are consumed, and what outputs are generated? Managers have historically optimized raw material inputs, for example, but they have tended to take energy and water for granted because there is little financial incentive today to do otherwise. And although companies such as Monsanto have focused on toxic waste in the past, true eco-efficiency will require better measures of all waste. Carbon dioxide, for instance, may not be toxic, but it can produce negative environmental effects. Ultimately, Monsanto's goal is to pursue eco-efficiency in all its interactions with suppliers and customers.

The Full-Cost Accounting Team. This team is developing a methodology to account for the total cost of making and using a product during the product's life cycle, including the true environmental costs associated with producing, using, recycling, and disposing of it. The goal is to keep score in a way that doesn't eliminate from consideration all the environmental costs of what the company does. With better data, it will be possible to make smarter decisions today and as the underlying economics change in the future.

The Index Team. This team is developing criteria by which business units can measure whether or not they're moving toward sustainability.

They are working on a set of metrics that balance economic, social, and environmental factors. Units will be able to track the sustainability of individual products and of whole businesses. These sustainability metrics will, in turn, be integrated into Monsanto's balanced-scorecard approach to the management of its businesses. The scorecard links and sets objectives for financial targets, customer satisfaction, internal processes, and organizational learning.

Three teams are looking externally to identify sustainability needs that Monsanto might address.

The New Business/New Products Team. This team is examining what will be valued in a marketplace that increasingly selects products and services that support sustainability. It is looking at areas of stress in natural systems and imagining how Monsanto's technological skills could meet human needs with new products that don't aggravate—that perhaps even repair—ecological damage.

The Water Team. The water team is looking at global water needs—a huge and growing problem. Many people don't have access to clean drinking water, and there is a worsening shortage of water for irrigation as well.

The Global Hunger Team. This team is studying how Monsanto might develop and deliver technologies to alleviate world hunger. That goal has been a core focus for the company for a number of years. For example, Monsanto had been studying how it might use its agricultural skills to meet people's nutritional needs in developing countries.

The final team develops materials and training programs.

The Communication and Education Team. This team's contribution is to develop the training to give Monsanto's 29,000 employees a common perspective. It offers a framework for understanding what sustainability means, how employees can play a role, and how they can take their knowledge to key audiences outside the company.

Can you give me some examples?

One of the seven sustainability teams is discussing how to gain a deeper understanding of global water needs and whether we at Monsanto might meet some of those needs with our existing capabilities. That is an example of a conversation that might not have occurred—or might have occurred much later—if we weren't focused on sustainability. Agricultural water is becoming scarcer, and the salination of soils is an increasing problem. In California, for example, they do a lot of irrigation, and when the water evaporates or flushes through the soil, it leaves small amounts of minerals and salts. Over time, the build-up is going to affect the soil's productivity.

Should we address the water side of the problem? Or can we approach the issue from the plant side? Can we develop plants that will thrive in salty soil? Or can we create less thirsty plants suited to a drier environment? If we had plants that could adapt, maybe semidesert areas could become productive.

Another problem is drinking water. Roughly 40% of the people on earth don't have an adequate supply of fresh water. In the United States, we have a big infrastructure for cleaning water. But in developing countries that lack the infrastructure, there might be a business opportunity for in-home water-purification systems.

I realize this is still early in the process, but how do you know that you're moving forward?

One interesting measure is that we keep drawing in more people. We started off with 80; now we have almost 140. And a lot of this response is just one person after another saying, "I want to be involved, and this is the team I want to be involved in." It's infectious. That's the way most good business processes work. To give people a script and tell them, "Your part is on page 17; just memorize it" is an archaic way to run institutions that have to regenerate and re-create themselves. It's a dead end.

Today, in most fields I know, the struggle is about creativity and innovation. There is no script. You have some ideas, some activities, some exhortations, and some invitations, and you try to align what people believe and what people care about with what they're free to do. And you hope that you can coordinate them in ways that aren't too wasteful—or, better still, that they can self-coordinate. If an institution wants to be adaptive, it has to let go of some control and trust that people will work on the right things in the right ways. That has some obvious implications for the ways you select people, train them, and support them.

Would it be accurate to say that all of your sustainability teams have been self-created and self-coordinated?

Someone asked me recently whether this was a top-down exercise or a bottom-up exercise. Those don't sound like very helpful concepts to me. This is about *us*. What do *we* want to do? Companies aren't machines anymore. We have thousands of independent agents trying to self-coordinate because it is in their interest to do so.

There is no top or bottom. That's just a metaphor and not a helpful one. People say, Here is what I think. What do you think? Does that make sense to you? Would you like to try it? I believe we must see what ideas really win people's hearts and trust that those ideas will turn out to be the most productive.

People in large numbers won't give their all for protracted periods of time—with a cost in their overall lives—for an abstraction called a corporation or an idea called profit. People can give only to people. They can give to their coworkers if they believe that they're engaged together in an enterprise of some importance. They can give to society, which is just another way of saying they can give to their children. They can give if they believe that their work is in some way integrated into a whole life.

Historically, there has been a bifurcation between who we are and the work we do, as if who we are is outside our work. That's unhealthy, and most people yearn to integrate their two sides. Because of Monsanto's history as a chemical company, we have a lot of employees—good people—with a recurrent experience like this: their kids or their neighbors' kids or somebody at a cocktail party asks them what kind of work they do and then reacts in a disapproving way because of what they *think* we are at Monsanto. And that hurts. People don't want to be made to feel ashamed of what they do.

I don't mean to disparage economic motives—they're obviously important. But working on sustainability offers a huge hope for healing the rift between our economic activity and our total human activity. Instead of seeing the two in Marxist opposition, we see them as the same thing. Economics is part of human activity.

What are the organizational implications of that?

Part of the design and structure of any successful institution is going to be giving people permission to select tasks and goals that they care about. Those tasks have to pass some kind of economic screen; but much of what people care about will pass because economic gain comes from meeting people's needs. That's what economies are based on.

The people who have been working on sustainability here have done an incredible job, not because there has been one presiding genius who has organized it all and told them what to do but because they want to get it done. They care intensely about it and they organize themselves to do it.

I don't mean to romanticize it, but, by and large, self-regulating systems are probably going to be more productive than those based primarily on control loops. There are some institutions that for a short period can succeed as a reflection of the will and ego of a single person. But they're unlikely to survive unless other people resonate with what that person represents.

We're going to have to figure out how to organize people in ways that enable them to coordinate their activities without wasteful and intrusive systems of control and without too much predefinition of what a job is. My own view is that as long as you have a concept called a job, you're asking people to behave inauthentically; you're asking people to perform to a set of expectations that someone else created. People give more if they can figure out how to control themselves, how to regulate themselves, how to contribute what they can contribute out of their own authentic abilities and beliefs, not out of somebody else's predetermination of what they're going to do all day.

How will you measure your progress toward sustainability? Do you have milestones?

For something at this early level of exploration, you probably want to rely for at least a year on a subjective sense of momentum. People usually know when they're going someplace, when they're making progress. There's a pace to it that says, yes, we're on the right track. After that, I would like to see some quantitative goals with dates and very macro budgets. As the teams begin to come to some conclusions, we will be able to ignite the next phase by setting some specific targets.

This is so big and complicated that I don't think we're going to end up with a neat and tidy document. I don't think environmental sustainability lends itself to that.

As your activities globalize, does the issue of sustainability lead you to think differently about your business strategy in different countries or regions of the world?

The developing economies can grow by brute force, by putting steel in the ground and depleting natural resources and burning a lot of hydrocarbons. But a far better way to go would be for companies like Monsanto to transfer their knowledge and help those countries avoid the mistakes of the past. If emerging economies have to relive the entire industrial revolution with all its waste, its energy use, and its pollution, I think it's all over.

Can we help the Chinese, for example, leapfrog from preindustrial to postindustrial systems without having to pass through that destructive middle? At the moment, the signs aren't encouraging. One that is, however, is China's adoption of cellular phones instead of tons of stuff: telephone poles and copper wire.

The fact that India is one of the largest software-writing countries in the world is encouraging. You'd like to see tens of millions of people in India employed in information technology rather than in making more stuff. But there's an important hurdle for companies like Monsanto to overcome. To make money through the transfer of information, we depend on intellectual property rights, which let us reconcile environmental and economic goals. As the headlines tell you, that's a little problematic in Asia. And yet it's critically important to our being able to figure out how to be helpful while making money. Knowledge transfer will happen a lot faster if people get paid for it.

Will individual companies put themselves at risk if they follow sustainable practices and their competitors don't?

I can see that somebody could get short-term advantage by cutting corners. At a matter of fact, the world economy *has* seized such an advantage—short-term in the sense of 500 years—by cutting corners on some basic laws of physics and thermodynamics. But it's like asking if you can gain an advantage by violating laws. Yes, I suppose you can—until they catch you. I don't think it is a good idea to build a business or an economy around the "until-they-catch-you principle." It can't be the right way to build something that is going to endure.

The multinational corporation is an impressive invention for dealing with the tension between the application of broadly interesting ideas on the one hand and economic and cultural differences on the other. Companies like ours have gotten pretty good at figuring out how to operate in places where we can make a living while remaining true to some fundamental rules. As more countries enter the world economy, they are accepting—with greater or lesser enthusiasm—that they are going to have to play by some rules that are new for them. My guess is that, over time, sustainability is going to be one of those rules.

Doesn't all this seem far away for managers? Far enough in the future for them to think, "It won't happen on my watch"?

The tension between the short term and the long term is one of the fundamental issues of business—and of life—and it isn't going to go away. Many chief executives have gotten where they are in part because they have a time horizon longer than next month. You don't stop caring about next month, but you also have to think further ahead. What's going to happen next in my world? If your world is soft drinks, for example, you have to ask where your clean water will come from.

How do you react to the prospect of the world population doubling over the next few decades? First you may say, Great, 5 billion more customers. That is what economic development is all about. That's part of it. Now, keep going. Think about all the physical implications of serving that many new customers. And ask yourself the hard question, How exactly are we going to do that and still live here? That's what sustainability is about.

I'm fascinated with the concept of distinctions that transform people. Once you learn certain things—once you learn to ride a bike, say—your life has changed forever. You can't unlearn it. For me, sustainability is one of those distinctions. Once you get it, it changes how you think. A lot of our people have been infected by this way of seeing the world. It's becoming automatic. It's just part of who you are.

Executive Summaries

Strategy and the New Economics of Information

Philip B. Evans and Thomas S. Wurster

We are in the midst of a fundamental shift in the economics of information—a shift that will precipitate changes in the structure of entire industries and in the ways companies compete. This shift is made possible by the widespread adoption of Internet technologies, but it is less about technology than about the fact that a new behavior is reaching critical mass. Millions of people are communicating at home and at work in an explosion of connectivity that threatens to undermine the established value chains for businesses in many sectors of the economy.

What will happen, for instance, to dominant retailers such as Toys "R" Us and Home Depot when a search through the Internet gives consumers more choice than any store? What will be the point of cultivating a long-standing supplier relationship with General Electric when it posts its purchasing requirements on an Internet bulletin board and entertains bids from anybody inclined to respond?

The authors present a conceptual framework for approaching such questions—for understanding the relationship of information to the physical components of the value chain and how the Internet's ability to separate the two will lead to the reconfiguration of the value proposition in many industries. In any business where the physical value chain has been compromised for the sake of delivering information, there will be an opportunity to create a separate information business and a need to streamline the physical one. Executives must mentally deconstruct their businesses to see the real value of what they have. If they don't, the authors warn, someone else will.

Clusters and the New Economics of Competition

Michael E. Porter

Economic geography in an era of global competition poses a paradox. In theory, location should no longer be a source of competitive advantage. Open global markets, rapid transportation, and high-speed communications should allow any company to source any thing from any place at any time. But in practice, Michael Porter demonstrates, location remains central to competition.

Today's economic map of the world is characterized by what Porter calls *clusters:* critical masses in one place of linked industries and institutions—from suppliers to universities to government agencies—that enjoy unusual competitive success in a particular field. The most famous examples are found in Silicon Valley and Hollywood, but clusters dot the world's landscape.

Porter explains how clusters affect competition in three broad ways: first, by increasing the productivity of companies based in the area; second, by driving the direction and pace of innovation; and third, by stimulating the formation of new businesses within the cluster. Geographic, cultural, and institutional proximity provides companies with special access, closer relationships, better information, powerful incentives, and other advantages that are difficult to tap from a distance. The more complex, knowledge-based, and dynamic the world economy becomes, the more this is true. Competitive advantage lies increasingly in local things—knowledge, relationships, and motivation—that distant rivals cannot replicate.

Porter challenges the conventional wisdom about how companies should be configured, how institutions such as universities can contribute to competitive success, and how governments can promote economic development and prosperity.

The End of Corporate Imperialism

C.K. Prahalad and Kenneth Lieberthal

As they search for growth, multinational corporations will have no choice but to compete in the big emerging markets of China, India, Indonesia, and Brazil. But while it is still common to question how corporations will change life in those markets, Western executives would be smart to turn the question around. The authors assert that the multinationals themselves will be transformed by their experience. In fact, they say, MNCs will have to rethink every element of their business models in order to be successful.

During the first wave of market entry in the 1980s, MNCs operated with what might be termed an imperialist mind-set. They assumed, for example, that the big emerging markets would be new markets for their old products. As a result of this mind-set, multinationals have achieved only limited success in these markets.

The authors guide readers through five questions that companies must answer to compete effectively. First and foremost, MNCs must define the emerging middle-class markets—which are significantly different from those in the West—and determine a business model that will serve their needs.

The transformation that multinationals must undergo is not cosmetic— simply developing greater cultural sensitivity will not do the trick. In order to compete in the big emerging markets, multinationals must reconfigure their resource base, rethink their cost structure, redesign their product development process, and challenge their assumptions about the cultural mix of their top-level managers. MNCs that recognize the need for such changes will likely reap the rewards of the postimperialist age.

Strategy under Uncertainty

Hugh Courtney, Jane Kirkland, and Patrick Viguerie

At the heart of the traditional approach to strategy lies the assumption that by applying a set of powerful analytic tools, executives can predict the future of any business accurately enough to allow them to choose a clear strategic direction. But what happens when the environment is so uncertain that no amount of analysis will allow us to predict the future? What makes for a good strategy in highly uncertain business environments?

The authors, consultants at McKinsey & Company, argue that uncertainty requires a new way of thinking about strategy. All too often, they say, executives take a binary view: either they underestimate uncertainty to come up with the forecasts required by their companies' planning or capital-budgeting processes, or they overestimate it, abandon all analysis, and go with their gut instinct.

The authors outline a new approach that begins by making a crucial distinction among four discrete levels of uncertainty that any company might face. They then explain how a set of generic strategies—shaping the market, adapting to it, or reserving the right to play at a later time—can be used in each of the four levels. And they illustrate how these strategies can be implemented through a combination of three basic types of actions: big bets, options, and no-regrets moves.

The framework can help managers determine which analytic tools can inform decision making under uncertainty—and which cannot. At a broader level, it offers executives a discipline for thinking rigorously and systematically about uncertainty and its implications for strategy.

Strategy as a Portfolio of Real Options

Timothy A. Luehrman

In financial terms, a business strategy is much more like a series of options than like a single projected cash flow. Executing a strategy almost always involves making a sequence of major decisions. Some actions are taken immediately while others are deliberately deferred so that managers can optimize their choices as circumstances evolve.

While executives readily grasp the analogy between strategy and real options, until recently the mechanics of option pricing was so complex that few companies found it practical to use when formulating strategy. But advances in both computing power and our understanding of option pricing over the last 20 years now make it feasible to apply real-options thinking to strategic decision making.

To analyze a strategy as a portfolio of related real options, this article exploits a framework presented by the author in "Investment Opportunities as Real Options: Getting Started on the Numbers" (*Harvard Business Review* July–August 1998). That article explained how to get from discounted-cash-flow value to option value for a typical project; in other words, it was about reaching a number. This article extends that framework, exploring how, once you've worked out the numbers, you can use option pricing to improve decision making about the sequence and timing of a portfolio of strategic investments. Timothy Luehrman shows executives how to plot their strategies in two-dimensional "option space," giving them a way to "draw" a strategy in terms that are neither wholly strategic nor wholly financial, but some of both. Such pictures inject financial discipline and new insight into how a company's future opportunities can be actively cultivated and harvested.

Fair Process: Managing in the Knowledge Economy

W. Chan Kim and Renée Mauborgne

Unlike the traditional factors of production—land, labor, and capital—knowledge is a resource that can't be forced out of people. But creating and sharing knowledge is essential to fostering innovation, the key challenge of the knowledge-based economy. To create a climate in which employees volunteer their creativity and expertise, managers need to look beyond the traditional tools at their disposal. They need to build trust.

The authors have studied the links between trust, idea sharing, and corporate performance for more than a decade. They have explored the question of why managers of local subsidiaries so often fail to share information with executives at headquarters. They have studied the dynamics of idea sharing in product development teams, joint ventures, supplier partnerships, and corporate transformations. They offer an explanation for why people resist change even when it would benefit them directly.

In every case, the decisive factor was what the authors call *fair process*—fairness in the way a company makes and executes decisions. The elements of fair process are simple:

- Engage people's input in decisions that affect them directly.
- Explain why decisions are made the way they are.
- Make clear what will be expected of employees after the changes are made.

Fair process may sound like a soft issue, but it is crucial to building trust and unlocking ideas. Without it, people are apt to withhold their full cooperation and their creativity. The results are costly: ideas that never see daylight and initiatives that are never seized.

Covert Leadership: Notes on Managing Professionals

Henry Mintzberg

The orchestra conductor is a popular metaphor for managers today—up there on the podium in complete control. But that image may be misleading, says Henry Mintzberg, who recently spent a day with Bramwell Tovey, conductor of the Winnipeg Symphony Orchestra, in order to explore the metaphor. He found that Tovey does not operate like an absolute ruler but practices instead what Mintzberg calls *covert leadership.*

Covert leadership means managing with a sense of nuances, constraints, and limitations. When a manager like Tovey guides an organization, he leads without seeming to, without his people being fully aware of all that he is doing. That's because in this world of professionals, a leader is not completely powerless—but neither does he have absolute control over others.

As knowledge work grows in importance, the way an orchestra conductor really operates may serve as a good model for managers in a wide range of businesses. For example, Mintzberg found that Tovey does a lot more hands-on work than one might expect. More like a first-line supervisor than a hands-off executive, he takes direct and personal charge of what is getting done. In dealing with his musicians, his focus is on inspiring them, not empowering them. Like other professionals, the musicians don't need to be empowered—they're already secure in what they know and can do—but they do need to be infused with energy for the tasks at hand. This is the role of the covert leader: to act quietly and unobtrusively in order to exact not obedience but inspired performance.

The Dawn of the E-Lance Economy

Thomas W. Malone and Robert J. Laubacher

Will the large industrial corporation dominate the twenty-first century as it did the twentieth?

Maybe not. Drawing on their research at MIT's Initiative on Inventing the Organizations of the 21st Century, Thomas Malone and Robert Laubacher postulate a world in which business is not controlled through a stable chain of management in a large, permanent company. Rather, it is carried out autonomously by independent contractors connected through personal computers and electronic networks.

These electronically connected freelancers—*e-lancers*—would join together into fluid and temporary networks to produce and sell goods and services. When the job is done—after a day, a month, a year—the network would dissolve and its members would again become independent agents.

Far from being a wild hypothesis, the e-lance economy is, in many ways, already upon us. We see it in the rise of outsourcing and telecommuting, in the increasing importance within corporations of ad-hoc project teams, and in the evolution of the Internet.

Most of the necessary building blocks of this type of business organization—efficient networks, data interchange standards, groupware, electronic currency, venture capital micromarkets—are either in place or under development. What is lagging behind is our imagination. But, the authors contend, it is important to consider sooner rather than later the profound implications of how such an e-lance economy might work. They examine the opportunities, and the problems, that may arise and anticipate how the role of managers may change fundamentally—or possibly even disappear altogether.

The Post-Capitalist Executive
An Interview with Peter F. Drucker

T George Harris

For half a century, Peter F. Drucker has influenced senior executives across the globe with his rare insight into socioeconomic forces and practical advice for navigating often turbulent managerial waters. In his latest contribution to the *Harvard Business Review,* Drucker discusses the impact of the ideas in his latest work, *Post-Capitalist Society,* on the day-to-day lives and careers of managers.

Drucker argues that managers must learn to negotiate a new environment with a different set of work rules and career expectations. Companies currently face downsizing and turmoil with increasing regularity. Once built to last like pyramids, corporations are now more like tents. In addition, businesses in the post-capitalist society grow through many and varied complicated alliances often baffling to the traditional manager.

Confronted by these changes, managers must relearn how to manage. In the new world of business, information is replacing authority as the primary tool of the executive. And, Drucker advises, one embarks on the road toward information literacy not by buying the latest technological gadget but by identifying gaps in knowledge.

As companies increasingly become temporary institutions, the manager also must begin to take individual responsibility for himself or herself. To that end, the executive must explore what Drucker calls competencies: a person's abilities, likes, dislikes, and goals, both professional and personal.

If executives rise to these challenges, a new organizational foundation will be built. While a combination of rank and power supported the traditional organization, the internal structure of the emerging organization will be mutual understanding and trust.

Values in Tension: Ethics Away from Home

Thomas Donaldson

What should managers working abroad do when they encounter business practices that seem unethical? Should they, in the spirit of cultural relativism, tell themselves to do in Rome as the Romans do? Or should they take an absolutist approach, using the ethical standards they use at home no matter where they are?

According to Thomas Donaldson, the answer lies somewhere in between. Some activities are wrong no matter where they take place. Dumping pollutants for unprotected workers to handle is one example of a practice that violates what Donaldson calls *core human values:* respect for human dignity, respect for basic rights, and good citizenship. But some practices that are unethical in one part of the world might be ethical in another. What may feel like bribery to an American, for example, may be in keeping with Japan's long-standing tradition of gift giving. And what may seem like inhumane wage rates to citizens of developed countries may be acceptable in developing countries that are trying to attract investment and improve standards of living.

Many business practices are neither black nor white but exist in a gray zone, a *moral free space* through which managers must navigate. Levi Strauss and Motorola have helped managers by treating company values as absolutes and insisting that suppliers and customers do the same. And, perhaps even more important, both companies have developed detailed codes of conduct that provide clear direction on ethical behavior but also leave room for managers to use the moral imagination that will allow them to resolve ethical tensions responsibly and creatively.

The Power of Virtual Integration
An Interview with Dell Computer's Michael Dell

Joan Magretta

Michael Dell started his computer company in 1984 with a simple business insight. He could bypass the dealer channel through which personal computers were then being sold and sell directly to customers, building products to order. Dell's *direct model* eliminated the dealer's markup and the risks associated with carrying large inventories of finished goods.

In this interview, Michael Dell provides a detailed description of how his company is pushing that business model one step further, toward what he calls *virtual integration.* Dell is using technology and information to blur the traditional boundaries in the value chain between suppliers, manufacturers, and customers.

The individual pieces of Dell's strategy—customer focus, supplier partnerships, mass customization, just-in-time manufacturing—may all be familiar. But Michael Dell's business insight into how to combine them is highly innovative. Direct relationships with customers create valuable information, which in turn allows the company to coordinate its entire value chain back through manufacturing to product design. Dell describes how his company has come to achieve this tight coordination without the "drag effect" of ownership.

Dell reaps the advantages of being vertically integrated without incurring the costs, all the while achieving the focus, agility, and speed of a virtual organization. As envisioned by Michael Dell, virtual integration may well become a new organizational model for the information age.

Fast, Global, and Entrepreneurial: Supply Chain Management, Hong Kong Style
An Interview with Victor Fung

Joan Magretta

Li & Fung, Hong Kong's largest export trading company, has been an innovator in supply chain management—a topic of increasing importance to many senior executives. In this interview, chairman Victor Fung explains both the philosophy behind supply chain management and the specific practices that Li & Fung has developed to reduce costs and lead times, allowing its customers to buy "closer to the market."

Li & Fung has been a pioneer in "dispersed manufacturing." It performs the higher-value-added tasks such as design and quality control in Hong Kong, and outsources the lower-value-added tasks to the best possible locations around the world. The result is something new: a truly global product. To produce a garment, for example, the company might purchase yarn from Korea that will be woven and dyed in Taiwan, then shipped to Thailand for final assembly, where it will be matched with zippers from a Japanese company. For every order, the goal is to customize the value chain to meet the customer's specific needs.

To be run effectively, Victor Fung maintains, trading companies have to be small and entrepreneurial. He describes the organizational approaches that keep the company that way despite its growing size and geographic scope: its organization around small, customer-focused units; its incentives and compensation structure; and its use of venture capital as a vehicle for business development.

As Asia's economic crisis continues, chairman Fung sees a new model of companies emerging—companies that are, like Li & Fung, narrowly focused and professionally managed.

Growth through Global Sustainability
An Interview with Monsanto's CEO, Robert B. Shapiro

Joan Magretta

Robert Shapiro asks a tough question: How do we face the prospect that creating a profitable, growing company might require intolerable abuse of the natural world? Monsanto—with its history in the chemicals industry—is an unlikely candidate to be creating cutting-edge environmental solutions, but that is precisely what it is doing. The need for sustainability is transforming the company's thinking about growth.

Changes in global environmental conditions will soon create an unprecedented economic discontinuity. To invent new businesses around the concept of environmental sustainability, Shapiro begins with a simple law of physics: A closed system like the earth's cannot support an unlimited increase of material things. It can, however, withstand exponential growth in information. So Monsanto is exploring ways to substitute information for "stuff" and services for products.

In its agricultural business, the company is genetically coding plants to repel or destroy harmful insects. Putting the right information in the plant makes pesticides unnecessary. Information replaces stuff; productivity increases and waste is reduced. Monsanto also is looking at its carpet business. Today it costs too much to reuse carpets. But Monsanto realized that if the manufacturer owned the carpet and merely leased it to customers, it might be feasible to put in more cost up front and make the carpet more recyclable. Monsanto is reexamining the total life cycle of all its products and asking, What do people really need to buy? Do they need stuff or do they need a service? And what would be the economics of providing that service?

About the Contributors

Hugh Courtney is a Management Consultant in McKinsey & Company's Washington, D.C. office. One of the leaders of McKinsey's Strategy Practice, he has served clients on a broad range of strategic issues in the chemicals, health care, energy, and telecommunications industries. His current client service and research interests focus on applied game theory and strategy development under uncertainty. Dr. Courtney was an academic economist before joining McKinsey.

Thomas Donaldson is the Mark O. Winkelman Professor at the Wharton School of the University of Pennsylvania and Director of the Wharton Ethics Program. He has lectured and consulted to many corporations including Walt Disney, Motorola, AT&T, J. P. Morgan, Johnson & Johnson, EDS, Shell International, IBM, Axel Johnson, Inc., Western Mining Company-Australia, NYNEX, American Medical Association, the IMF, Bankers Trust, and World Bank. Professor Donaldson's articles have appeared in publications such as *The Academy of Management Review, Ethics,* and *Economics and Philosophy.* He is also the author and editor of several books, including *Ties that Bind: A Social Contracts Approach to Business Ethics,* coauthored with Thomas W. Dunfee; *Ethical Issues in Business,* 6th Edition, coedited with Patricia Werhane; and *Ethics in International Business,* which won the 1998 SIM Academy of Management Best Book Award.

Peter F. Drucker is a writer, teacher, and consultant whose 32 books have been published in more than 20 languages. He is the cofounder of the Peter F. Drucker Foundation for Nonprofit Management, and has counseled numerous governments, public service institutions, and major corporations. In addition, Mr. Drucker has published more than 30 articles in the *Harvard Business Review,* has been a frequent contributor to magazines such as *The Atlantic Monthly,* and was a columnist for the *Wall Street Journal* from 1975 to 1995.

Philip B. Evans is a Senior Vice President of The Boston Consulting Group in its Boston office, and worldwide coleader of BCG's Media and Convergence Practice Group, which focuses on the strategic implications of the economics of information. He writes on business strategy, and is the coauthor of "Strategy and the New Economics of Information" (*Harvard Business Review*), which was awarded a McKinsey Prize. He is also coauthor (with Thomas Wurster) of the forthcoming *Blown to Bits: How the New Economics of Information Transforms Strategy.*

W. Chan Kim is the Boston Consulting Group Bruce D. Henderson Chair Professor of Strategy and International Management at INSEAD and Fellow of the World Economic Forum at Davos. Prior to joining INSEAD, he was a professor at the University of Michigan Business School. He has published numerous articles on strategy and managing the multinational in *Academy of Management Journal, Management Science, Organization Science, Strategic Management Journal, Journal of International Business Studies, Sloan Management Review, Harvard Business Review,* and others. He is also a contributor to the *Wall Street Journal,* the *Wall Street Journal Europe,* the *Financial Times,* the *New York Times,* and the *International Herald Tribune.*

Jane Kirkland is Director of Knowledge Management at McKinsey & Company. She is responsible for the firm's knowledge management technology and its global research and information services organizations; she also has oversight of knowledge management professionals who reside in industry or functional practices. Previously she was a Principal in the Cleveland/Pittsburgh office of McKinsey, where she served clients in the financial services and electronics industries. Her work with these clients focused primarily on strategy.

Robert J. Laubacher is a Research Associate with the "Inventing the Organizations of the 21st Century" initiative at MIT's Sloan School of Management. The initiative's Scenarios project, which he heads, attempts to envision the range of alternative organizational forms that may emerge over the next 20 years. Mr. Laubacher has also undertaken research on the social aspects of highly flexible, project-based work organizations. Prior to joining the 21st Century initiative, he worked as a strategy consultant and was researcher for *The Prize,* a Pulitzer Prize–winning history of the international oil industry. He was also Executive Producer of the independent feature film *Home Before Dark.*

Kenneth Lieberthal is the William Davidson Professor of Business Administration and Professor of Political Science at the University of Michigan, where he has been on the faculty since 1983. Professor Lieberthal has published about a dozen books and more than five dozen articles, mostly focused on Chinese politics and economic decision-making. He is currently on leave from the University of Michigan while serving in Washington, D.C. as Special Assistant to the President and Senior Director for Asia on the National Security Council.

Timothy A. Luehrman is a Principal in the Boston office of PricewaterhouseCoopers's Corporate Value Consulting practice. He is the Director of PwC's newly formed Global Technical Center, serving PwC professionals and their clients engaged in business valuation. Prior to joining PwC, Luehrman was Professor of Finance at Thunderbird, the American Graduate School of International Management in Glendale, Arizona. He also has held faculty appointments at MIT's Sloan School of Management, Harvard Business School, and IMD International in Lausanne, Switzerland. Luehrman's publications focus on applied corporate finance, particularly business valuation, real options, capital budgeting, and international corporate finance. His article, "Strategy as a Portfolio of Real Options" shared the second place 1998 McKinsey Award.

Joan Magretta is a consultant and writer based in Cambridge, Massachusetts. She is a Contributing Editor of the *Harvard Business Review* and was its principal strategy editor for the past five years. Before that, she was a partner at the management consulting firm of Bain & Company in Boston. She won the McKinsey Award for the best article to appear in *Harvard Business Review* in 1998.

Thomas W. Malone is the Patrick J. McGovern Professor of Information Systems at the MIT Sloan School of Management. He is the founder and director of the MIT Center for Coordination Science and one of two founding codirectors of the MIT research initiative "Inventing the Organizations of the 21st Century." Professor Malone's research focuses on how computer and communications technology can help people work together in groups and organizations, and on how new organizations can be designed to take advantage of the possibilities provided by information technology. Before joining the MIT faculty, Professor Malone was a research scientist at the Xerox Palo Alto Research Center (PARC). He has been a cofounder of three software companies and has consulted and served as a board member for a number of other organizations. He has published over 50 research papers and book chapters and has been frequently quoted in publications such as *Fortune, Scientific American,* and the *Wall Street Journal.*

Renée Mauborgne is the INSEAD Distinguished Fellow and Affiliate Professor of Strategy and Management at INSEAD and Fellow of the World Economic Forum at Davos. She is also president of ITM Research, a research group committed to discovering ideas that matter in the knowledge economy. She has published numerous articles on strategy and managing the multinational in *Academy of Management Journal, Management Science, Organization Science, Strategic Management Journal, Journal of International Business Studies, Sloan Management Review, Harvard Business Review,* and others. She is also a contributor to the *Wall Street Journal,* the *Financial Times,* the *New York Times,* and the *International Herald Tribune.*

Henry Mintzberg jointly holds the positions of Cleghorn Professor of Management Studies at McGill University in Montreal, Canada, and Professor of Organization at INSEAD in Fontainebleau, France. His research deals with issues of general management and organization, focusing on the nature and styles of managerial work, as well as on forms of organizing and the strategy-formation process. He is the author of over one hundred articles and nine books, including most recently *Strategy Safari.*

Michael E. Porter is the C. Roland Christensen Professor of Business Administration at the Harvard Business School and a leading authority on competitive strategy. He has served as a counselor on competitive strategy to many leading U.S. and international companies and speaks widely on issues of international competitiveness to business and government audiences throughout the world. Professor Porter is the author of 14 books including *Competitive Advantage: Creating and Sustaining Superior Performance,* which won the Academy of Management's 1985 George R. Terry Book Award, as well as *The Competitive Advantage of Nations.* Actively involved in economic policy initiatives, his most recent work focuses on the development of America's inner cities.

C.K. Prahalad is the Harvey C. Fruehauf Professor of Business Administration at the University of Michigan Business School. His research focuses on the role of and the value added to top management in large, diversified, multinational corporations, and he has consulted with numerous firms worldwide. Mr. Prahalad is the coauthor, with Gary Hamel, of *Competing for the Future*, named by *Business Week* as one of the year's best management books in 1994. He is also the author of many award-winning articles, such as "Strategic Intent" and "The Core Competence of the Corporation," which won McKinsey Prizes in 1989 and 1990, respectively.

Patrick Viguerie is a Principal in the Atlanta office of McKinsey & Company, where he serves clients in a wide range of industries, including telecommunications, electronics, and chemicals. As one of the leaders of McKinsey's Strategy Practice, he has led the firm's thinking in the area of strategy under uncertainty. Mr. Viguerie is also the leader of McKinsey's Microeconomics Practice, which brings leading-edge analytical capabilities, such as game theory, to client applications.

Thomas S. Wurster is a Vice President in The Boston Consulting Group's Los Angeles office, where he heads up the office, and worldwide coleader of BCG's Media and Convergence Practice Group. He has extensive experience consulting to leading media and consumer companies, and to a wide variety of other clients in the areas of information, entertainment, telecommunications, and computing. He is a graduate of Cornell University, where he earned an A.B. in economics and mathematics with distinction and was elected to Phi Beta Kappa. He received his M.B.A. with honors from the University of Chicago and earned his Ph.D. in economics from Yale University. Mr. Wurster writes on media and strategy and is coauthor (with Philip Evans) of the forthcoming *Blown to Bits: How the New Economics of Information Transforms Strategy*.

Index

cash flow, xv, 74, 225
centralized structures, 149, 150, 225
channels. *See* distribution/distribution
   networks
Charles Schwab, 21
chemicals/chemical industry, 83, 235,
   243, 248
   agricultural use of, 237, 238, 239–240,
      242
   standards for safe use of, 178
China. *See* emerging economies
Ciba-Geigy, 184–185
Circle K stores, 214
Citibank, 7
Citicorp, 62, 63
civil rights in foreign business settings,
   173, 176, 179–180
"close to the market" buying strategy,
   219–220
clusters, xiii–xiv, 25–48
Coca-Cola, 54, 188
codes of conduct. *See* business ethics in
   foreign settings
collective action, 45–46, 48
colocation of companies. *See* clusters
comanagement, 142–143
command-and-control management,
   129, 160
commitment of employees, 117, 128–
   129, 131
communication, as competency, xviii,
   165–166, 169
communications technologies, 149
Compaq, 194
comparison shopping, 21
competencies, in knowledge economy,
   163, 167
competition
   analysis of competitor's conduct, 111
   analysis of competitor's costs and
      capacities, 74
   in bookselling, 20
   comparative advantage, 26
   between Encyclopædia Britannica and
      Microsoft Encarta, 3–4
   between Federal Express and UPS, 80–
      81
   for information, 5–6
   between Kodak and Hewlett-Packard,
      67, 77
   of multinational corporations in
      emerging economies, 49–51, 62–
      65
   and the paradox of location, 25–26,
      47
   in standards for electronic cash
      transactions, 83–85

competitive advantage
   in clusters, 30–36, 38–39, 44
   innovation and, xiii–xiv, 170–171
   location as, xiv, 25–26
   productivity and, xiii–xiv, 30–34
   sources of, and the new economics of
      information, 19–23
   technology as, 40
competitive intelligence systems, 85
complementarities, 32–33
complexity, as management
   responsibility, 160
compliance issues. *See* business ethics in
   foreign settings
computer industry, xvii, 68, 171, 193,
   194–195
   market, 80
   risk in, 197–198
   standards, 208
   See also specific companies
connectivity, 3, 6, 23
consulting, global, 155
consumer education, 54
consumer goods and services. *See*
   demand for consumer goods and
   services
Consumer Reports, 21
contractors, independent. *See*
   independent contractors
cooperation
   within clusters, 30
   voluntary, 122, 128–129
coordination technologies, xvii, 148–149.
   See also computer industry; electronic
   networks
core competence, 22
core values, 179–180. *See also* business
   ethics in foreign settings
corporate culture
   core values in, 179–180
   in foreign business settings, 179–183,
      187
   leadership levels and, 140–141
   multinational corporations and, 59
corporations, evolution of, 161–162
corruption. *See* business ethics in foreign
   settings
cost structures, 5–6
covert leadership, xvi–xvii, 133–144. *See
   also* leadership
cross-selling, 14, 21–22
cultural differences. *See* business ethics in
   foreign settings
cumulative volatility metric, 94
customer relationships, 5, 193, 195, 204–
   206
   in foreign business settings, 187